*exploring*

# DREAMWEAVER 8

James L. Mohler

Kyle Bowen

THOMSON

DELMAR LEARNING

United States

**THOMSON**

**DELMAR LEARNING**

# Exploring Dreamweaver 8

## James L. Mohler and Kyle Bowen

**Vice President, Technology and Trades, ABU**
David Garza

**Director of Learning Solutions**
Sandy Clark

**Senior Acquisitions Editor**
James Gish

**Product Manager**
Jaimie Weiss

**Marketing Director**
Deborah Yarnell

**Channel Manager**
William Lawrensen

**Marketing Coordinator**
Mark Pierro

**Production Director**
Mary Ellen Black

**Senior Production Manager**
Larry Main

**Production Editor**
Benj Gleeksman

**Technology Project Manager**
Linda Verde

**Editorial Assistant**
Niamh Matthews

**NOTICE TO THE READER**

Publisher does not warrant or guarantee any of the products described herein or perform any independent analysis in connection with any of the product information contained herein. Publisher does not assume, and expressly disclaims, any obligation to obtain and include information other than that provided to it by the manufacturer.

The reader is expressly warned to consider and adopt all safety precautions that might be indicated by the activities herein and to avoid all potential hazards. By following the instructions contained herein, the reader willingly assumes all risks in connection with such instructions.

The publisher makes no representation or warranties of any kind, including but not limited to, the warranties of fitness for particular purpose or merchantability, nor are any such representations implied with respect to the material set forth herein, and the publisher takes no responsibility with respect to such material. The publisher shall not be liable for any special, consequential, or exemplary damages resulting, in whole or part, from the reader's use of, or reliance upon, this material.

# contents

# *preface*

## INTENDED AUDIENCE

You might wonder why we'd set out to write yet another book on Dreamweaver, given the slew of books that already exist for Macromedia Dreamweaver. The primary purpose of this book is to provide a succinct text that covers the "need-to-know" information in a concise manner. Throughout this book you will find condensed information about the Dreamweaver software with a concentration of information that beginning web design students need to know. We don't delve into every detail or facet of the software. Often books that follow this path provide so many diatribes that students quickly lose interest. Rather, this text focuses on the critical features and functions and their use.

When writing this we have focused on the primary audience—that is, educational institutions with a two- or four-year focus. By virtue of its design, Dreamweaver is a tool that is often central to web design and development activities. Thus, this book should adequately provide enough content for a beginning course in web development.

## EMERGING TRENDS

We don't think anyone can argue that Dreamweaver is a tool that has established itself as the favorite for many web designers—both novice and professional. This is generally because the tool is specifically designed to meet the needs of the web designer—providing tools the same way that designers think about them. However, to achieve continued success, the tool must constantly change. As we all know, the technology available for web designs continually changes at a rapid pace. So, as the technology continues to evolve, so must the development environment. Fortunately, this type of growth and refinement can already be seen in each new release of Dreamweaver.

So, what can we see as the future of web technology? Our guess is that the future technologies are already here—we just need to find new and creative uses for them. For example, using CSS for layout is not really a new idea. But we are just now beginning to see this technique hit mainstream web design. We would certainly look for continued growth and interest in using CSS to establish visual web designs.

Another major area for expansion will be in dynamic technologies. As many of these technologies are introduced, only the programmer at heart will really start to work with them. However, as tools such as Dreamweaver continue to expand and improve, implementing dynamic technologies as part of a web design will become a reality for anyone.

The other major technology to watch out for is Flash. Don't take us the wrong way, Flash is already very much successful. However, the future of this format will be very different from the unprofessional-looking animations that can be seen on some sites. Look for future web designs to include more and more Flash elements that provide dynamic content and application-like features.

## BACKGROUND OF THIS TEXT

The whole reason for this book is to provide a "need-to-know" approach to web design within Dreamweaver. While other books talk about every feature and function of the software, our approach here is to boil it all down to the most important points and placing emphasis there. Information found in this book is a compendium of our experience using the tool within professional development environments. As well, this information is tempered through the eyes of two people with much classroom experience (about 15 years in total) and classical training in instructional design.

We believe this book meets a need within the education market. While most of us educators likely "make due" with a volume that is either overkill (which often leads many students to throw their hands up in the air, believing they will never learn to use a tool) or too skimpy (which often yields the same frustration as the former as well as questions along the lines of "Why did you make us buy this book?"), in this book we have attempted to hit the right balance. We have constantly asked ourselves the question, "Is this important at this stage for the student to know?" While only time will tell whether we have met our goal, our aim in this book has remained focused on that question.

# TEXTBOOK ORGANIZATION

## Chapter 1—A Discovery Tour

The opening chapter provides an introduction and tour of the Dreamweaver work environment. The reader becomes familiar with the basic interface components and customizing the Dreamweaver GUI to their liking.

## Chapter 2—Web Design Basics

Although Dreamweaver provides a great number of tools to expand your web design, there are still foundational skills that must first be mastered. This chapter introduces the reader to how Dreamweaver handles some of the fundamental aspects of web design, such as working with text, images,and color.

## Chapter 3—Creating Structure with Tables

There are times when a designer needs to lend visual structure to a design. The most battle-tested method of establishing layout within a web page is to use tables. In this chapter, the reader will explore the basics of tables and the tools that Dreamweaver provides to create them.

### Chapter 4—Adding Interactivity with Forms

Providing a web page doesn't always have to be a one-way street of communication from designer to user. By implementing forms and form elements, the viewing public is given the opportunity to "talk" with the designer in a multitude of ways. Thus this chapter explores the available objects that can be implemented as part of a form.

### Chapter 5—Dividing Pages with Frames

While Frames are no longer commonly used, there are still situations where they can provide you with design advantages over other technologies. This chapter explores the aspects of using frames as part of a design. In addition, it also covers the different techniques for creating a "frames design" within Dreamweaver.

### Chapter 6—Site Management

There is more to becoming a top-notch web developer than just design. There are organizational principles involved with pulling pages and images together to create an entire on-line presence. The chapter explores the fundamentals of how a site's files are managed using Dreamweaver. The key to achieving organization, is understanding Dreamweaver's model of creating local and remote sites— and the movement of files between the two.

### Chapter 7—Automating Web Development with Templates

With an understanding of how to define and manage a site, the reader moves on to learn about the template creation tools available within Dreamweaver. This chapter introduces how Dreamweaver templates can be used design, build, and deploy pages efficiently. Here the reader learns about how templates are created and the principles behind their design and use.

## Chapter 8—Managing Assets and Building Libraries

Also related to site management, Chapter 8 explores two tools that enable web designer's to effectively manage and maintain their designs. First, this chapter covers how the Dreamweaver Assets panel is used to view and manage assets such as images, URLs, colors, or media elements. Next, like using templates, the reader will explore how Dreamweaver library items are built and used to enable efficient web design and development.

## Chapter 9—Formatting Text with CSS

A key aspect of modern web design is working with Cascading Style Sheets (CSS). This chapter opens with a description of CSS and the different elements that are used to build a style. Following a basic understanding of CSS, the reader will explore the tools that Dreamweaver provides to build and apply styles to a web design.

## Chapter 10—Developing Layouts with CSS

Chapter 10 delves into one of the hottest topics in modern web design—the use of CSS to establish visual layout. Because HTML tables are not really intended to be used as a layout mechanism, creating "tableless" designs using CSS can provide a number of advantages. This chapter begins with a discussion of CSS positioning, before moving on to explore many of the aspects that are used in combination to create visual layouts. Finally, the chapter wraps up with an explanation of how CSS layout techniques can be achieved using Dreamweaver.

## Chapter 11—Adding Interactivity with Behaviors

Chapter 11 provides in introduction to the use of behaviors to add interactivity to web designs. It covers the use of the Behaviors panel as well as many of the basic things designers want to know how to do.

## Chapter 12—Working with Dynamic Pages

While database-driven pages can be difficult to construct, this chapter provides an unintimidating overview of how to prepare and utilize dynamic technologies within Dreamweaver. It discusses some of the high-level issues associated with designing dynamic pages, as well as how to build pages that can display content stored within a database.

## Chapter 13—Working with Macromedia Flash and Multimedia

An extremely common technique for adding visual interest to a web design is to implement multimedia elements such as Macromedia Flash. Even though Flash is typically authored within its parent application of the same name, Dreamweaver provides several tools that allow you not only to work with Flash, but to create small movies that serve a practical purpose within a web design. This chapter explores the options for working with Flash elements, in addition to other types of multimedia elements such as digital video.

## Chapter 14—Integrating with Macromedia Fireworks

The book concludes with an overview of various methods by which Dreamweaver's image editing capabilities can be extended using Fireworks. This chapter discusses methods of moving images back and forth between Dreamweaver and Fireworks, as well as the creation and implementation of new graphics.

# FEATURES

The following are some of the salient features of the text:

- Learning goals are listed at the beginning of each chapter.

- Written to meet the needs of design students and professionals for a visually oriented introduction to basic design principles and the functions and tools used within Dreamweaver.

- Client projects involve tools and techniques a designer might encounter on the job to complete a project.

- Full-color section provides stunning examples of design results that can be achieved using Dreamweaver.

- "Exploring on Your Own" sections offer suggestions and sample lessons for further study of content covered in each chapter.

- "In Review" sections are provided at the end of each chapter to quiz a reader's understanding and retention of the material covered.

# HOW TO USE THIS TEXT

The following features can be found throughout the book:

## ↗ Charting Your Course and Goals

Each chapter begins with the sections *Charting Your Course* (a brief summary of the intent of the chapters) and Goals (a list of learning points). These section describe the competencies the reader should achieve upon working through and understanding the chapter.

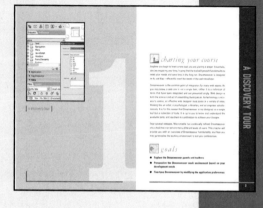

## ↗ Don't Go There

Material with the heading *Don't Go There* appears throughout the text, highlighting common pitfalls and explaining ways to avoid them.

**DON'T GO THERE**

In the prior process, you will note that I had you create two swatches of the same color with varying alphas. This was purposeful. If you blend two different colors with two different alphas some pretty strange things can happen. Typically you end up with some haloing effects—where there are hints of one or the other color in the transparency. To avoid haloing, anytime you are creating a gradient that gradates Alpha, use the exact same RGB values in the two chips.

## ↗ Try This

Boxed sections entitled *Try This* present tasks for the reader to experiment with. Following along with these will give the reader hands-on experience working with Flash.

**TRY THIS**

Try creating various linear gradients and saving them as swatches. Try doing something real-world. For example, try creating a multicolor gradient that could be used to simulate the look of highly reflective metal (add a lot of sharp whites and blacks). Or, try to add a simulated horizon line (integrate some blue for a sky and brown for the gr

## In Review and Exploring on Your Own

*In Review* and *Exploring on Your Own* are sections found at the end of each chapter. These allow the reader to assess his or her understanding of the chapter. The section *Exploring on Your Own* contains exercises that reinforce chapter material through practical application.

## Adventures in Design

These spreads contain client assignments showing readers how to approach a design project using the tools and design concepts taught in the book.

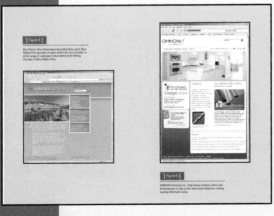

## Color Insert

The color insert presents work that can be achieved when working with Macromedia Dreamweaver.

## E.RESOURCE

An instructor's guide on CD is available to assist instructors in planning and implementing their instructional programs. It includes sample syllabi for using this book in either an 11 or 15 week course. It also provides answers to the end of chapter review questions, Powerpoint slides highlighting the main topics, and additional instructor resources. Order Number: 141801611X .

## ABOUT THE AUTHORS

**James L. Mohler** is a Senior Research Scientist and Associate Professor at Purdue University. He has authored or coauthored over 20 texts, presented over 40 papers and workshops, written 25 academic and trade publications, and taught over 15 different courses at Purdue, ranging in size from 22 to over 400 students. Currently James is working with the Information Technology group at Purdue, leading a group of highly talented artists and programmers who are building Purdue's next generation web presence. He also served as the SIGGRAPH 2005 Conference Chair.

**Kyle D. Bowen** is currently a Web Application Programmer at Purdue University. He has contributed to, or served as technical editor for, over 20 texts within the web design, development, or usability area. His broad range of experience includes developing web strategies, instructional media, and providing faculty training within higher education.

## ACKNOWLEDGMENTS

James and Kyle would like to especially thank the wonderful team at Delmar for all their support on this book. The authors are only a part of a much larger team, and thanks go to Senior Acquisitions Editor, Jim Gish; Product Manager, Jaimie Weiss; Production Editor Benj Gleeksman; and Editorial Assistant, Niamh Matthews. Thanks also go to Carol Leyba for composition and Daril Bentley for copy-editing.

James would like to thank his wife Lisa, who has been patient and loving while he has spent endless hours in the office. In addition,

Kyle Bowen would like to thank his wife Kelli for providing endless support and inspiration.

Thomson Delmar Learning and the author would also like to thank the following reviewers for their valuable suggestions and expertise:

**GARY CROSSEY**
Digital Media Department
Blue Ridge Community College
Brevard, North Carolina

**BRUCE HUFF**
Department Chair, Visual
Communications Department
Dakota County Technical College
Rosemount, Minnesota

**MELISSA COGSWELL**
Focus Media
Haslett, Michigan

**DEBBIE ROSE MYERS**
Senior Instructor, Graphic
   Design Department
The Art Institute of Ft.
   Lauderdale
Ft. Lauderdale, Florida

**CECILIO ACOSTA**
Digital Media Department
Texas State Technical
   College—Waco
Waco, Texas

# QUESTIONS AND FEEDBACK

Thomson Delmar Learning and the authors welcome your questions and feedback. If you have suggestions that you think others would benefit from, please let us know and we will try to include them in the next edition.

To send us your questions and/or feedback, you can contact the publisher at: Media Arts & Design, Thomson Delmar Learning, Executive Woods, 5 Maxwell Drive, Clifton Park, NY 12065, 800-998-7498, or

James Mohler at: Purdue University, Purdue West Plaza Suite D, 1404 W. State Street, West Lafayette, IN 47907, *jlmohler@purdue. edu*

Kyle Bowen at: Purdue University, Purdue West Plaza Suite D, 1404 W. State Street, West Lafayette, IN 47907, *kbowen@purdue.edu*

A Discovery Tour

*charting your course*

Anytime you begin to learn a new tool, you are placing a wager. Essentially, you are wagering your time, hoping that the tool will provide functionality to meet your needs and save time in the long run. Dreamweaver is designed to do just that—efficiently meet the needs of the web developer.

Dreamweaver is the common point of integration for many web assets. As you may know, a web site is not a single item; rather, it is a collection of items that have been integrated and are presented singly. Web design is both the science and art of assembling these pieces. As technology continues to evolve, an effective web designer must serve in a variety of roles, thinking like an artist, a psychologist, a librarian, and an engineer simultaneously. It is for this reason Dreamweaver is not designed as a single tool but a collection of tools. It is up to you to know and understand the available tools, and to use them in combination to achieve your designs.

Over several releases, Macromedia has continually refined Dreamweaver into a tool that can service many different levels of users. This chapter provides you with an overview of Dreamweaver functionality, and how you may personalize the working environment to suit your preferences.

 *goals*

- Explore the Dreamweaver panels and toolbars
- Personalize the Dreamweaver work environment based on your development needs
- Fine-tune Dreamweaver by modifying the application preferences

# MANEUVERING IN THE ENVIRONMENT

Macromedia uses standardized user interfaces for their software. By unifying the design of their products, Macromedia has made it easier for those people who are already familiar with a particular product to learn new Macromedia products. For this chapter, we will start at the beginning to provide an introduction for those new to the tools, and a possible refresher for those who may already have experience with other Macromedia applications, such as Flash or Fireworks.

## What's Your Pleasure?

figure | 1-1 |

The first time you start Dreamweaver, you can select your preference for how the workspace will be configured.

After the initial installation of Dreamweaver, running the application for the first time will force you to make a decision: are you a designer or a coder? Choosing one of these options, as indicated in Figure 1-1, will edit the Dreamweaver workspace to provide more direct access to functionality typically used by persons in these roles. It is important to note that all of the same functionality will exist despite the option you may choose. For this book, we are going to explore Dreamweaver using the Designer interface. Just keep in mind that as your web development skills continue to evolve Dreamweaver provides an additional workspace layout.

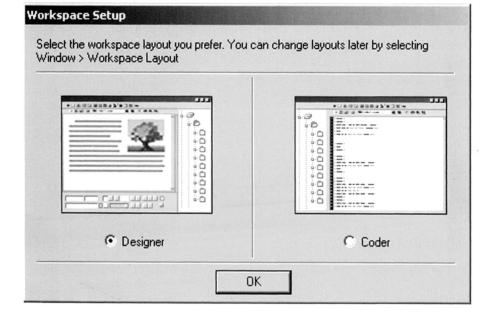

TIP: You can change your workspace layout at any time by accessing Window | Workspace layout.

## The Start Page

Each time Dreamweaver is opened, you will be presented with the start page, shown in Figure 1-2. The start page is designed to provide you with single-click access to either edit a recently opened document or to create a new document based on a particular technology or template. Additionally, the start page provides access to Macromedia Dreamweaver Exchange and to interactive features such as the Dreamweaver quick tour and tutorials.

To start our tour of the Dreamweaver workspace, we are going to create a new document. Because each item under the Create New heading offers slightly different interface options based on the functionality offered by the specific technology, you should click on the HTML option so that we can explore the most fundamental features of the Dreamweaver workspace.

figure | 1-2 |

The start page provides you with single-click access to edit or create new documents.

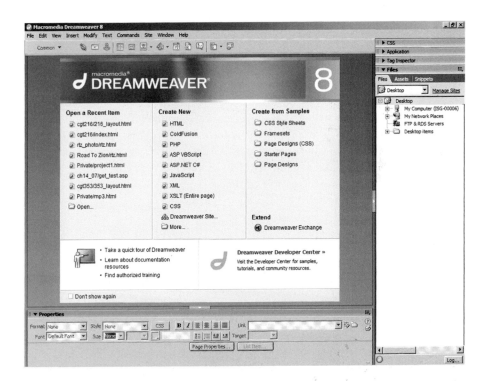

## The Dreamweaver Interface

figure | 1-3 |

The Dreamweaver
workspace.

Figure 1-3 shows the basic Dreamweaver interface. While this interface shares many of the hallmarks of a standard application, there are five primary components worth exploring individually. The Document window, Insert bar, Property Inspector, Tag Selector, and panel groups comprise the core elements of the Dreamweaver workspace.

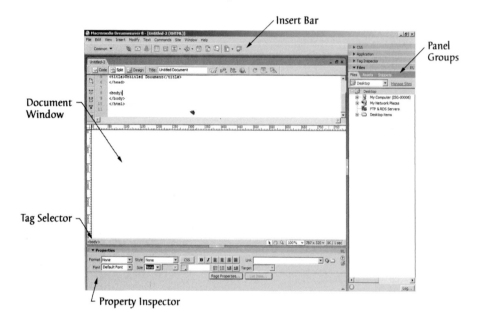

WYSIWYG

Tools such as Dreamweaver are commonly referred to as WYSI-WYG (What You See Is What You Get) editors. Simply, this means that as you design your web page within Dreamweaver you will be able to see your design changes as you make them. This is a big step up from the days of editing code, saving the document, and viewing the saved code in the web browser.

The Document window is where all of your web design will take place. Working within the Document window is not all that dissimilar to working with your favorite word processing package. Through this window, you can add and lay out all of the visual elements that make up the current document. Based on how you arrange the design elements within the Document window, Dreamweaver will determine how the web page will be viewed through the web browser—with some exceptions. We will discuss these exceptions as we encounter them throughout the book.

## Changing Your View

While the Document window can show your page as it will appear in the browser, it can also expose elements that would normally be invisible. The Document toolbar offers a number of viewing options that modify what appears in the Document window, as shown in Figure 1-4. The most popular of these options are the Code, Split, and Design buttons on the left of the Document toolbar. Typically, when designing within Dreamweaver you will have the Design option selected. However, by clicking on the Code option you can view and edit the underlying code for your current page. An additional twist to this relationship is the Split view, which will allow you to view the design and code views simultaneously (as shown in Figure 1-4). While using split view, selecting elements in the Design window will highlight the associated source in the Code window (and vice versa).

figure | 1-4 |

The Split view will show both the design and code views.

— Document Toolbar

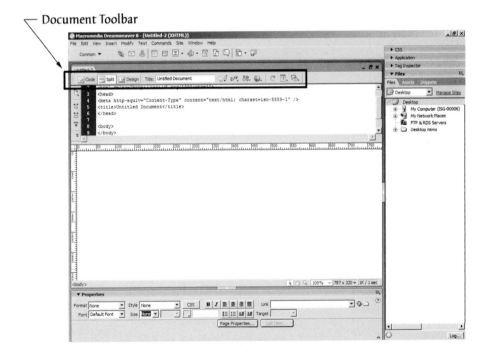

## Window Size

When you begin to design for the Web, something to keep in mind is that there are a great number of variables that are beyond your control. Working with web pages is not like working in a page layout program—things are not absolute, per se. One such variable we must take into account is the viewing resolution (or "browser window size") your audience may be using. To meet the needs of your audience, many times you must design a site to fit the greatest number of users. Dreamweaver has included a feature that allows you to resize the Document window, so that a page can be viewed as it would appear with different window sizes.

For this feature to be available, make certain the Document window is not currently maximized (it will be by default). To resize the Document window, click on the Window Size button (shown in Figure 1-5), which is located along the bottom of the Document window (refer to Figure 1-4 for location). From the pop-up menu, select a window size you would like to use. Note that there are two sets of dimensions listed for each option. The first set is the actual pixel dimension of the document's viewing area. The second dimension refers to the size of a browser maximized to a specific resolution. Now you may be asking, "Why are there two sets of dimensions?" The first resolution is slightly smaller, to account for the buttons, toolbars, and scroll bars commonly found around the viewing area of a web browser. In the next chapter we will discuss further how best to use this feature.

figure | 1-5 |

Using the "resize window" feature will allow you to design your pages for common window sizes.

The Insert Bar

figure | 1-6 |

The Insert bar holds a number of different objects that can be inserted into your design.

The Insert bar, shown in Figure 1-6, provides direct access to those items most often used when designing any web page. A wide variety of objects (including images, tables, and hyperlinks) may be found on the Insert bar. When you click on an item to insert, the associated HTML code for that object will be inserted into the current page. In many instances, Dreamweaver may prompt you for additional information about the object before insertion. The

Insert bar is actually divided into many different sets of options, called categories, which will vary depending on the technology selected when the page was created. We will explore the Insert bar more closely in the next chapter.

## Property Inspector

The Property Inspector is Dreamweaver's version of "mission control." Whether you are emphasizing text, adding a URL for a hyperlink, or changing the display properties for a Flash movie, the Property Inspector allows you to modify the characteristics of virtually any object selected within the Document window. The available properties will change (some more dramatically than others) based on the nature of the selected item. As Figure 1-7 illustrates, selecting an image will display a different set of options than will selecting text. Additionally, changing the properties of any given item will immediately be reflected within the Document window.

figure | 1-7 |

The Property Inspector will change depending on the item selected.

While the Property Inspector may be viewed in either standard or expanded modes, I suggest setting it to the expanded mode now (expanded mode is shown in Figure 1-7). Even if you are a beginner, you will quickly outgrow the standard mode. To set the Property Inspector to expanded mode, click on the small white triangle in the lower right-hand corner. This will cause the Property Inspector to expand to show more options.

## Tag Selector

The Tag Selector feature, shown in Figure 1-8, is intended for those of you who are comfortable with reading and editing source code associated with elements in the Document window. The Tag Selector works by displaying the tags that surround the current selection. By selecting each individual tag you can expand the current selection, edit a particular tag, or remove a tag entirely. The advantage of this feature is that you can make changes at a code level without having to leave the design view.

figure | 1-8 |

You can select, edit, or delete tags associated with elements within the Document window.

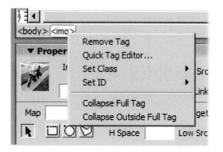

## Panel Groups

Dreamweaver is a very different application than you may have worked with in the past. While designed to serve a goal of helping you to design, develop, and deliver a web site, how this is accomplished may differ entirely from site to site. The delivery of content on the Web may take many different forms, involving any one of a number of different technologies. For one project you may need HTML only; for others you may need JavaScript, ASP, or Cascading Style Sheets (CSS).

Dreamweaver is a very robust package that delivers an entire catalog of tools for developing in most web environments. To provide this level of functionality, Dreamweaver employs panel groups to organize the available options. Panel groups, like those shown in Figure 1-9, are designed to improve efficiency by allowing you to streamline and customize your work environment. If you are working on a site that uses CSS extensively, you would probably want to have the CSS Styles panel open at all times. Conversely, if you have a question about a particular tag, you might look it up in the Reference panel, and then close the panel when finished. No matter what the specific need, effectively using panel groups can save you considerable time and energy.

figure | 1-9 |

Panel groups can be open or closed based on your needs.

## Files Panel

While there are many different panels available in Dreamweaver, the Files panel (shown in Figure 1-10) is of particular importance. Simply described, the files panel is (as the name suggests) a listing of files and directories. Most commonly, this listing is of those files and directories associated with the site you are working on. However, this is not a requirement. Using this panel provides you with direct access to open files without having to go through the File | Open procedure for every document. Because a web site may contain hundreds of documents, using the Files panel can really save you some time.

In addition to helping you manage the files on your workstation, the Files panel can also help you to manage files on the web server. This includes managing the movement of files back and forth from these locations.

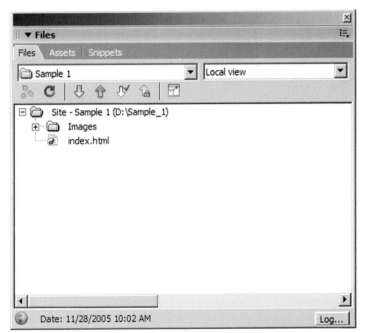

figure | 1-10 |

The Files panel can help you manage the files associated with your site.

## History Panel

Since we are just getting started learning about Dreamweaver, this is a good opportunity to introduce the History panel. The History panel catalogs all of the actions you perform to a particular file. So, as you enter text, create hyperlinks, insert images, and so on, the

History panel will take note of the change and display a list of steps you have taken in the panel. An example of this listing is shown in Figure 1-11.

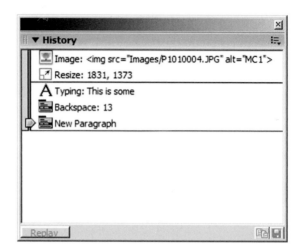

figure | 1-11 |

The History panel can help you step back through the changes you have made to a document.

This History panel is like the "Undo" command on steroids. Rather than hitting Edit | Undo several times to find where you may have gone wrong, the History panel will allow you to pinpoint the exact step, and then back yourself up. To reverse your steps, click and drag the slider on the left of the History panel. The most recent steps will appear at the bottom of the list. As you drag the slider upward, you are stepping back in the life of the current file. Once you locate the specific step where things went awry, move the slider to the step immediately preceding. Any action you perform with the current file at this point will remove all subsequent steps shown in gray within the History panel. This panel also has a number of other interesting features, discussed in subsequent chapters.

## Working with Panels

Once you start working closely with Dreamweaver, you will quickly find those panels you interact with regularly. Typically, these are the panels you constantly leave open, ready to do work at a moment's notice. For panels you use less frequently, there are a number of different options for arranging them in your workspace.

One method for working with panels is to take advantage of their expanded or collapsed state. To expand or collapse a panel, click on the expander arrow next to the name of the panel. This is a helpful feature for those panels you may refer to from time to time but don't want waste screen real estate on by keeping open. While panels and panel groups can be closed, collapsing a panel may work slightly better because it can still be readily accessed within the workspace. To close a panel, click on the Options menu button to the far right of the panel name and select Close Panel Group.

### Docking and Undocking

In addition to opening and closing panels, they may also be positioned in different locations within the Dreamweaver workspace. By default, when working with the Designer layout many of the panels are docked on the right-hand side of the screen. Docked panels are those physically attached to the workspace. As opposed to being docked, a panel may also appear floating (or undocked), so that you can move it around the workspace as needed. To undock a panel, click on the panel's gripper (the dotted lines in the blue panel title bar to the left of the toggle arrow) and then drag the panel to the desired location. You will see that the panel has been removed from its docked position and is now floating over your workspace (see Figure 1-12). To dock the panel, grab the panel's gripper and drag to the desired location with the other panels. As you drag the panel near other panels, a black line will appear. This line is the position where the panel will appear docked when you release the mouse.

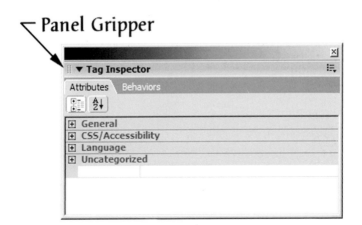

figure | 1-12 |

By using a panel's gripper you can dock and undock panels as needed.

In addition to docking with other panels, it is also important to note that panels may also be docked to the left of the workspace. To dock a panel on the opposite side of the workspace, click on the panel's gripper and drag to the side of the workspace. As you approach the edge, a black outline will appear. This outline is the area where the panel will be docked when you release the mouse.

Something to keep in mind as you are arranging your panels: when you exit out of Dreamweaver, the location and state of your panels will be saved. The next time you start Dreamweaver, all of the panels will be where you last left them, and any panels you expanded will appear open on screen.

While Dreamweaver provides a great number of options for customizing your workspace, just try to keep it simple. Remember, you have to work within this environment. If you go too crazy with the panels you will spend endless amounts of time searching for panels within the workspace.

TIP: If you can't remember where a panel is located or lose track of one, click on the Window menu and then the panel name. This will surface the panel to the top.

## Working with Panel Groups

Now that you have a feel for the different panels, you will soon discover that not all panels are created equally. Some panels require a great amount of space, where others require very little. To make the most of the space you have available, panel groups may be resized or renamed dependent upon your particular needs.

To resize a panel group that has been undocked, just click and drag the corner of the window. You will find that working with undocked panel groups is similar to working with windows in any other application.

For docked panel groups, click and drag the title bar up and down as needed. If you want one panel group to consume the entire vertical area, the Maximize feature may be used. To maximize a panel group, click on the Options menu button and select *Maximize panel groups*. Maximizing can be particularly useful when working with the Files panel. Panel groups may also be expanded horizontally. To do this, click and drag the bar that separates the panels and the Document window. Note that there is also an Arrow button in the center of the separator bar. Click on this button to minimize the entire panel group area.

## TRY THIS

Now that we have discussed many of the available options for working with panels, take some time to experiment with docking and undocking. Also, while you are at it, explore the panels available under the Window menu. Here you will find several panels that are not displayed in Dreamweaver by default.

# CUSTOMIZATION AND PREFERENCES

Since you have now been completely immersed in the details of maneuvering in the Dreamweaver workspace, we can now begin to explore some of the available application preferences.

## Application Preferences

Within Dreamweaver there are a great number of preferences that may be modified (actually, 20 different categories in all). A majority of the time, you will probably just use the default settings. Many of the available configurations deal with how Dreamweaver will write (or help you write) and display the code that makes up your site. If you are the type that enjoys a little hands-on coding from time to time and want to get involved in the nitty-gritty of how best to utilize the code-editing features of the application, you might want to check out many of the Preference options that are not covered by this chapter. For the rest of us, I am going to touch on just a few of the more commonly used configurations. To access and edit the application preferences, select Edit | Preferences and then select from the categories on the left.

### General Preferences

The General category of preferences, shown in Figure 1-13, is used to determine some of Dreamweaver's global configurations. It is important to note that I will not be covering every option within this category. If you want more information on a particular option or feature, consult the Dreamweaver help file by selecting Help | Using Dreamweaver. The following is a sampling of options available in the General category of preferences.

● *Show start page:* As we discussed earlier in this chapter, the start page is presented each time you start Dreamweaver. If you wish to disable this page, deselect this option.

● *Reopen documents on startup:* This feature allows you to leave documents open when you exit Dreamweaver. Once you restart the application, those files you left open will automatically be presented. If there are one or two files you find yourself constantly editing, enabling this can option can save you some time.

● *Maximum number of history steps:* Earlier in this chapter, we explored some of the functionality of the History panel. The maximum number of steps determines how many steps will be available through the panel. Once you begin to exceed the maximum number, the History panel will discard the oldest steps. The default number of steps is set at 50, and the maximum value possible is 99,999. Quite honestly, the default number of steps should be more than enough to meet your development needs. Once the number gets above 50, I am not sure I could remember back that far anyway.

figure | 1-13 |

The General category of preferences is for making global configuration changes within Dreamweaver.

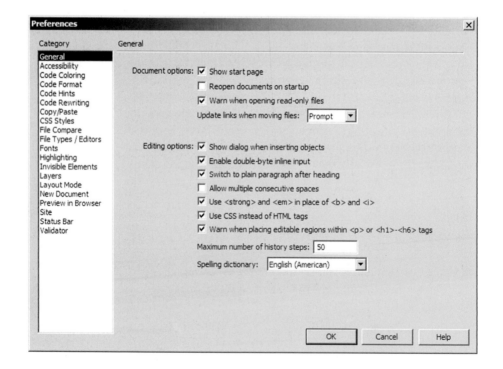

Your first inclination might be to dial up the maximum number of history steps to the 99,999, thinking, "What could it hurt; I can't have too much insurance." In fact, the higher the number of history steps used the greater the amount of computer memory needed to run Dreamweaver. If you set the maximum number of steps too high, the performance of your computer (and Dreamweaver, for that matter) will be affected.

## Invisible Elements

When discussing the Document window, I mentioned that it is a WYSIWYG-style editor. This is only partially true. There are a number of elements that will never visually appear in either Dreamweaver or the web browser, but this doesn't mean they aren't there. To make it easier to work with invisible elements, Dreamweaver adds graphic icons in the locations where these elements exist. The Invisible Elements category of the Preferences, shown in Figure 1-14, lists all invisible elements available. Once you begin to spend more time working with Dreamweaver, you will learn which of these elements you will find useful, and which you will find an annoyance.

figure | 1-14 |

You can enable or disable Invisible Elements by clicking on the checkbox corresponding to each of the elements.

**Preferences**

| Category | Invisible Elements |
|---|---|

General
Accessibility
Code Coloring
Code Format
Code Hints
Code Rewriting
Copy/Paste
CSS Styles
File Compare
File Types / Editors
Fonts
Highlighting
**Invisible Elements**
Layers
Layout Mode
New Document
Preview in Browser
Site
Status Bar
Validator

Show: ☑ Named anchors
☐ Scripts
☐ Comments
☐ Line breaks
☐ Client-Side image maps
☑ Embedded styles
☑ Hidden form fields
☑ Form delimiter
☐ Anchor points for layers
☐ Anchor points for aligned elements
☑ Visual Server Markup Tags (ASP, CFML, ...)
☐ Nonvisual Server Markup Tags (ASP, CFML, ...)
☐ CSS display: none

Show dynamic text as: {Recordset.Field}

Server-Side includes: ☑ Show contents of included file

OK   Cancel   Help

## Preview in Browser

From a design standpoint, the Preview in Browser category of preferences is extremely important. A key aspect of any web design is the ability of that design to translate to multiple browsers. While Internet Explorer is by far the most popular web browser in use, there are still a number of people who use Netscape, and alternative browsers such as Opera and Mozilla. While it is not my intention to launch into an argument over the merits of each of the browsers, it is important that we understand that each browser has its own idiosyncrasies. To help ensure that your design will be cross-browser compatible, Dreamweaver provides the Preview in Browser feature. Simply explained, this feature allows you to take a page you have designed in Dreamweaver and instantly view it in the appropriate web browser (and it assumes that you have that browser installed). The Preview in Browser option, shown in Figure 1-15, allows you to set which browsers you want to use to directly view your pages.

figure | 1-15 |

Dreamweaver can be configured to use any number of different browsers to view your web page designs.

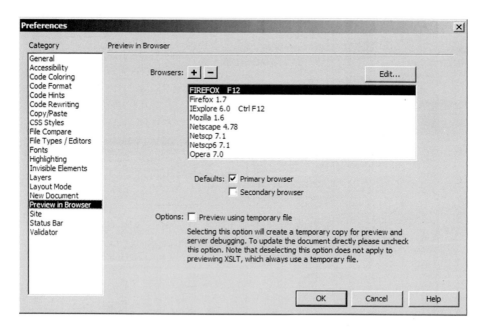

To add a browser to the list of available browsers, click on the Plus (+) button. Then, using the Add Browser dialog box, provide a name for the browser and a path to the browser application on your workstation. Through this dialog box, you can also set the new browser as the Dreamweaver default by selecting either the Primary or Secondary browser option. Once you click on OK, the browser will be added to the list.

## TRY THIS

Take a few minutes and add entries for any browser on your machine that may not already appear in this list. Don't have any other browsers besides Internet Explorer? Then get one! Most alternatives to IE (such as Netscape, Mozilla, or Opera; web page URLs for which follow) have an available version that may be downloaded and used free of charge.

● Netscape: *http://www.netscape.com/download/*

● Mozilla: *http://www.mozilla.org/*

● Opera: *http://www.opera.com/*

## Customizing Shortcuts

Another, slightly less common, feature to customize is Keyboard Shortcuts, which Dreamweaver uses to circumvent many of the menu items. By selecting Edit | Keyboard Shortcuts, you have access to the entire list of shortcuts used by Dreamweaver (see Figure 1-16). While some shortcuts are common to most other applications (for example, Ctrl + S or Command + S for save), others are entirely specific to Dreamweaver and can be relatively awkward. If there is a command you use regularly, and you can't quite hit that last key with your little finger, you can edit the shortcut to

figure | 1-16 |

Using the Keyboard Shortcuts editor, you can create, modify, or delete Dreamweaver's default shortcuts.

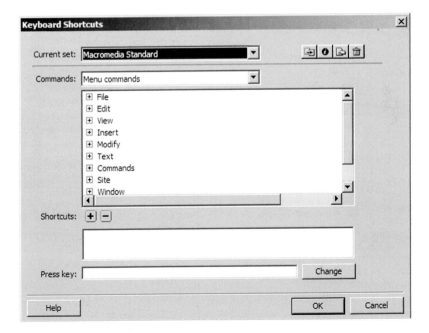

something a little more basic. In addition to editing shortcuts, you can add your own. This will be particularly helpful when we discuss snippets in later chapters.

## Customizing the Insert Bar

Because there is a large number of objects that may be inserted into your design using the Insert bar, it would be impossible to develop a system of categories that would meet everyone's needs. So, if you find yourself constantly using the same objects from different categories you can group them using the Favorites category. You can add any of the objects to the Favorites category by right-clicking on the Insert bar and selecting Customize Favorites. This brings up the dialog box shown in Figure 1-17, which allows you to move available objects to the Favorites category. While many of these objects may seem new to you now, not long after using Dreamweaver you will discover those items that meet your needs.

figure | 1-17 |

Using the Favorites category, you can group many of objects you may commonly use.

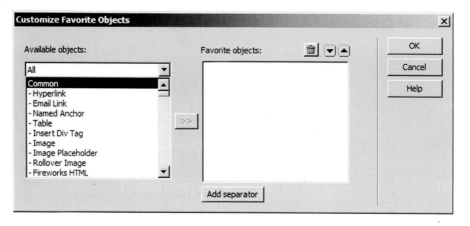

# SUMMARY

In this chapter we have taken our first steps in exploring Dreamweaver. While developing a familiarity with the Dreamweaver workspace may not be greatly exciting, it is an important step in becoming an efficient user of the application. Coming away from this chapter, you should have a good understanding of how the Property Inspector, the panel groups, the Insert bar, and Document toolbars all work. Also important is an understanding of how Dreamweaver may be customized to meet your specific needs.

As we move forward, keep in mind that Dreamweaver is not a single tool but a set of tools. It is your ability to know, understand, and leverage these tools that will save considerable time and energy down the road.

## in review

1. How can you add objects to the Insert bar's Favorites category?

2. How do you switch from the Document window's design, code, and split views?

3. What is the Tag Selector used for?

4. What does the Property Inspector do?

5. What is the Files panel used for?

6. How can you use the History list to undo changes?

7. How do you dock and undock a panel?

8. How do you configure the Preview in Browser option?

## ➚ EXPLORING ON YOUR OWN

NOTE: Two of the following reference materials are available only through the Dreamweaver start page. To access these elements, make sure you have the start page enabled, as discussed earlier in this chapter. You may need to close any open documents to display the start page.

1. Via the Dreamweaver start page, click on the Take a quick tour of Dreamweaver option. This will open your web browser and provide you with a short presentation in Dreamweaver functionality.

2. Via the Dreamweaver start page, click on Take a Dreamweaver Tutorial. This will open Dreamweaver's Getting Started window. Read through the material in the first two sections: "Welcome to Dreamweaver" and "The Dreamweaver Workspace."

3. Visit the Macromedia Dreamweaver support site at *www.macromedia. com/support/dreamweaver/* and familiarize yourself with some of the help resources available.

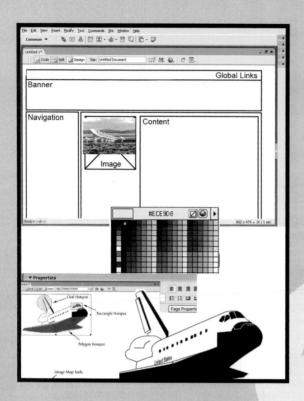

| Web Design Basics |

*charting your course*

Before you can run, you must first learn to walk. Before you can build that top-ten site visited by millions, you must first walk through the basics of developing new pages and content within Dreamweaver. Many of the topics discussed in this chapter will quickly become second nature to you. Many elements of this chapter deal with foundational skills that any web designer needs to master. And, while you may have some familiarity with these concepts by using other tools keep in mind that how they are implemented with Dreamweaver may vary slightly. With that said, let's take our first steps.

 *goals*

- **Learn about creating new web documents**
- **Explore how to work with text**
- **Learn about web graphics and formats**
- **Find out about web-safe colors**
- **Discover how hyperlinks are created**

# CREATING NEW PAGES

Anytime you type an address into a web browser, somewhere on the other end is a file that contains a description of the page you are requesting. These pages are then returned to your web browser and displayed. In reality, a web site is nothing more than a string of pages that have been interconnected with hyperlinks. It is also these same pages that integrate all of the text, images, and multimedia featured on the web site.

At this point you are probably asking, "How does your browser know what to display?" A majority of the pages displayed in your web browser are constructed using HyperText Markup Language (HTML). HTML pages provide a description of the layout, structure, and content for a given page. Many of you may already have a great amount of experience writing HTML from scratch, so I am not going to explain all of the ins-and-outs of the language. In addition, the reason for using Dreamweaver is so that you don't have to write the code yourself. However, if you plan on making web design your profession I highly encourage you to learn the language. I promise that it is not all that difficult once you know a few basics.

## Creating New Documents

In this chapter, and for a majority of this book, we are going to create and work with static HTML pages. Disregarding the Dreamweaver start page for a moment, to create a new HTML page select File | New. This will open the New Document window, shown in Figure 2-1. On the left of this window is the General category listing of pages you can create. To create an HTML page, click on the Basic page category. Unless you are building a dynamic page that makes use of a database, most of the time you will be working with the Basic page category. In the Basic page list, select the HTML option, and then click on the button labeled Create. This will open a new blank document window within the Dreamweaver workspace.

NOTE: As you probably noticed, there are a number of other file types available in the Basic page category. Most of these are for specialized purposes that are beyond the scope of this book. However, we will be taking a look at the HTML template and Cascading Style Sheet (CSS) page types in the chapters to come.

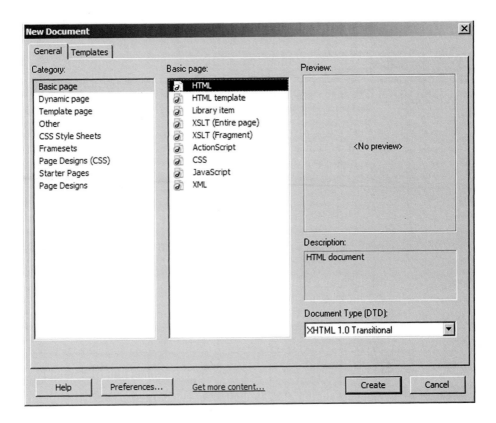

figure | 2-1 |

Using the New Document window, you can start new documents that utilize many different technologies.

## Page Properties

Now that we have started our very own HTML page, we can explore some of the global properties of the document. The properties set within the Page Properties dialog box will apply to everything on the current page. To open the Page Properties dialog box (shown in Figure 2-2), select Modify | Page Properties. This dialog box is broken into five separate categories of properties. It is important to note that I will not be covering all of the options. Since the MX 2004 release of Dreamweaver, the application has been changed to use CSS for many of the settings. It is for this reason I will only be touching on a few of the options briefly here. I will be covering some features much more in depth in later chapters.

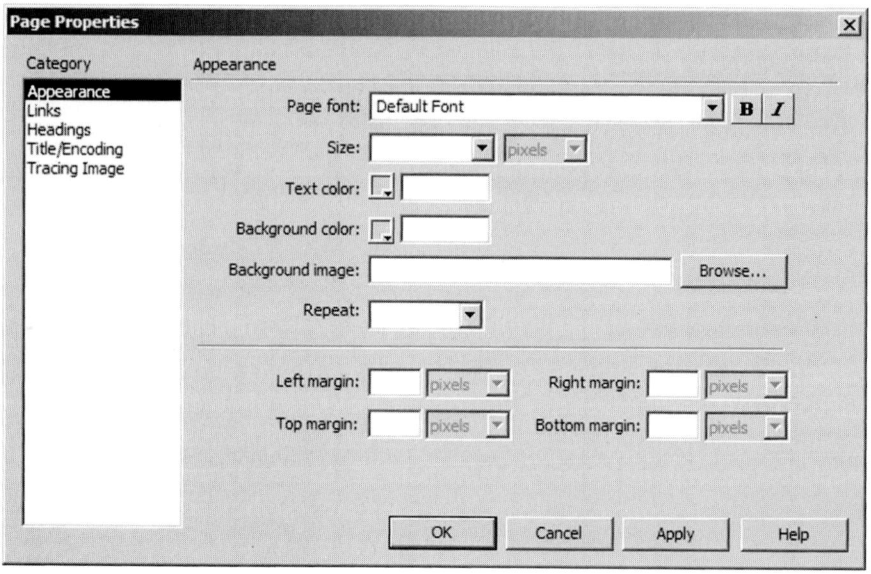

figure | 2-2 |

The Page Properties dialog box will help you apply settings to an entire HTML page.

### Appearance

The Appearance category of page properties allows you to assign global visual properties to the text, background, and layout of the page. To get a better feel, let's explore each option individually.

- *Page Font, Size, and Text Color:* As the names of these three settings imply, this is where you can define the default font, text size, and text color for your page. By making this selection, any text you add to the page will automatically adopt these settings unless you specify otherwise.

- *Background Color:* By default, Dreamweaver will set the background of your page to white. If white is a little too uninteresting, modifying this setting can change your background color to something different. Later in this chapter, I will explain what to think about when selecting colors.

- *Background Image and Repeat:* This defines an image that will appear in the background of your page (see Figure 2-3) and how it will repeat (if at all). If you define a background image with the repeat options, it will be tiled to fill the entire browser window. It is possible to set both a background color and image for your page. However, the background image will override the color, unless the image is unavailable.

- *Margins:* This defines the distance between the elements on your page and the edge of the browser window. I should also note that this setting does not affect the background images or color. A popular effect is to set the margins to zero. This will push all of your page elements right up to the edge of the browser window.

Be *very* careful when using a background image or a background color with your page design. While you may enjoy tiling your baby picture in the background of the page or choosing fuchsia for the background color, your visitors may not appreciate the sentiment. If you are going to use a background image, make certain it is a simple graphic, with subtle colors. If choosing a different background color, consider its effect on the ease of reading the page. What you put in the background (color or image) can drastically detract from the readability and visual impact of the page (shown in Figure 2-3).

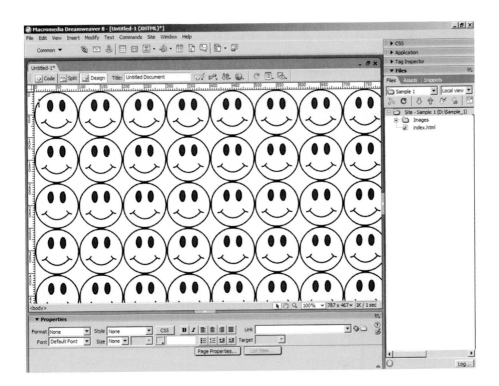

figure | 2-3 |

Tiling the wrong image in the page's background can be extremely ugly.

### Links

The Links category of properties sets the visual appearance of all hyperlinks on your page unless specified otherwise.

- *Link Font and Size:* This setting defines the font and size that will be used for the hyperlinks on your page. Typically, this setting will be left in the default value of what you set for the page font.

- *Link Color:* This defines the color of a link when first viewed on your page and before anyone interacts with it. By default, the color is set to blue.

- *Visited Links:* This defines the color of a link that has already been clicked. By default this color is set to purple.

- *Active Links:* This defines the color of a link as it is being clicked. By default, this color is set to red.

- *Rollover Links:* This defines the color when the mouse hovers over the link. I should also note that this feature will not work in older browsers, most commonly versions of Netscape prior to 6.0.

- *Underline Style:* This setting controls how (or if) an underline will appear on a hyperlink. The available options are relatively self-explanatory.

There are many schools of thought on the best use of hyperlink color and underlining. Design purists will tell you that hyperlinks are always blue and underlined, and thus should never be changed. Moderates will tell you that hyperlinks should be either blue or underlined. And still other designers think that it really doesn't matter what the color is; it is the functionality that matters. No matter what you decide for your site, make certain of two things. First, make sure there is a great amount of contrast between the link color and the background color. Second, make certain the visited and rollover link color is different from the background color. If these colors are the same, your links will disappear when hovering or clicked. I know it sounds strange, but it has been known to happen.

### Title and Encoding

The most important feature of this category is the Title field. The Title field defines the text that will appear in the web browser's title bar. By default, the page has the illustrious name of "Untitled Document." When building your site, take special care in titling your pages. Not only does a page title appear with the browser but it will appear in the search results when found by web search engines such as Google.

The Encoding option defines the character set that should be used when displaying the page in the web browser. As you know, some languages use the same A-Z alphabet that English uses, whereas other languages (such as Japanese) use many different characters. Unless you are working with languages other than English, you will probably never change this setting.

## Tracing Images

An interesting advantage of using visual editors such as Dreamweaver is that you can use tracing images to help you with your design. As part of the web design process, many designers will produce page mock-ups using raster imaging tools such as Adobe Photoshop or Macromedia Fireworks. Using the tracing image option, you can import an image (such as a page mock-up) and place it in the background of your page (shown in Figure 2-4). This

figure | 2-4 |

Using a tracing image can help you visualize your design.

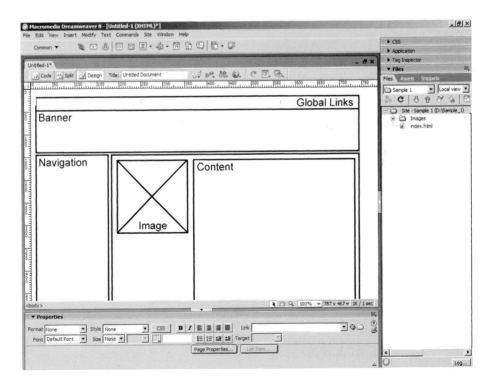

can help you make design decisions on content sizing and layout. The tracing image is different from the background image because it will not appear when the page is viewed in the browser. In reality, the tracing image is typically removed when you are finished designing the page. If you are having difficulty visualizing portions of the page, the tracing image's transparency can be modified.

## Saving Your Work

Now that we have made some changes to our HTML page, we will want to save it for later use. Saving a document out of Dreamweaver is not all that different than it is for many other applications. To save your page, select File | Save. Since the page has not been saved yet, this will open the Save As dialog box. Here you can assign a file name to your page. If there is ever a time where you are editing more than one page at a time (which is common in fairly large sites), the Save All feature can be used. By selecting File | Save All, you can save all currently opened files.

Here comes the big question, "What should I name the file?" There are near endless possibilities for what your file should be named. The following are some general guidelines.

- *Don't use spaces.* If the file name absolutely needs some type of visual separator, use the underscore (_).

- *Type it all lowercase.* Dependent on the type of web server where your site will be hosted, the file names may be case sensitive. To try to make this a non-issue, just type your file names in all lowercase.

- *Keep it short.* You, or a visitor to your site, may have to type in this file name as part of the web address. Do everyone a favor and try to keep the name at a reasonable length of eight characters or less.

- *Use the correct file extension.* When a file name is entered, an extension will be required. Because we are creating an HTML file, the most common file extensions are *.htm* or *.html*. By default, Dreamweaver for Windows tacks on the *.htm* extension, whereas the Macintosh version will use *.html*. Dependent on your web server, and technologies used, you may have to use a different file extension. Contact the system administrator of your web host to learn the file extension that should be used.

# Viewing Your Work

While you are designing your site, it will be important to take a step back and view your work. Because Dreamweaver is a visual editing tool, it is possible to get a feel for your design within the development workspace. However, to get the most accurate depiction of what your audience will see you need to view the page in a web browser.

## View Your Work Within Dreamweaver

One of the largest time-saving benefits to Dreamweaver is your ability to view a page as you design it. Before visual editors, designers would need to painstakingly edit lines of HTML code one at a time, save the page, and then open it in a browser. Viewing your page this way many times, as you design a site, can take a little while.

There are two techniques for receiving an approximate view within the Dreamweaver workspace. First, by selecting View | Visual Aids | Hide All you can turn off all of the extra artifacts that are added for your benefit. For example, table borders and invisible element icons will no longer be visible. Clicking on Hide All again will return the elements to their normal display mode.

The second option for viewing your page in the workspace is by using the Window Size option, discussed in the previous chapter. Part of successful web design is coloring inside the lines, while thinking outside the box. This means that you must learn to develop cutting-edge designs, but at the same time understand the constraints you must work with. One of these constraints is that not everyone has their monitor resolutions set on the highest level, or has their web browser maximized all of the time. The Window Size feature will allow you to view your design with typical browser sizes.

What browser size should I design with? There is no one-size-fits-all solution to this problem. In reality, you can design a site to any size. However, the point of designing to a particular browser size is twofold. First, you should strive to eliminate horizontal scrolling. This is where your design is so wide that the visitor must scroll sideways to view the entire site. The second is somewhat abstract, but it is important to know what parts of your design will appear "above the fold." When a visitor first approaches your site, make sure the most important parts of the page are available at the top. Thus, the user will not need to scroll down to the lower portion of the page to find the primary message of the page.

I still haven't answered the question what size should a page be designed to? Currently (and this changes occasionally) the general rule of thumb is to design your page to be in the neighborhood of 760 pixels wide. This will fit neatly into a browser window used at a screen resolution of 800 x 600. Current screen resolution trends suggest that 800 x 600 and 1,024 x 768 are by far the most common screen resolutions. Figure 2-5 shows common design sizes comparatively.

figure | 2-5 |

Several common design sizes and how they stack up proportionally.

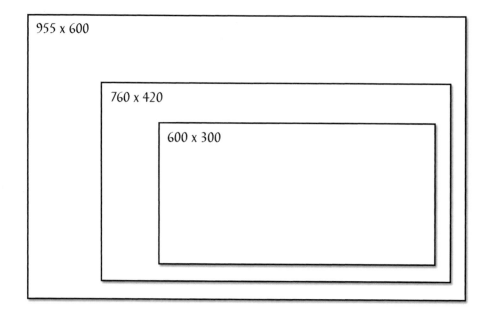

955 x 600

760 x 420

600 x 300

**DON'T GO THERE**

As you are thinking about designs, keep in mind that your pages will not always be viewed from a computer. Today there are a number of options for surfing the Web, including PDAs and cell phones. These devices present some interesting problems because their aspect ratio (the ratio of width to height) is totally different from computer monitors. As you progress in your web development skills, you should consider these as viable options for content viewing as well.

## Previewing Your Page

As you design your page within Dreamweaver, the application will do its best to approximate how the page will appear. The most significant drawback is that much of the functionality you build into a page, such as hyperlinks, will not be available. To obtain a quick idea of how your design is shaping up, the current page can be previewed within a web browser.

Previewing a page will create a temporary file that will be displayed in the browser. The temporary file is a replica of what the file would look like if you were to actually save the file. Previewing a file is useful if you are making many design changes and you want to take a look before committing the changes to a saved document.

To preview your page, select File | Preview in Browser and then select from the list of browsers you have configured. This will automatically start the browser and display your current page. For more information on how to configure additional browsers, see Chapter 1.

## Testing with the Browser

It is now time to see where the rubber hits the road. Viewing your saved page design within the web browser will give you a very clear indication of how site visitors will view your design. The process of opening an HTML page will vary slightly, based on the browser.

1. Using Dreamweaver, save your HTML file.

2. Start your web browser. In this case I will be using Microsoft Internet Explorer.

3. Select File | Open. If you are using Internet Explorer, this will summon the Open dialog box. If you are using Netscape, File | Open will take you directly to the browse window (go to step 5).

4. Click on the button labeled Browse.

5. Locate the file you saved to your workstation in step 1.

6. Click on the button labeled Open.

I cannot stress this enough. You must test your pages in more than one web browser. In addition, if you are a PC user find a friend with a Mac and let them take a look as well.

# WORKING WITH TEXT

There is a saying in web design that "Content is king." Without content, a web site is an empty shell with very little use. All web sites serve the same singular goal of communicating some message to the visitor. The most common mechanism for providing this message is through using text. Typically, textual content makes up the largest portion of content for any site. While Dreamweaver functions very similarly to your typical word processing package, there are a number of idiosyncrasies that need to be discussed.

## Adding Text: Everything You Thought It Could Be

For this section, I am not going to pretend to teach you how to enter text into your computer. Instead, we should explore some of those subtle differences when working with type on the Web. The following are a few things to keep in mind as you are entering text.

- *Paragraph breaks and line breaks:* As you are entering your text and you want to move down to the next line, you are probably conditioned to hit the Enter key. While in Dreamweaver this still works, you are actually creating a paragraph break. If you want the text to continue onto the line directly below your current line of type, press Shift + Enter (or select Insert | HTML | Special Characters | Line Break).

- *Spaces:* Keep in mind that as you type you only get one space at a time. You can hit the space bar until you are blue in the face, but the browser will only ever show one space. If you need to insert more than one space, you must use what is called a non-breaking space. To insert a non-breaking space, press Ctrl + Shift + Space (or select Insert | HTML | Special Characters | Non-Breaking Space). More than one non-breaking space can be used.

- *Tabs:* Typically in word processor applications, when the tab key is pressed at the beginning of a paragraph the first line is indented by five spaces. This is not so when working on the Web. There are a number of workarounds for this dilemma. The most common method is to simply leave the tab out. However, if an indent is required you can insert five (or more) non-breaking spaces. This is kind of messy (from an HTML code standpoint), but it works.

- *Special characters:* Sometimes you need a character that cannot be found on the typical keyboard. For example, the copyright symbol (©) or that funny-looking upside-down question mark (¿) may be needed from time to time. To view the available characters and insert them into your documents, select Insert | HTML | Special Characters | Other.

## Lists

When you have several items that need to be formatted, lists may be used. There are two types of lists: unordered and ordered (shown in Figure 2-6). Unordered lists, more commonly known as bulleted lists, are used for items that should appear in no specific order (see Figure 2-6a). Ordered lists are used when you have several items that come in sequential order that need to be ordered numerically or alphabetically (see Figure 2-6b). To create a list:

1. Enter the text for the words or phrases that make up the list. Press the Enter key after each item, which will insert a paragraph break that will be removed later.

2. Highlight the text that makes up your list.

3. Click on the Unordered List or Ordered List button in the Property Inspector.

figure | 2-6

4. If any of the items on the list have subitems, highlight the subitems and click on the Text Indent button on the Property Inspector.

Lists can be either (A) unordered or (B) ordered.

A
- Unordered Lists
- Ordered Lists
- Indented Text

B
1. Add the text.
2. Highlight the text.
3. Click the Ordered List Button.

# HYPERLINKS AND NAVIGATION

The one thing that makes the Web the Web is hyperlinks. The ability of a user to click on a link and then be instantly routed to a new piece of information is relatively powerful. The hyperlink is what can connect you to sites anywhere else in the world, and at the same time connect the world to you.

## Linking

The process of creating a link within Dreamweaver is very simple. The problem is that there are a number of different types of hyperlinks. The only real complication in creating a hyperlink is deciding what technique is best for the given scenario. Now we are going to walk through the different types of hyperlinks and when they should be used.

## Link to Your Pages

Probably the most common type of hyperlink you will work with is the relative link. Relative links are used to link to pages within your site. While other types of links may be used to perform the same operation, using a relative link is most efficient. The following are the steps for creating a hyperlink to a page on your site.

1.  If you have not already done so, save your file. This may seem strange, but by saving the file first Dreamweaver will automatically use the correct file path for the link.

2.  Type or highlight the text to be used as a hyperlink.

figure | 2-7 |

3.  In the Property Inspector, shown in Figure 2-7, click on the Folder icon to the right of the Link field. This will open the Select File dialog box.

Using the Property Inspector, you can add link information for any selected text.

4.  Select the page you wish to link to and click on OK. Note that the text now appears as a hyperlink, and the path to the file has been entered into the Link area of the Property Inspector.

There are many different ways to type the file path used for relative links. Later in the book we will discuss the different linking models that can be used.

## Links to Other Pages

As I mentioned earlier, hyperlinks can connect your site to sites anywhere else in the world. To make this connection, an absolute link is used. Absolute links provide the browser with an exact location for another site, document, or location on the Internet. In most instances, a hyperlink will appear something like this: *http://www.websitename.com*. You are probably already familiar with absolute links; they show up on television or in magazines all the time. To insert a link to another site, type or highlight the text you want to use as the link, and then enter the full URL into the Link area of the Property Inspector.

### Target Links

Target links are the same as most other types of hyperlinks, but with a special twist. While there are four different types of targets you can add to a hyperlink, I am only going to touch on one now. The _blank_ target can be used in conjunction with any hyperlink to open the requested page in a new browser window. This is slightly different than those irritating "pop" windows you see used for advertisements on commercial sites. Using the _blank_ target will open a browser window with the same size and buttons as the orig-inating browser window. To add the _blank_ target to your hyper-link, create your hyperlink as discussed previously, and then select _blank_ from the Target pull-down list in the Property Inspector. In the chapter dealing with frame sets, we will discuss the other three types of targets.

While it can be handy to use the _blank_ target to open new brows-er windows, this should be done in moderation. It can grow very tiresome for a visitor to your site if every link opens in a new win-dow. Good uses for the _blank_ target might be for linking to alter-native types of content such as PDF files or for providing links to sites you may only be referencing.

## Named Anchors

Now that we have looked at creating links to other pages, the next step is to create links within the same page, or named anchors. Named anchors are used to define (or anchor) a specific location on a page. Then, when a user clicks on a hyperlink they can be taken directly to where the anchor has been inserted. If you are dealing with a large amount of content on a single page, named anchors may be particularly useful so that your users can avoid some scrolling. I should also mention that a named anchor may also be used to link to a specific point on a separate page.

Creating a named anchor is a two-part process. First, you must cre-ate the anchor point. Then you add a hyperlink to the anchor. To create the named anchor:

1.  Put your cursor on the part of the page to where you would like to insert the named anchor.

2.  Select Insert | Named Anchor, which will bring up the Named Anchor dialog box.

3.  Assign an anchor name. To avoid issues later, anchor names should only contain letters and numbers. Dreamweaver will provide a warning if illegal characters are used. Once you click on OK, an anchor icon will appear in the Document window.

To create a link to a named anchor:

1.  Type or highlight the text you would like to use as a link.

2.  In the Link area of the Property Inspector, type a pound sign (#) followed by the name you assigned the anchor in step 3 of the previous steps. For example, if the anchor's name is *top*, the link should appear as *#top*.

## ▶ TRY THIS

Now that we have covered the basics of working with pages and text, take some time to create new documents and tinker with the page properties. Try adding some text to the page and previewing it in a web browser. Once you get a feel for how you can control the visual appearance, create some hyperlinks that will click you through from page to page, or to another site on the Web.

## GRAPHICS AND COLOR

The inclusion of graphics on any page will open an infinite number of design possibilities. Unfortunately, not all of these possibilities are good. If you think back to some of the worst web sites you have ever visited, it was most likely their poor choices regarding images that doomed the site. Who was the person that thought having an animated dancing hamster at the top of their site was a good idea anyway? Effectively using graphics on your site takes special planning and an understanding of the available file formats.

The use of color on your site can have a similarly negative effect. The colors you choose with a design can create a physical and emotional response for the user. It is this response that sets the overall tone for your site. A good web design will set a tone that complements the primary message you want to convey. Additionally, there are physical factors that can determine your color choices. For example, green text on a red background (other than being seriously ugly) will appear almost invisible to any user that suffers from color blindness. There are entire books devoted to the discussion of color, and best practices for use. For this chapter, I am going to discuss the mechanics of using color on your pages within Dreamweaver.

## Web Graphic Formats

There are three primary graphics formats used on the Web today. The GIF, JPEG, and PNG formats can all be displayed within the web browser as part of your design. Each of these formats serves a particular purpose that when used correctly can help you preserve image quality while reducing download time.

### GIF Images

The Graphic Interchange Format, more commonly known as GIF, was one of the Web's earliest supported graphic formats. What makes the GIF format special is that it only supports 256 colors, and is most commonly used for images that have large areas of the same color, such as that shown in Figure 2-8. Cartoons, text, illustrations, black-and-white photos, and charts are types of images you may want to save as a GIF.

figure | **2-8** |

Graphics with areas of solid color are best saved in the GIF format.

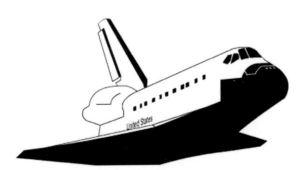

The GIF format also comes in additional flavor called the GIF89a. This format differs from the standard GIF in that it supports transparency and animation. The GIF89a format provides 1-bit transparency. This means that you can select one color (and only one)

to be transparent within the image. Unless the image is very simple, adding transparency may not be very useful. Additionally, creating an animated GIF is also relatively primitive. If you need to create animation for the Web, Macromedia Flash is really the way to go.

### JPEG Images

The JPEG format was specifically designed for use with photographic images (see Figure 2-9) because they can support millions of colors. In fact, the acronym JPEG stands for Joint Photographic Experts Group. The JPEG format is slightly different than the others because it uses "lossy" compression. This means that when an image is saved in this format some of the data that makes up the file is actually left out in order to make for a smaller file. The tradeoff is that with a smaller file comes a reduction in picture quality. Fortunately, when saving a JPEG file you can actually set how much the image should be compressed so that you can reach a happy balance between size and quality.

figure  2-9

Photographs are best saved in the JPEG format.

### PNG Images

Even though it has been around for several years, the PNG (Portable Network Graphic) format is a relative newcomer. Originally developed to replace the GIF format, PNG is an extremely versatile format with several advantages over both the GIF and JPEG. The most redeeming traits of this format are improved file compression, multiple levels of transparency, and a 2D interlacing. For more information on the specifics of the format, visit the official PNG site at *www.libpng.org*.

Why isn't everyone using the PNG, you might ask? Until version 4 of the major web browsers, the PNG format was not widely supported. It will take some time before all features of the format are supported, and web developers are ready to make the switch. Even though designers have been slow to adopt it, PNG is definitely the image format of the future.

## Working with Graphics

No matter what graphic format you are using, the process of inserting an image onto your page is the same. To insert an image, select Insert | Image, and then select the graphic you wish to place on the page. Now the image will appear within the Document window. Once on your page, there are a number of different properties that may be set using the Property Inspector (shown in Figure 2-10).

figure | 2-10 |

Modifying the options in the Property Inspector can change how the image will appear.

The options you can set for images include the following.

- *Width (W) and Height (H):* This sets the width and height (in pixels) of the selected image.

- *Source (Src):* This is the file path to the selected image.

- *Link:* Adding a file path or URL here will make the image a hyperlink.

- *Alternative Text (Alt):* This option should always be used to associate a description to the image. Visitors of your site that are visually impaired will be able to experience the images on your site based on the alternative text description. If the image is a design element of little consequence, the description should be set to a single space so that text readers will ignore it.

- *V Space and H Space:* This setting adds an extra space to either the top and bottom (v space) or the left and right (h space) edge of the image. If no value is added here, the image will "bump into" any adjacent text or images.

- *Low Source (Low Src):* This determines an image to present while the actual image is being downloaded. Typically, this property is used when you have a very large image that may take your user a little while to download over a slower connection.

● *Border:* This setting will add a color border around the edge of the image. If an image is being used as a hyperlink, you may want to set this option to zero.

● *Align:* This option is used to determine how the image will align with any adjacent text.

figure | 2-11 |

Images can have
several different
hotspots differing
in shape and size.

## Image Maps

In addition to an image serving as a single hyperlink, it can be divided into several clickable areas called "hotspots." Hotspots can be shaped as a rectangle, an oval, or a multisided polygon, as shown in Figure 2-11.

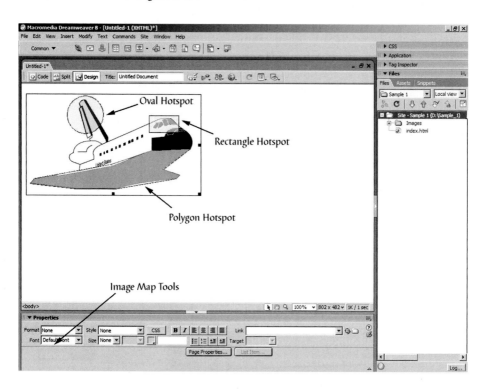

The following are the steps for creating an image map.

1. Insert an image to use for the image map.

2. Click on the appropriate Hotspot tool from the lower left of the Property Inspector.

3. Place your cursor over the image in the location of the hotspot. Click and drag to create the desired size and shape of the hotspot.

4. Add a file path or URL to the Link option in the Property Inspector.

## Web-safe Colors

Anytime web design is discussed, the topic of web-safe (or browser-safe) colors will soon be mentioned. If you have spent any time within the web development community, I am sure you will have heard someone mention this notion.

Back in the early 1990s a group of software engineers, who probably never spent a day of their lives designing anything with color, selected a palette of 216 colors that would be common among the major browsers on both the Mac and PC. The idea was that these colors would display consistently despite the user's browser or operating system. Needless to say, designing with these colors is certainly a challenge. As a matter of fact, the colors in the browser-safe palette aren't very good aesthetically as it relates to design. Nevertheless, having a palette of 216 colors was fine and dandy when video cards could only support 256 colors, but today monitors and video cards have made significant improvements.

Should you use the web-safe color palette? Well, there is nothing that should prevent you from using these colors in designs. Just keep in mind that unless you have a compelling reason (that is, unless you are designing for an audience who will have very old machines) you should not feel constrained to only the colors on this palette. It is important to realize that no matter what colors you use there will to some degree be differences in how they will be displayed with any given computer.

Now, to be completely fair the web-safe color palette is not entirely dead. Actually, the continued development of new pervasive computing devices such as PDAs and cell phones has given renewed life to the web-safe palette. While recent PDAs have extended their color palettes into the thousands, many new devices (such as cell phones) are just now making the switch from black-and-white to color displays. So, there is still some relevance to browser-safe palettes.

## Working with Color

Many page elements, ranging from text color to table cell background, can inherently have a defined color. Any color used on the

## System Color Picker

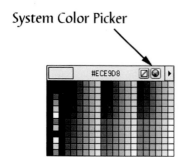

figure | 2-12 |

Using the Dreamweaver color picker, you can select from a web-safe color palette or mix your own color.

Web is specified by a six-character hexadecimal code. Fortunately, the Dreamweaver color picker (shown in Figure 2-12) can help you mix the proper color without having to do the math and find the hex number.

Any element in Dreamweaver you can associate a color with will use the same color picker. To access the color picker, click on the color box that will appear in the appropriate dialog box or Property Inspector. Once the picker is open, your cursor will turn into an eyedropper. This eyedropper will allow you to select a color either on the color palette or from some other element that appears anywhere on your screen.

When using a color from the palette, keep in mind that there are several different palettes available. By default, the palette will appear with web-safe colors. To change to a different palette, click on the Arrow button in the top right of the color picker. Selecting Windows OS, Mac OS, or Grayscale will expand the available set of colors.

If the palette colors will just simply not work, you can create your own. Clicking on the System Color Picker button will open the Color dialog box. Here you can custom mix the exact color you are looking for. However, keep in mind that not all colors you create here will display similarly on other computers. It is also important to note that Windows users and Mac users will see a different dialog box to mix colors with.

## SUMMARY

In this chapter we have covered many of the basics related to web design. The key points you should take from this chapter are setting page properties, viewing your pages in a web browser, creating hyperlinks, and understanding the available image formats and when each should be used. Now you are armed with just enough knowledge to begin creating and populating HTML pages with content. The concepts you learned in this chapter will carry over in each of the chapters that follow.

## in review

1. What is HTML?

2. Where will a page title appear on the web browser?

3. What should you keep in mind when naming an HMTL file?

4. What is the difference between a line break and a paragraph break?

5. What are the two types of lists?

6. How do you open a link in a new browser window?

7. What are named anchors used for?

8. What are the major graphic formats? When should each of them be used?

9. What is meant by web-safe color?

## ✦ EXPLORING ON YOUR OWN

1. Create several new HTML pages that will compose a mini web site. Assign each of them the appropriate page properties. On each page, add hyperlinks to all of the other pages. Once finished, view your mini site in a web browser.

2. Using an image-editing tool such as Macromedia Fireworks or Adobe Photoshop, create some new graphics. Export the graphics in the appropriate format and insert them in an HTML page.

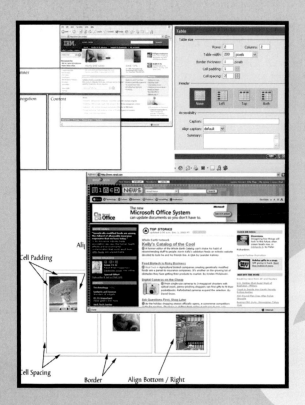

# | Creating Structure with Tables |

*charting your course*

One of the biggest time-saving features offered by visual editing tools is the ability to create tables. If you have ever hand-coded a table on your own, you will know that the process can take considerable time and is often frustrating. In fact, even the most ardent of HTML hand coders will often use tools such as Dreamweaver to create their tables.

When starting down the path of learning to create and use tables, it is important to realize that tables aren't just for data. Using tables to visually structure the content on your page can be extremely powerful. Suddenly your designs can take on an entirely new appearance, allowing you to create pages that arrange content in ways that are unique and relatively consistent. There are several "must-have" skills for modern web designers, and the ability to create tables is certainly one of them.

 *goals*

- Learn about the mechanics of tables
- Learn how to create tables
- Explore how tables may be adjusted
- Explore creating tables in layout mode
- Find out how tables can help give structure to your design

# ANATOMY OF THE TABLE

If you have ever worked with a spreadsheet before, working with tables is not all that much different. All tables are constructed of the same basic pieces. These are the row, column, and cell, which together make up the overall structure of any table (see Figure 3-1). The table row runs across the table horizontally, whereas columns are vertical table elements. The point where a row and column intersect is the cell. The table cell is where you will do most of your business. In general, table cells can contain virtually any type of element that can be inserted into a page. Also included on this list are separate tables, called nested tables, which we will discuss later in this chapter. The cardinal rule to remember when working with table cells is that they will expand to fit whatever content is placed within them.

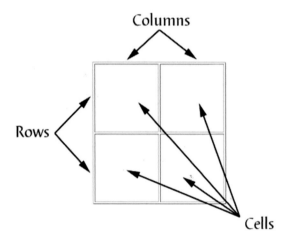

figure | 3-1 |

All tables are con-
structed of the same
basic elements:
rows, columns, and
cells.

In addition to the physical construction of a table, there are four common properties, shown in Figure 3-2, used to adjust the appearance of the table. These settings may all be modified by using the Property Inspector.

● *Border:* This property is used to determine the width of the border that surrounds the edges of the table and cells.

● *Cell Padding (CellPad):* This property, as the name may suggest, determines the minimum amount of space between the inside edge of a cell and any content the cell may contain.

● *Cell Spacing (CellSpace):* This property sets the distance between table cells.

● *Alignment:* This property, which comes in both horizontal (Horz) and vertical (Vert) flavors, specifies how content will be aligned within each table cell. Content can be horizontally aligned to the left, right, or center. You can also choose the browser default; usually to the left. In addition, content can also be vertically aligned to the top, middle, bottom, or baseline. Using the baseline setting, you can align the first text line of different cells in the same row. Just like the horizontal alignment, you can also choose the browser default, which is usually in the middle.

figure | 3-2 |

By editing the properties of the table, you can affect how the content in the cells will be displayed.

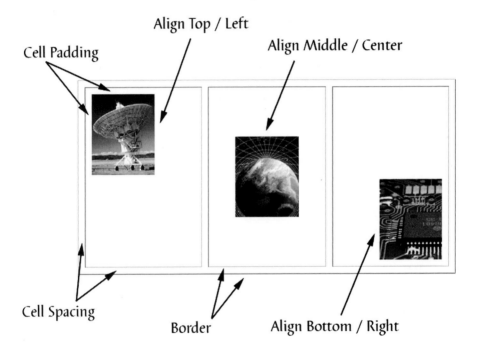

Something to keep in mind as you are working with these attributes is that other than the alignment properties once applied they will affect the entire table and not just certain cells. Later in this book, we will discuss how you can maintain greater control by using Cascading Style Sheets (CSS).

# WORKING WITH TABLES

Dreamweaver offers two modes for creating tables: standard mode and layout mode. In this section we are going to explore the standard mode for creating tables because it will help to explain how tables are constructed. And regardless of the mode that may be used, the HTML code for the resultant tables will be the same.

## Creating Tables

Creating a table is a simple process. However, it can take some planning. Sketching out your table on paper first can save you some time later down the road. Your sketch need not be anything fancy, just enough to help you calculate how many rows and columns you will need. Once you know this information, you are ready to create the table.

As with most other elements in Dreamweaver, there is more than one way to create a table. For this chapter we are going to use the Insert bar, discussed in Chapter 1. If it is not already, set the Insert bar to show the layout options. To create the table, click on the Table button on the Insert bar. This will open the Table dialog box (shown in Figure 3-3), where you define many of the table's attributes. These attributes are as follows.

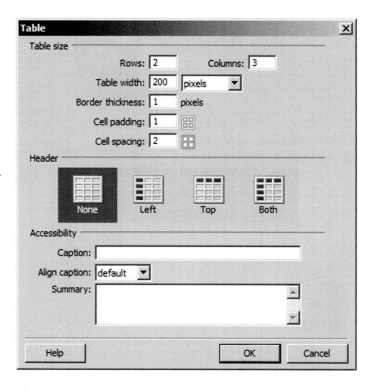

figure | 3-3 |

The Table dialog box is used to set the initial properties of your new table.

● *Rows and columns:* This is why I say to sketch out your table first. Before you can get too far, the first thing that needs to be defined is how many rows by how many columns will be needed. While rows and columns can be added later, you can save yourself some energy by getting it right at this step.

- *Table width:* This setting will determine how wide the table will appear within the browser. The width of a table may be set as either a percentage or pixel width. A percentage width will allow the table to scale to fit the area provided.

- *Border thickness:* This specifies the width of the border that defines the edges of the table and cells. I should also note that this may be set to zero to make the table border invisible. When you use tables to lay out pages, this is how you hide the table.

- *Cell padding and cell spacing:* These options allow you to set the cell padding and cell spacing values that were discussed earlier in this chapter. If left blank, the table will display a default value of 1 for cell padding and 2 for cell spacing. Also, both of these values may be set to zero, similar to the border option.

- *Header:* The header option is typically used with tables that contain organized tabular data. For example, if you were inserting a table with monthly rainfall for the last year, each of your columns would use a heading corresponding to each of the months. Headings are not a required feature of tables, but they should be used to aid the visually disabled visitors of your site.

- *Accessibility:* In addition to providing headings, there is additional description information that can be added to your table. This information, also typically used for data tables, will aid visually impaired visitors of your site that use screen readers. The Caption option will add a title to your table that will visually appear within the browser. The Summary feature should be used to provide a description of the data in the table. This table summary will not appear in the browser window, but will be read by screen readers.

## Adjusting Table Elements

Now that there is a new table in the Document window, chances are it isn't exactly what you had in mind. There are a number of different things you can do to modify the structure of the table, or how content appears within the table.

### Adding Rows or Columns

Change your mind about how many rows or columns that were needed? There are several ways to add new rows or columns on the fly as you work on your page design. The quickest way to add table elements is to use the functionality provided by the Insert bar. To add a column to your table, click in a table cell adjacent to where the column should be added, and then click on the Insert Column to the Left button or the Insert Column to the Right button on the Insert bar. Each time you press one of these buttons, additional columns will be added. In addition to columns, rows can be added by using the Insert Row Above and Insert Row Below buttons. If you know precisely how many rows or columns that need to be added, selecting Modify | Table | Insert Rows or Columns will allow you to add several table elements simultaneously.

If you get a little overly zealous and add too many rows or columns, they can be deleted. To delete a row or column, place the cursor in a cell within the row or column you wish to delete and then select Modify | Table | Delete Row or Modify | Table | Delete Column. Keep in mind that if you have merged or split (we will discuss this next) many table cells, deleting a row or column may provide unexpected results.

### Merging and Splitting Cells

As you gain more experience with tables, just creating new rows and columns will not always meet your needs. You may also need to take two table cells and merge them. For example, by merging cells in adjacent columns one cell can span two columns (as shown in Figure 3-4). To merge cells, select the cells you wish to merge by clicking in the first cell and then dragging to the last cell. Once the cells are highlighted, click on the Merge Cells button on the Property Inspector or select Modify | Table | Merge Cells.

figure | 3-4 |

Table cells in adjacent rows or columns may be merged or split.

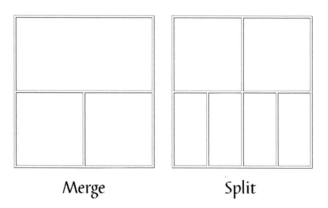

Merge          Split

In addition to merging cells, a single cell can be split into several cells. This simply works the exact opposite of merging cells. To split a cell, click in the cell you wish to split, and then click on the Split Cell button on the Property inspector (or select Modify | Table | Split Cell). This will open the Split Cell dialog box, where you can define how many rows or columns to split the cell into.

### Adjusting Width and Height

While working in the standard table design mode, you can adjust the physical width and height of the table, rows, and columns. To reshape the table, first select the table by clicking on one of the outside borders. Then, click and drag the resizing handles to resize the table to the width and height you had in mind. In addition to adjusting table size, the columns and rows can be resized. To adjust the width of a column or height of a row, click on the border between cells and drag to the desired location. In addition to dragging to resize, you can have more accurate sizing by using the width and height options in the Property Inspector. Later, we will discuss how Dreamweaver's layout mode can be used to more closely control tables used with page design elements.

## ▶ TRY THIS

Now that you have just enough information about creating tables to be dangerous, take a few moments to create a table on your own. Get acquainted with how tables can be adjusted by merging or splitting several table cells. Also, take a shot at working with the table properties, such as cell padding and cell spacing.

# WORKING IN LAYOUT MODE

Quite often in web design, tables are used to add structure to how content appears on the page. This structure is determined by how table columns and rows can be used in conjunction to provide the best possible visual layout. By default, HTML pages will only align all of the page's content in one big column. To create multicolumn designs, tables are often used. Understanding this problem, Dreamweaver has a layout mode for creating tables that are used to contain page design elements. To turn on the layout mode, click on the Layout mode button on the Insert bar. A blue bar will be added to the top of the Document window to denote that layout mode is currently enabled and to provide a link to exit back to standard mode.

**NOTE:** The tables you create in layout mode can also be created in standard mode. The difference is that layout mode has additional functionality that is commonly used when designing tables used for layout. Also, tables that are created in standard mode may be edited using layout mode, and vice versa.

## Creating a Layout Table

figure | 3-5

Using layout mode can help you build complex tables used to visually arrange the content of the page.

When working in layout mode there are two primary elements that can be added: the layout table and layout cell (shown in Figure 3-5). The layout table defines outside edges of the table that will contain the layout cells. Typically, the layout table you draw will be a similar size and shape to your overall page design. There are many different strategies for using layout tables. While it is possible to create many separate tables, the most common strategy is to use one table that will contain all of the elements on the page.

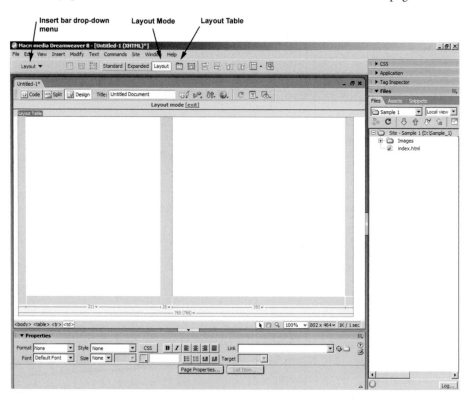

Follow these steps to create a layout table:

1. Select Table from the Insert bar drop-down menu (see Figure 3-5) and then click on the Layout mode button.

2.  Click on the Layout Table button on the Insert bar.

3.  Position the crosshair on the location of the page where the table should be created. It is important to note that if you are creating more than one table they may not overlap. However, as we will discuss later, a table can be "nested" completely inside another table.

4.  Click and drag to draw the table to the needed size and shape.

## Creating Layout Cells

Layout cells are used to define areas of content where they will appear on the page. For example, you might draw a layout cell along the left-hand side of your page to contain the navigation, and layout cell on the right to contain your page content. You may also want to draw a layout cell spanning the entire page at the top to contain a banner image and navigation, or a cell spanning the bottom to contain footer and copyright information. Obviously, there are seemingly an infinite number of combinations regarding how the cell can be added. There are two rules to keep in mind as you are drawing your layout cells. First, a cell may not be placed on the page without a companion layout table. If you draw a layout cell outside a table, a layout table will automatically be inserted for you. Second, much like layout tables cells may not overlap. To create a layout cell, follow these steps:

1.  Make sure the Insert bar drop-down is set on Layout.

2.  Click on the Draw Layout Cell button on the Insert bar.

3.  Position the crosshair on the location of the page, or within the layout table, where the cell should be created.

4.  Click and drag the cell to the size and shape you desire. Note that the cell will automatically snap to the edges of the table, rows, or columns. If you plan on drawing more than one cell, hold down the Ctrl key. This will allow you to draw multiple cells without having to hit the button each time.

While you can draw in cells in endless ways, try to avoid very complex designs that involve a great number of rows and columns. Keep in mind that as you add content the table cells will expand. The expanding table cells may result in an alignment that is less than favorable.

## Adjusting Layout Cells

You may discover that you have added a cell in the wrong place and want to move it to a different location. To move a layout cell, click on the edge of the cell and drag to the desired location. The cell will appear in outline until you release the mouse button and the cell has been placed. The same rules that applied when drawing a cell also apply to adjusting the layout of a cell.

In addition to moving a cell, it may be resized. To resize a cell, click once on the border of the cell. Then you can click and drag with the handles to expand the cell. Keep in mind that increasing the size of one cell may require you to decrease the size of adjacent cells.

## Working with Widths

In previous chapters we have discussed the importance of taking width into account when designing a page. A delicate balance when working with width issues is how you maintain control and still maximize the available space within the browser window. When working within the layout mode, you can use a width of a table column to help establish this control. The two width options available in layout view are Fixed-Width and Autostretch.

Fixed-width columns, as the name implies, will fix the width of a table column to a specific number of pixels. To ensure that the column will be presented at the intended width, Dreamweaver will automatically insert a spacer image. In general, a spacer image (also sometimes called a "glass block" or "pixel shim") is a completely transparent GIF image that is normally 1 pixel by 1 pixel. To set a column as fixed width, access the Column Header menu by clicking on the number that indicates the column's width and selecting Make Column Fixed-Width (see Figure 3-6). This will fix the table column at its current width. You may need to adjust the width value in the Property Inspector to reach the exact intended size.

figure | 3-6 |

Using the Column Header menu you can set a column width as a fixed width or auto-stretched.

Comparatively, autostretched columns will expand to fill any available space, dependent on the width of the browser window. For example, when inserting layout cells we talked about inserting a column on the left for navigation and a column on the right for content. If we were actually building a page like this, we might set the navigation bar to be fixed width and the content area to be autostretched. To set a column as autostretched, click on the Column Header menu (shown in Figure 3-6) and select Make Column Autostretched. When this selection is made, you may be asked to select an image to use as a spacer image. If you don't already have a spacer image, Dreamweaver can create one for you.

## TRY THIS

Before moving on, switch Dreamweaver into layout mode and create a new table on your own. Try creating several different layout cells of varying sizes and shapes. Also, explore how cell width can affect your design by switching cells back and forth from fixed width to autostretched.

# DESIGNING WITH TABLES

Now that you have a good feel for the mechanics of building tables, let's talk a little about how tables can be used to develop effective web designs. The funny thing about web design is that every designer will have their own techniques. For the next couple of topics I am going to discuss some commonly used techniques that can be further extended to use with your own web designs.

## Page Design Structure

As was mentioned throughout this chapter, tables are often used to provide a visual structure to the design elements and content on your pages. Effective web designers can use tables to compartmentalize and segregate portions of the design, navigation, and content that appear on their pages.

Even though there is any number of potential designs that can be created with tables, there is a particular layout so commonly used that it is worth mentioning here. If you spend any amount of time browsing on the Web you will probably come across a page, like that shown in Figure 3-7, that uses a left-hand style of navigation. This layout is relatively simple to pull off using tables. Typically,

figure | 3-7 |

Sites such as ibm.com use a very common left-hand style of navigation.

this design calls for three separate areas, or table cells. At the top of the page is usually a cell that contains a graphical banner and some global navigation for the site. The next element of this design is a cell that runs from the banner down the left of the page to contain navigation links. And last, there is a large area on the right that is used to hold the main body of content for the page.

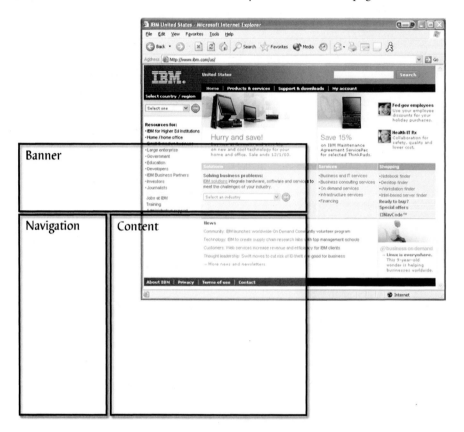

## Width: To Fix or Not To Fix

In this chapter we have looked at a number of different ways to set the width of a table column. This was certainly no accident. Ask any web designer and they will tell you their opinion on how web pages should be designed with respect to the width of the layout. There are two basic schools of thought on this subject (see Figure 3-8). On one side, some designers believe that page designs should always use a flexible layout that will fit the browser window no matter how wide it might be. So, if a user has their browser maximized to 1,280 pixels the layout should scale to fit. This is a good method because the design will always make the most out of the available screen real estate. In addition, this type of design can be forgiving to those people who don't have a large amount of space to work with. The downside of this design is that you will be giving up a great deal of control over how the page will look in a browser.

The other side of this debate is for the fixed-width layout. This type of layout, as you probably guessed, will fix the width of the entire page to a specific number of pixels. The advantage to this design is that you can maintain a greater amount of control over how the page will appear within the user's browser. The major weakness to this design methodology is that it will not be optimized for those people whose resolution or browser window is set either lower or higher than the width you designed for.

figure | 3-8 |

Sites such as wired.com use a flexible width layout, whereas yahoo.com uses a fixed width.

## Nesting Tables

A common technique for organization of content in a specific cell is to insert an additional table. Commonly referred to as nesting a table, this process is simply creating a table within a table cell (shown in Figure 3-9). For example, in a left-hand navigation scheme you would probably have one large table that defines the overall structure for the page. Then a separate nested table could be used as a left-hand table cell for the navigational options. By nesting tables, you can set separate padding, spacing, and border attributes for the table that contains all of your navigation options. The process of nesting a table is exactly the same as creating any other table. The only difference is that you need to create a new table within an already-created table cell.

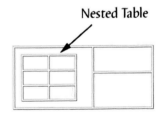

**Nested Table**

figure | 3-9 |

Using nested tables can help you further control how your content will lay out on screen.

While it is possible to nest tables several layers deep, I caution against it. Nesting multiple tables can have several adverse affects. First, it will greatly complicate your HTML code. Second, it can slow (albeit fractions of a second) the time a browser takes to download and render your page. And third, it can really add extra time when you need to make additions to your content or change your table structure. If you need tighter control over your tables, Cascading Style Sheets may provide the options you need.

## Adding the Aesthetic

The visual attributes of a table don't have to be just the stuff you drop in the cells. Tables can also have color or images applied to each cell. Adding color to a table cell can be a good low-cost way of adding visual interest to your page. By low-cost I mean that you don't have to spend any time creating graphics, and almost no file weight is added to affect download time. Cell color can also be used with data tables to help separate lines of data, or to separate the table heading from the rest of the table. To add a background color to a table cell, follow these steps:

1. Select the cell or cells you wish to color.
2. In the Property Inspector, select the Background color box next to the Bg label.
3. Use the color picker to select the desired color.

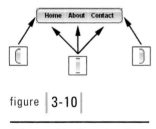

figure | 3-10 |

Using graphics in conjunction with table cell backgrounds can provide interesting visual elements.

In addition to adding color, you can add images to the background of a table cell. When an image is added to the background of a table cell, it will be tiled in a contiguous pattern to fill the entire cell. Using background images can be helpful when using design elements that are designed to be flexible. One common technique is to develop a graphic banner or button bar that uses a background image to give the illusion that the graphic fills a given area. Figure 3-10 shows a button bar that uses two graphics and a cell background graphic to give the impression that this is one solid component.

## SUMMARY

In this chapter we explored how to build tables that can be used to give visual structure to your data and content. As you continue to gain experience with this tool, you will discover new ways to implement tables with your design. The key elements to take from this chapter are what tables can be used for, how tables are constructed, and how tables can be adjusted to meet the needs of your design.

## in review

1. What are the three primary elements of a table? Also, describe how each is used to define the structure of a table.

2. What modes exist for working with tables in Dreamweaver? What are possible scenarios where you would use each?

3. What are the two types of widths that can be applied to layout cells?

4. What is a spacer image, and what type of layout is it typically used with?

5. What does it mean to merge or split a table cell?

6. Why is column width important?

7. What are nested tables?

## ↗ EXPLORING ON YOUR OWN

1. Create a new table designed to contain a data set of your choosing. Use the available heading options and background colors to make the table easy to understand.

2. Create a new page that utilizes tables as the main structural element.

3. Browse the Web and locate a page that uses a visual structure you like. Using Dreamweaver, try to imitate the structure of that page.

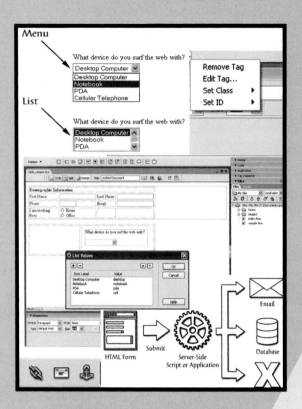

| Adding Interactivity with Forms |

*charting your course*

If there is one point I can't belabor enough it is that the Web is a medium designed to communicate. As you design and build your web sites, this communication is generally in one direction, from you to your audience. However, implementing forms provides a mechanism that allows your audience to communicate back with you. A form is an interface to a communication pipeline that exists between you (the designer, creator, or owner of a site) and the user. Anytime you wish to solicit a response from your end user, forms will certainly be involved. While forms are really nothing more than a series of interactive text boxes, checkboxes, or buttons, it is the information received from these forms that is of importance.

Forms can be implemented in many different ways, including creating surveys, shopping carts, or collaborative venues such as discussion forums. As we go through this chapter, we will explore the available building blocks you can use to build your web-based forms.

 *goals*

- **Learn about forms and how they can be created**
- **Discover the available form objects and how they are used**
- **Find out how to effectively design forms**

# FORMS: THE BIG PICTURE

All by itself, a web form serves very little purpose. Sure, the user can input text and click on buttons, but the information has nowhere to go. To capture your audience's responses, an additional server-side script or application is needed. While creating forms is not all that difficult—at least from the HTML perspective (you can devote an entire career of study concerning survey question development)—implementing forms is a little trickier because there are various options for where you can send your data, in addition to the mechanisms by which you implement those options.

Figure 4-1 illustrates the relationship between the form a user sees inside the web browser and the server application. These applications can be written in a number of different languages. Several years ago, most form-processing applications were provided as Common Gateway Interface (CGI) applications, which is nothing more than a bridge between two dissimilar technologies. However, today's forms are enabled by languages such as Active Server Pages (ASP), Java Server Pages (JSP), or ColdFusion. Later in this book, we will discuss developing dynamic applications that will allow you to take form input and store it in a database.

figure | 4-1 |

The HTML form is just one component of a system intended to accept input from the audience.

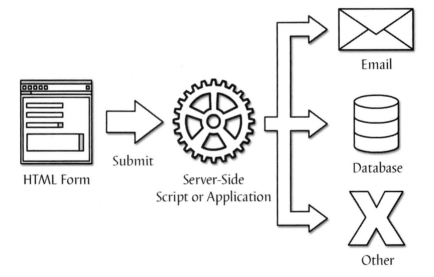

Email

HTML Form

Submit

Server-Side
Script or Application

Database

Other

So how does this work? The process is relatively simple, but the implementation can be complicated, depending on your particular needs. First, the end user enters the required information into the web form. Next, upon clicking on a "submit" button the information is sent to a server application for processing. How this information is processed varies from form to form. Some applications, commonly referred to as mail scripts, will simply take the responses and e-mail them to a predetermined location. Other forms can serve more complex needs, such as storing the data in a database or sending a confirmation e-mail to the person submitting the form. No matter how your server application will handle the information from the form, the objects used to create the forms will be the same.

**NOTE:** So where do you get a server-side script or application to process your form? As I mentioned earlier, there are several different options for these. The best first step is to contact the system administrator for your web server. This person should be able to tell you what technology is available to build a form-processing application. You may also want to ask if there are already existing scripts or applications you can use. Some web servers will provide a very simple server-side script (such as a mail form script) you can implement within your site—rather than having to scour the Web for one or attempting to write one yourself.

## Creating the Form

To kick off the construction of any form, the first thing that must be done is to define the form itself. In Dreamweaver, place the cursor on the page where you would like to start your form and click on the Form button on the Forms Insert bar. Clicking on this button will add a dashed red outline (shown as a dashed gray line in Figure 4-2) to your page. This outline serves as a container that defines the outer edges of the form. Any form objects you add within this form outline will then "belong" to this form. It is important to note that the outline that appears in the Document window will not appear in any way when the form is viewed in the browser. This outline element is provided so that you can visually see where the form exists on the page in Dreamweaver. I should also note that this outline cannot be scaled larger or smaller, but will continue to expand to fit the form object as you add elements (text boxes, radio buttons, and so on) to it.

Once a form has been added, there are several options that may be set using the Property Inspector. In the case of the form object, properly setting these attributes can be critical to the successful implementation of the form. The following properties can be set for the form object.

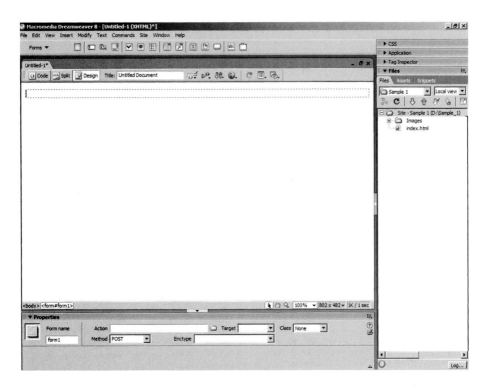

figure | 4-2 |

Adding a form to your page will appear as a dashed red outline in the Document window.

- *Form Name:* This setting allows you to add a unique name for your form. If you are using more than one form on a single page, adding a form name can help separate the forms. Adding a name attribute to the form will also allow you to reference the form using Dreamweaver behaviors.

- *Action:* This allows you to define the script or application that will process the form; that is, where the data will be sent. Upon submission of the form, the location specified here will receive the form data. If you have created your own script to handle the form processing, add the file name here. If you are using a "canned" script you have downloaded or received form your web administrator, it will likely include instructions for the location that should be entered here.

- *Target:* This property works exactly like the target property for hyperlinks that was discussed in Chapter 2. Typically, this option will be left blank unless you have a specific need to target a new browser window or frame.

- *Class:* This property, which is available for most of the form objects, allows you to specify a style that has been defined using Cascading Style Sheets (CSS). We will discuss CSS later in this book.

- *Method:* Defining this property specifies how the form's data will be transmitted to the server-side script or application. The method used here will be dictated by the script or application that will handle the processing. There are two options for this property:

  - ○ *Post:* The Post method is one of the more common methods, but can be the most difficult to comprehend. When submitting a form using the Post method, the data for each form object will be transmitted via the HTTP request. If this doesn't make any sense to you, that is perfectly okay. The real thing to understand is that the form data will be sent completely behind the scenes, without the end user ever really seeing anything.

  - ○ *Get:* The Get method is less common, but no less powerful. Using this method, the form data is actually added to the URL you are requesting. For example, if you have a single text field named *textfield1* containing the text sample, this information will be added to the end of the URL and will appear as *?textfield1=sample*. Dependent on the server-side script, this data may be visible to the end user.

- *Enctype:* This property determines how the forms data will be encoded when transmitted. Typically, this option will be left blank unless your script or application requires its use.

## Text Field

Probably the most common and versatile form object is the text field. The text field object is used when you want your user to provide input in the way of text or numbers. This form object is often used to capture simple text information such as names or e-mail addresses, but can also be used in conjunction with web applications to include search-keyword fields or log-in and password fields.

To add a text field to the form, place the cursor inside the form outline and click on the Text Field button on the Insert bar. The following detail the text field options that may be set using the Properties panel.

● *Name:* This property is used to provide an identifying name for the text field. It is important that each text field on your form be named uniquely in order for the form to function properly. Dreamweaver will automatically assign a unique name to a new text field, but you should get into the habit of naming your form elements now. Keep in mind that a form object's name cannot contain spaces or special characters. It is also important to know that the name you provide here will be used as the identifier when the field's content is submitted to the server-side script or application for processing.

● *Character Width:* This property will set the total number of characters wide the text field can display at once on screen.

● *Max Characters:* This property will set the total number of characters (including spaces) a text field can contain. The maximum number of characters can be more or less than the value used with the character width.

● *Type:* This property is used to determine how the text field will function and display on screen. There are three possible options (shown in Figure 4-3).

### Single Line Text Field

figure | 4-3 |

### Password Text Field

Using the Properties panel, a text field can be set to one of three different types.

### Multi Line Text Area

○ *Single line:* This type is used for information that is relatively short, such as a name, e-mail address, or phone numbers.

○ *Password:* This type is specifically intended when you want to capture a user's password. Because you never know who is looking over your shoulder, this text type of text field will display all asterisks or bullets as characters when the user types data into it.

○ *Multi line:* This type is technically not a text field at all, but is considered a text area. We will cover the particular options available with text areas a little later on.

● *Initial Value:* The information you add for this property will be used as the default value of the text field when the form is first displayed in the web browser. For example, if you are requesting that the user enter a date you may want to pre-populate the text field with the current day's date.

## Hidden Field

Interestingly enough, the hidden field form object is actually the text field's distant cousin. By this I mean that the hidden field is treated exactly the same way as the text field when submitted to the server. In fact, you can think of the hidden field as a text field with an initial value that cannot be changed by the end user. Other than the form element itself, the hidden field is the only form object your audience will never interact with. In reality, they will never really know that it is there—unless of course they use the View Source option in the browser to view the HTML code of the page.

So, if you can't see it and you can't interact with it, what good is it? The hidden form element is often used to send information about the form that will be used by the server-side application to change how the form data is processed. For example, many canned e-mail scripts will use a hidden field to determine where form responses will be e-mailed rather than hard-wiring the e-mail address into the script itself. This allows scripts and applications to remain flexible and reusable.

To add a hidden field to your page, place the cursor inside the form outline and click on the Hidden Field button on the Insert bar. Because the hidden field is, well… hidden, it will appear in the Document window as one of Dreamweaver's invisible element icons (see Figure 4-4). The following detail the few hidden field options that may be set using the Properties panel.

● *Name:* Just like the text field, each hidden field must have a unique name to identify the information submitted.

● *Value:* The information provided here will be stored within the hidden field and sent to the server when the form is submitted.

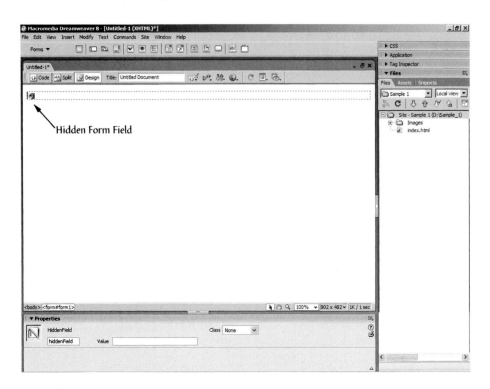

figure | **4-4** |

The hidden form element is used to store values that are invisible to the end user.

## Text Area

If your form calls for the user to provide copious amounts of textual information, the text area is the form object for you. While it is very similar in nature to the text field object, it has one big difference. You can define the physical display attributes of the text area (shown in Figure 4-5). However, there is no maximum number of characters.

To add a text area to your page, place the cursor inside the form outline and click on the Text Area button on the Insert bar. The following detail the text area options that may be set using the Properties panel.

● *Name:* If you haven't got the point yet, each form element should have a unique name. Put it here.

● *Character Width:* Just like the text field, this determines how many characters wide the text box will display at once. The one difference is that this value also determines when the text will wrap, dependent on the selected wrap option.

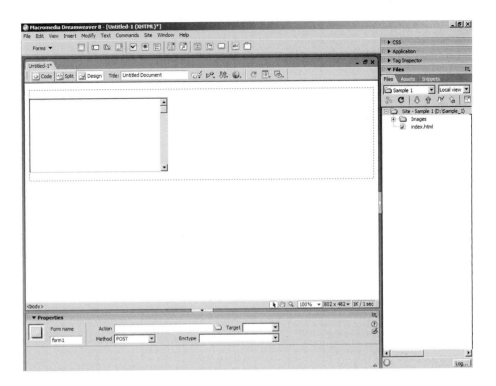

- *Type:* By default, the text area object will have the *Multi line* option selected. If either the *Single line* or Password options are selected, the text area object will automatically convert itself to a text field.

- *Number of lines:* This property determines how many lines of text will be visible at once. If the total number of lines is exceeded, vertical scroll bars will be enabled.

- *Wrap:* This property determines how text will wrap inside the text area object. There are four primary settings.

  ○ *Default:* While the default wrap value was originally intended to be off, in reality it will vary dependent on the browser. Best practice is to select from one of the next three options.

  ○ *Off:* A text area using this option will not wrap text when it reaches the edge of the text area. The line will continue to expand to the right until the user hits Return (or Enter) to move to the next line. If this is your desired effect, make certain a character width value has been added.

  ○ *Virtual:* This option will make the text inside the text area appear as though the text wraps from one line to the next.

figure | 4-5 |

The text area is used when one line simply will not do.

When a line of text reaches the right edge of the text area, it will visually wrap down to the next line. However, when this information is submitted no line breaks will be added, and the information will be submitted as one long string of text.

○ *Physical:* Within the browser, the physical text wrap will visually appear the same as the virtual wrapping option. The difference is that physical wrapping will insert line breaks for each line when the information is submitted.

● *Initial Value:* Just like the text field object, this determines the default value of the form object when it is first displayed in the web browser.

## Checkbox

The checkbox form object is just like a light switch: it is either on or off—no in-between state. Typically there are two types of questions that checkboxes are used with. First is the simple true/false question. For example, "Check here if you like pizza." Using a checkbox here will allow your user to answer the question with a single click of the mouse. The second, and possibly more common implementation, is to use the checkboxes in groups (shown in Figure 4-6). For example, you may ask a question that has several responses. This would be a "select all that apply" type of scenario.

figure | 4-6 |

What are your favorite colors? (select all that apply)

☐ Red

☑ Blue

☑ Yellow

☑ Green

Using checkboxes in groups will allow users to select several items.

To add checkboxes to your page, place the cursor inside the form outline and click on the Checkbox button on the Insert bar. The following detail the checkbox options that may be set using the Properties panel.

● *Name:* While you already know that it is important to provide unique names for your form objects, the checkbox has one additional consideration. You may, on occasion, have two identical sets of checkbox groups. For these situations you may want to adopt a clear naming convention for your form objects.

- *Checked Value:* The information provided for this option will be submitted as the value of the checkbox if it is checked (selected). If the checkbox is not selected, no information will be submitted.

- *Initial State:* This option determines if the checkbox will be checked or unchecked by default.

## Radio Button

If checkboxes are used to allow users to select more than one item from a group of options, how do you constrain the user to just one? This is where radio buttons come into play. Sometimes you will find a situation where you want to ask the user a multiple-choice question, to which there should only be a single response. Radio buttons achieve this by only allowing one button in a group to be selected at any given time (shown in Figure 4-7). A key concept to remember is that radio buttons should always be used in groups of two or more (because if they are used individually a checkbox should be used instead).

What is 2 + 2?

- ○ 1
- ○ 2.5
- ○ 3
- ◉ 4

figure | 4-7 |

___

Radio buttons should always be used in groups.

Radio buttons can be added to your page in one of two different methods. First, to add a single radio button to your page place the cursor inside the form outline and click on the Radio Button button on the Insert bar.

The second method of adding radio buttons is by adding an entire group of buttons at once. Clicking on the Radio Group button on the Insert bar will summon the dialog box shown in Figure 4-8, where you can add the names and values of the radio group's buttons. In this dialog box you can define the name of the radio group in the Name field, use the Add (+) and Remove (-) buttons to add additional radio buttons, or use the Up Arrow and Down Arrow buttons to reorder the options. As each radio button is added to the group, you will need to define the label and value. The label is simply the text that appears next to the button, which has no effect on how the button functions. In addition, the Value field determines what information is transmitted for this option when the form is submitted. The last set of options in this dialog box allows you to lay out the radio button group using either line breaks or tables.

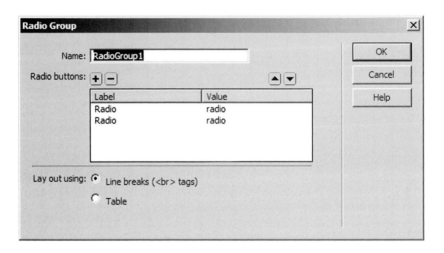

figure | 4-8 |

Using the Radio Group dialog box, you can add several radio buttons at once.

No matter which method you use to add radio buttons, the names and values are altered the same way (using the Properties panel). The following detail the radio button options that may be set.

● *Name:* Nowhere on your form is the assigning of names more important than it is for radio buttons. The name you choose here is what makes a single radio button belong to a group of buttons. All buttons in the same group need to have the exact same name. It will be the values of the radio buttons that are unique within each named set.

● *Checked Value:* The information provided here will be transmitted if this radio button has been selected. For a group of radio buttons, there will only be one value submitted.

● *Initial State:* This property will determine whether the radio button is selected by default when first viewed inside the browser.

## List/Menu

Radio buttons work well when you have multiple-choice questions, but what happens when you have a large number of options? The inherent drawback to using radio buttons on a form is that they can consume a fair amount of screen real estate. So, if space is a concern and you have a significant number of possible responses the list or menu form object is the solution. The menu form object works by collapsing all of the possible options into one compact list that expands when clicked (see Figure 4-9). This provides just enough functionality to the user, allowing them to make their selection and then remove the remainder of the options from view.

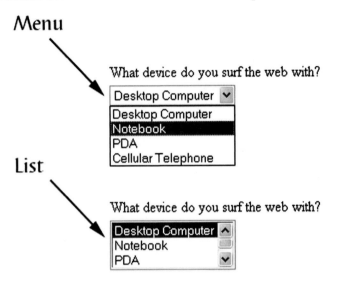

figure | 4-9 |

Selecting either the Menu or the List option will provide two different appearances.

This form object also comes in an additional flavor, referred to as a list. The list object is used when you have a very large number of options where multiple responses may be possible. The main drawback of this object is that it can take up considerably more space than the menu type of the same object. However, the trade-off is that you can pack quite a bit of information into a list object.

To add a list or menu to your page, place the cursor inside the form outline and click on the List/Menu button on the Insert bar. The Properties panel will provide slightly different options based on whether a list or menu type is being used. If a particular property is not available, it will appear grayed out. The following detail the list/menu options that may be set using the Properties panel.

- *Name:* Just like any other form element, a unique name is necessary.

- *Type:* This is where you make the separation. Do you want a menu or a list?

- *List Values:* Clicking on the List Values button will summon a dialog box (shown in Figure 4-10) you can use to define the possible options for this form element. Just like the radio group dialog box, use the Add, Remove, and Up and Down arrow options to modify the available options. The information you provide as the Item Label is what will appear in the list or menu. What you enter as the value will be submitted for the selected item.

● *Initially Selected:* This property allows you select the item that will first appear selected when the form is displayed in the browser.

● *Height:* This property, which is only used by the list object, defines how many items will be viewable at once. If you have more items than room to display them, scroll bars will be provided.

● *Allow Multiple:* This property, which is only available to list form objects, will allow your audience to select and submit more than one option. For a user to make multiple selections, they will need to hold down the Shift or Ctrl key while clicking on the desired items.

figure | 4-10 |

List Values dialog box.

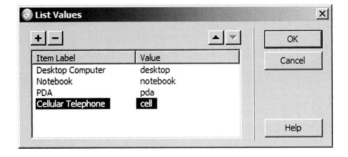

There are two things to remember when using a list or menu. First, keep your item labels short. The length of the longest label determines the total width of the list or menu form object. The longer the form object, the more space you are losing. Another helpful tip for using a list form object with multiple selections enabled is to provide some type of instructions. This type of form element is relatively rare, so don't automatically assume that your audience will know how to use it.

## Jump Menus

Although not intended for this use, the menu form object has become a common navigational element found on many sites.

Dreamweaver refers to these objects as "jump menus," but in reality it is just a menu form object with some JavaScript attached to it.

This jump menu object works by assigning a location to each item on a menu form object. Then, when the user clicks on a particular item it acts as a hyperlink, sending the user to the intended destination. The jump menu can be an effective navigational tool if your site has several distinct areas of content or a handful of pages that are commonly visited by your audience. In practice there is any number of uses for this form element.

To create a jump menu in Dreamweaver, click on the Jump Menu button on the Insert bar. This will open the Insert Jump Menu dialog box (shown in Figure 4-11), where you can adjust the following options.

figure | **4-11** |

The Insert Jump Menu dialog box.

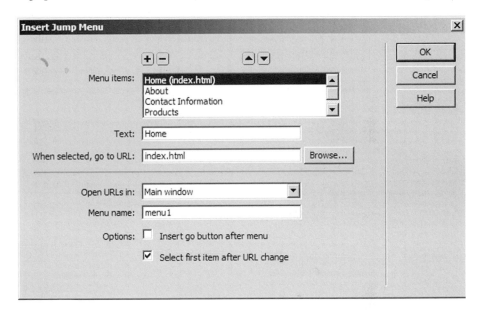

- *Menu Items:* Using the Add (+) and Remove (-) buttons, add the options you would like to have appear in the menu.

- *Text:* This option defines the text that will appear for each item in the menu. If you select the individual items in the Menu items area, you can modify the text for each.

- *When selected, go to URL:* This option defines where the browser will be pointed when each item is selected. This can be either an absolute or relative link.

- *Open URLs in:* If you are using frames (which we will discuss in a future chapter), this option determines within which frame the requested page will appear.

● *Menu name:* This defines the unique name for this form object.

● *Options:* There are two additional options for the jump menu objects.

○ Instead of having the menu item trigger the move to another page, you can have Dreamweaver add an adjoining Go button. Adding this Go button makes navigating with the menu a two-step process for the user. They must first select the desired destination and then click on Go.

○ A common method for designing a jump menu is to use the first item as some type of instruction, such as "Select a location." By selecting *Select first item after URL change* you can add some type of prompt as the first item in the list.

figure | 4-12 |

## File Field

Using the file field form object, you can select files from your local workstation.

The file field form object is one of those weird elements you may never actually use. This form object is intended for situations when the user needs to select a file from their local workstation and insert the file path into the text field (shown in Figure 4-12). While a practical use probably doesn't immediately jump into your

mind, it can be useful when developing server-based applications. For example, some people develop applications that allow their users to upload images or documents to the web server that necessitates the use of the form field form object.

To add a file field to the form, place the cursor inside the form outline and click on the File Field button on the Insert bar. The following detail the file field options that may be set using the Properties panel.

- *Name:* Use a unique name.

- *Character Width:* This property defines how many characters wide the adjoining text field will appear.

- *Max Characters:* This property defines how many characters the adjoining text field may contain.

## Buttons

I think by this point we all know what buttons are and what they usually look like. However, not all buttons are the same. When working with a form, there are three types of buttons (shown in Figure 4-13) that can be used.

The first type of button is the submit button. Whenever there is a form that sends data to the server, there is almost always a submit button. A submit button does just what it sounds like: it submits the form data to some location. Anytime you have a form that contains a submit type of button, it will automatically submit that form when clicked.

The next type of button, the reset button, is much like the submit button in that respect. A form that contains a reset type of button will automatically clear all the form objects to their default or starting values once clicked. This can be helpful for forms that are relatively long. It gives the user a quick way to clear the data in the form and "start over."

The last type of button is just a plain ordinary button. All by itself, a button that is not a submit or reset button really doesn't do anything. For this type of button to serve a purpose, coding will need to be added. Later in this book we will discuss Dreamweaver behaviors that can be added to buttons in order to give them life.

To add a button to your form, place the cursor inside the form outline and click on the Button button on the Insert bar. The following detail the button options that may be set using the Properties panel.

figure | 4-13 |

There are three
types of buttons.

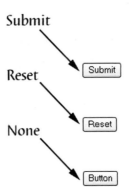

- *Name:* While a button's name should still be unique, it serves very little purpose as far as the form is concerned. The button name will be used if you use JavaScript or similar scripting to enhance interactivity.

- *Label:* This property determines what text will appear on top of the button. By default, this will be Submit, Reset, or Button. However, you can also enter your own text.

- *Action:* The option you select here will determine how the button will function with the form, as described earlier. The *Submit form* and *Reset form* options are relatively obvious. However, the None option is used to create plain buttons that initially have no function.

**DON'T**
**GO THERE**

While you may feel that the default button labels of *Submit* and *Reset* insult your creative integrity, it is important that you not stray too far from the concept. Many users of the Web have come to understand what buttons with particular labels have come to mean. If you are going to substitute your own names for these buttons, make certain it will be completely obvious to the user what the buttons will do when clicked.

## Accessibility Objects

Dotted throughout this book are suggested techniques for increasing the universal accessibly of your web designs. Designing and building HTML forms is certainly no exception. Dreamweaver provides two form objects used expressly for this purpose: *fieldset* and *label*. At the beginning of this book I mentioned that we wouldn't be going into the specifics of HTML coding. Unfortunately, Dreamweaver's implementation of this object is not as elegant as you might expect (and the documentation isn't much better), so we are going to quickly examine these two objects at the code level.

The *fieldset* element is used to group a series of form objects that may be related. For example, if you needed to ask for personal information such as name, address, and phone number you would create a *fieldset* to contain these items. To insert the *fieldset* HTML code, click on the Fieldset button on the Dreamweaver Insert bar. Next, move to Dreamweaver's code view and rearrange the *fieldset* tags to contain the form elements. If you look at the HTML code sample in Figure 4-14, you will see three form elements contained by an opening and closing *fieldset* tag. In addition to the *fieldset* tag, there is a tag called *legend*. This tag is used to name the *fieldset*. In this case the legend reads "Personal Information." For a person using a screen reader application to use this page the information contained within the legend tag will be read aloud.

figure | 4-14 |

The *fieldset* and *legend* HTML code.

The *label* element is used to identify each form object on the page. For people who use a screen reader application to use this form, the label information will allow them to know what information should be provided. To add this information using Dreamweaver, highlight the text you want to use as a label for the form object, and then click on the Label button on the Insert bar. Next, you will need to go into code view to add the *for* attribute. The *for* attribute is to determine which form object the label is labeling. The information used for the *for* attribute should be identical to the ID of the form object. Note in Figure 4-15 that the *label* tags have been added to all text field descriptions.

figure | 4-15 |

The *label* HTML tag with the appropriate *for* attributes.

# DESIGNING FORMS

The process of developing a form is both a science and an art. Just like anything else you do on the Web, plan out your form before you start to build. This will save you some time in the long run. The following are some questions you may want to ask before building your forms.

- *Why am I using a form?* While it may sound simple, sometimes the primary goal of a web form is lost. Most people very much dislike filling out forms—be they on the Web or elsewhere. This means that you need a compelling reason for someone to use your form.

- *Who do I want to fill out the form?* Even if you are opening your form for response from the general public, it is still important that you have an understanding of your intended audience. For example, if your form is intended for children, or possibly persons from other countries, you may want to adjust your form accordingly.

- *What information do I require from the form?* Take some time to list the questions you would like to place on the form. Then go through item by item and decide: (1) if the question is needed and (2) if the information is absolutely necessary for the successful submission of the form. Like I said, no one likes filling out a form, so keep it as short as possible.

- *What happens when the form is submitted?* After a user fills in all the blanks and clicks on the Submit button, your server-side script or application will take over. Possibly this script sends an e-mail or maybe it stores the responses in a database. In any event, take some time to plan what exactly needs to happen with the information. Also, don't forget about your user. When a user clicks on Submit, what do they see next?

## How to Choose the Proper Form Object

Once you have an understanding of what questions you need to ask, the next step is to figure out how to ask them. Figure 4-16 shows an example of five different ways of asking the same question. So which one works best? Unfortunately, there is no one-size-fits-all solution to selecting form elements. The following are a few concepts to help you choose the proper form objects.

- *Does the user need to choose more than one option?* The quickest way to narrow down the possible form objects to use is to rule out the ones that will not work. If you are allowing the user more than one response, either the checkboxes or list object will work the best.

● *What will require the fewest number of clicks?* The form should be as easy as possible for your audience to use. For the example in Figure 4-16, a menu form object would technically work. However, given that there are only two possible responses the menu object requires on additional click over using the radio buttons.

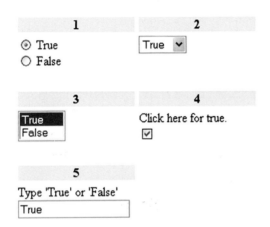

figure | 4-16 |

There is almost always more than one way to ask a question.

● *Would the user survey the possible options, or search for a specific option?* Sometimes your users will approach the form differently depending on the question. For example, if you have a question that is something like "Select the item that best describes your job:," the user will want to read and evaluate each possible response before making a selection. Conversely, if you ask a question such as "Select the state you live in:," the user will not need to evaluate the responses, they will just search for the exact item that corresponds to where they live.

● *What are the chances the user could make a mistake?* Even the savviest of Internet users will make mistakes when filling out a web form. Begin to think about how you can use the right form elements to reduce the likelihood of this happening. For example, having the user select the state they live in from a menu is better than having them type it into a text field. You never know what someone might type into a text field.

## Using Tables to Lay Out Forms

The next step in the form design process is to establish how each of the form elements will be positioned on the page. Tables are a great mechanism for creating effective form layouts. Using tables, you can help make the form easier to use, add some visual interest, and establish consistent alignment of form objects.

Figure 4-17 shows an example form that uses a table to establish a visual structure for the form. There are a few things to take note of in this example. First, note how the form has been visually broken into two parts: the "Demographic Information" and the "Issue Information." By grouping similar elements and adding appropriate heading information, this will clue the user as to the type of information that will be requested.

figure | 4-17 |

Using tables can help provide visual structure for your forms.

**Trouble Ticket**

| Demographic Information | | |
| --- | --- | --- |
| First Name: [            ] | Last Name: [            ] |
| Phone: [            ] | Email: [            ] |
| I am working from: ○ Home  ○ Office | |

| Issue Information | |
| --- | --- |
| I am having problems with my: | Computer ▾ |
| Additional Comments: | |
| [                                              ] | |
| Submit | |

Next, lean back and take a wider look at the form. Note how the table borders, background color, fonts, and font color all add visual interest to the form. Using these elements, you can make the form a little less daunting and tie it to the visual style of your site.

Last, examine how the Last Name and Email fields appear in a second column of the form. Both of these items align consistently to the right, even though the preceding elements (First Name and Phone) are of varying lengths. As you arrange form elements on the page, take some time to make sure that all of your form objects have a constant alignment to one another. This makes it easier for the user to figure out what fields go with what labels.

In the previous chapter we discussed how tables can be inserted and adjusted using Dreamweaver. The process is exactly the same when working with forms, but there is one key point to keep in mind. When populating tables with form elements, either the table needs to be completely inside the form outline or the form outline completely inside a table cell. Figure 4-18 shows an example of each scenario. While technically possible, it can be unwieldy to work with forms that only span a few cells, columns, or rows within a table. Thus, the example in the upper part of the page in Figure 4-18 is typically preferable.

figure | 4-18 |

Tables should be completely inside a form outline or the form outline should be completely inside a table cell.

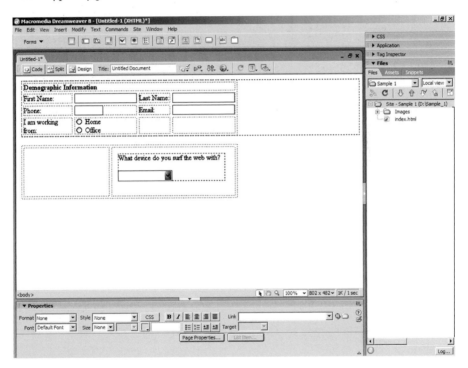

## SUMMARY

In this chapter we have explored how you can develop forms using Dreamweaver. The core concepts you should take away from this chapter are how a form works, the objects that make up a form, and things to think about when designing a form. While building web forms is not the most exciting thing you will do on the Web, just remember that forms are the only way your audience can communicate back to you.

## in review

1. What is a form, and how does it work?

2. What important properties are set when inserting a form?

3. What is the difference between a text field and a text area?

4. What is an instance where you should use radio buttons instead of checkboxes?

5. What is the difference between a menu and a list?

6. What is a jump menu, and how is it used?

7. What are some things to think about when selecting form elements?

8. Describe how tables can be used when designing forms.

## ↗ EXPLORING ON YOUR OWN

1. Think of a fictional company, and develop a product order form or customer satisfaction survey. Try to use many of the available form objects. Experiment with the available properties for each form item.

2. Create a set of simple HTML pages and add a jump menu that allows you to jump from page to page. Try making one of the options go to another site on the Web.

## notes

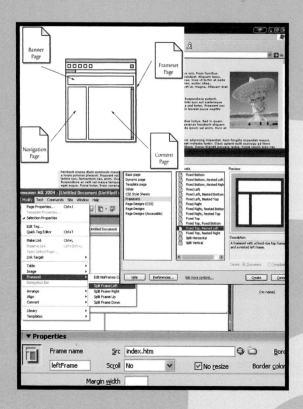

| Dividing Pages with Frames |

*charting your course*

Let me start this chapter by making a deal with you. We can explore how frames are created as long as you promise not to abuse or misuse the knowledge. Agreed?

At first glance, frames seem to be the solution to many design issues, but keep in mind that there are *huge* trade-offs—a lot of negatives that go along with the positives. When frames were first introduced in the mid 1990s, many web designers jumped on the bandwagon and began designing all their pages using frames. However, we quickly found that frames introduced a number of new challenges. It is these challenges that have made frames one of the most widely misused HTML capabilities. Frames are a tool that should be left in a glass case with a warning sign reading "Break glass only in case of emergency."

If frames are so bad, why use them at all? Frames have a very specific niche that only they alone can fill. Using frames when designing your pages allows you to divide the browser window into multiple compartments, each acting much like a small browser window in itself. So, as you can imagine, this type of technology does have practical applications. With all that said, we can now begin to explore how frame pages are built using Dreamweaver.

 *goals*

- Explore the parts needed to establish a frames page
- Discover how frames are built
- Explore the available options when working with frames
- Find out how to design your navigation to use frames
- Learn about the drawbacks to using frames

# FRAMESET ANATOMY 101

The first concept to understand is that a frames page is not one file. Actually, a frames page is constructed from many different HTML pages that are all displayed at once using a frameset (we call it that because the actual HTML code word that does it is <FRAME-SET>). Figure 5-1 illustrates how the component pages are used together to create a frames page.

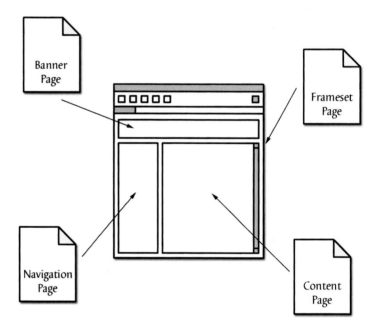

figure | 5-1 |

A frames page is constructed from multiple files.

Before we move on, let's first get the vocabulary down. All pages that use frames have two fundamental parts: the frame and the frameset. The frameset is a special HTML page that defines the overall layout of the frames and the pages that will appear in each frame. The pages that appear within a frame are nothing more than standard HTML pages that, in reality, have no real knowledge that they have been "framed." For this reason, you can frame almost any page, whether it was designed to be used with frames or not.

NOTE: If you are designing your entire site to use frames, the frameset page should be named with whatever is being used as the default document for each directory. For example, default pages are commonly named *index.html, default.html,* or *welcome.html.* Check with your web server administrator for the correct file name to use.

## Columns and Rows

As long as we are exploring frames vocabulary, let's add two more terms to the list. All framesets are divided into either rows or columns, much like you would divide a table. As you can see in Figure 5-2, adding rows to your frameset will create horizontal frames and adding columns will add vertical frames.

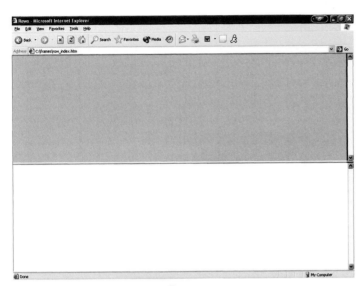

**Rows**

figure | 5-2 |

Framesets can be divided into rows or columns.

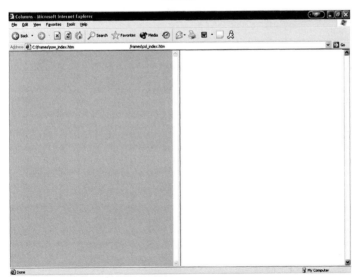

**Columns**

If splitting a page into rows and columns is not sophisticated enough, you can further divide frames using something called nested frames. Nested frames work just like nested tables, in that they are simply frameset documents within a frame. Nested frames, like those shown in Figure 5-3, are commonly used when you want multiple rows within one column, or vice versa.

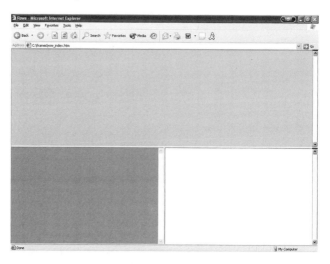

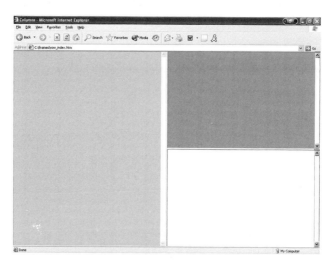

figure | 5-3 |

Using nested frames will create much more complicated framesets.

## Sizing and Scrolling

Something to keep in mind is that each time a frame is divided using rows and columns you will be reducing the total amount of browser space available to display the page in the frame. To overcome this problem, each frame can use resizing or scrolling. By default, all frames are resizable. This means that the end user can click and drag the border between frames to either shrink or expand the frame. In addition, each frame can utilize scroll bars that will act exactly like those on the browser window. By default, frames will have either horizontal or vertical scroll bars available if the page's content is more than can be displayed within the frame at once. If your page design takes into account the size of the frames, resizing and scrolling can be independently disabled or enabled for each frame.

# BUILDING FRAMES

A big advantage to using visual editing tools is that the creation of framesets is a simple process. Dreamweaver provides three separate ways to build a frames page: dragging a new frame, splitting a frame, or using a predefined frameset layout. Each of these methods is used in different ways depending on the needs of your design. No matter how you choose to build it, something to remember is that as you split your page into multiple frames the actual frameset file will be automatically coded and created for you.

## Dragging a New Frame

The first method for adding frames to your page is by dragging the frame border to the desired location of the Document window. Dragging new frames is often used to add simple rows or columns to your page on the fly. First, check that frame borders are enabled by selecting View | Visual Aids | Frame Borders. Next, to add a new frame on your page move the mouse over the outside border (shown in Figure 5-4) of the Document window until the pointer turns to a double-headed arrow. Now you can click and drag the frame border to the desired location. Dragging the top or bottom border will create new frame rows, and dragging the left-hand or right-hand border will create columns. In addition, you can also simultaneously add rows and columns to your page. To do this, move your mouse over the corner of the outside border until the pointer turns to a four-headed arrow. Now you can click and drag the border of your new column or row to the desired location on the page.

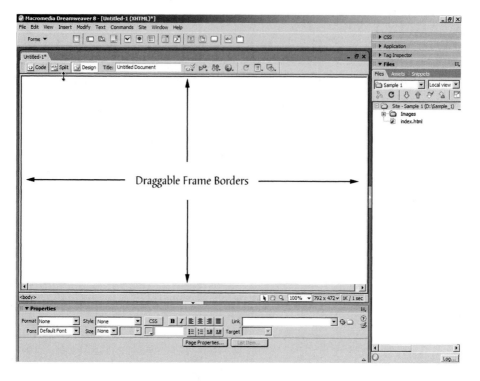

Draggable Frame Borders

figure | 5-4 |

By clicking and dragging the outside frame border, you can split your page into multiple frames.

## Splitting a New Frame

If your design calls for a slightly more complex frameset, you can "split" your page into frames or nested frames (see Figure 5-5). To split the page into multiple frames, place your cursor on the page or frame you want to split. To do so, select Modify | Frameset | Split Frame Left or Split Frame Right to add a new column. Or, you can add a new row by selecting Modify | Frameset | Split Frame Up or Split Frame Down. If you have an existing frame layout, this same process can also be used to add nested frames. In the case of nested frames, you will be splitting the frame wherever the cursor is currently located.

NOTE: If you need to create nested frames, keep in mind that there is no real way to "merge" two frames like you would with table cells. For this reason, create all of your rows or columns first, and then split these frames to add any nested frames you may need.

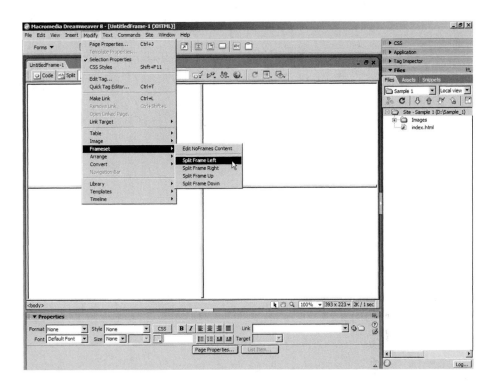

## Predefined Framesets

In addition to creating your own custom frameset, Dreamweaver offers a number of predetermined frameset layouts you can use. These framesets are provided as templates of the most common frame layouts used by web designers. In reality, if one of the predetermined framesets will not work you may want to reevaluate the complexity of your design. In addition, even though these framesets have already been established the design can still be modified to fit your particular needs.

There are two methods for using predetermined framesets. First, you can use the Insert bar to add a frameset for a new or existing document. To do this, click on the Frames button in the Layout category of the Insert bar. Then select from the list of options shown in Figure 5-6. Once the selection is made, the frameset will be added to the Document window.

In addition to the Insert bar, you can start a new page using a predetermined frameset template. To start a new page with this method, perform the following.

1. Select File | New. This will open the New Document dialog box, shown in Figure 5-7.

figure | 5-5 |

Using the split frame method, you can create custom framesets.

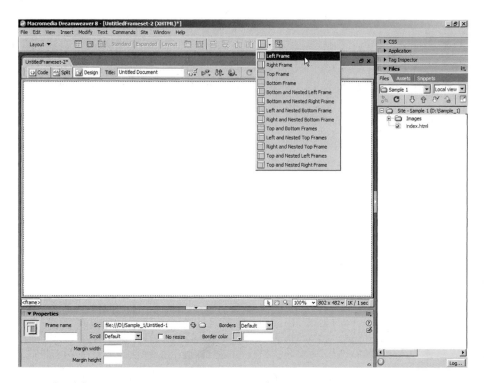

figure | 5-6 |

You can use the Frames button on the Insert bar to add a predefined frameset.

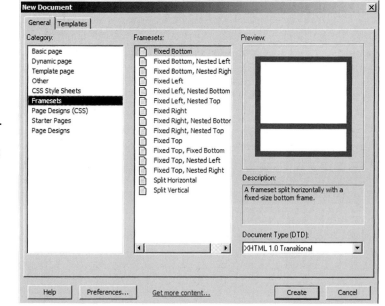

figure | 5-7 |

You can start a new page using a predefined frameset as a template.

2. Click on the Category named Framesets.

3. Click on the desired frameset template. If the names of the framesets don't make sense, a preview and description will appear on the right when each option is selected.

4. Click on the Create button. This will start a new frameset and associated files in the Document window.

## Removing Frames

Removing a frame is even easier than creating a frame. I should also note that the process for removing a frame is exactly the same regardless of how it was created. To delete a frame, click and drag the frame's border off the Document window. Or, in the case of a nested frame you can click and drag the frame's border to the border of the parent frame.

▶ **TRY THIS**

Before moving on, start a new document and add a few frames. Take a few minutes to experiment with the different methods for creating frames. Try adding frames in multiple ways on the same page. You may also want to explore the available predefined frameset layouts Dreamweaver offers.

# WORKING WITH FRAMES

Now that you can build the frameset, let's take a look at how it can be finely tuned to meet your design needs. This is where working with frames can get a little tricky. Even though there are only a handful of properties that can be set, the process is complicated because each frame's properties are set independently. In addition, even though the "simple" process of saving a file takes some extra planning when working with frames.

## Selecting Frames

Before you can do anything to a frame, it must first be selected. Because a frame is not a physical element on a page—it is really a structural element that defines the edges of several adjoining pages—the selection of just one frame can be a little awkward. Fortunately, Dreamweaver offers the Frames panel (shown in Figure 5-8) to make this process easier. The Frames panel can be summoned by selecting Window | Frames.

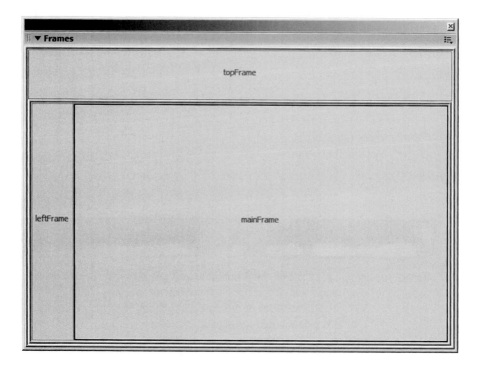

figure | 5-8 |

The Frames panel is a utility to help you tell what frame you are currently working with.

The Frames panel allows you to select frames, framesets, and nested framesets. To select a single frame using the Frames panel, click inside the box that represents the desired frame. Or, to select a frameset click on the thick outer border of the frames. This border will exist for nested framesets as well.

As different elements are selected, you will see two changes in the Dreamweaver workspace. First, a dotted line will appear around the frame or frames that have been selected. This will provide a visual clue as to what frame you are currently working with. The other significant change is with the Property Inspector. The available options within the Property Inspector will change depending on the chosen frame or frameset.

## Frameset Properties

In addition to separating the browser window into frames, the frameset also has several properties that can be used to adjust behavior based on the end user's browser size or based on the content within the frame. The following list details available options (shown in Figure 5-9) that may be set using the Property Inspector when a frameset has been selected.

- *Borders:* This property determines if borders are displayed for this frameset. The available options are Yes, No, and Default. The Default setting will allow the web browser to decide if borders are displayed. It is usually best, however, to set it to either Yes or No.

- *Border Color:* This property is used to set the color of the frameset borders.

- *Border Width:* This property specifies the width of the border that surrounds the frameset.

- *RowCol Selection:* This selection mechanism, which works similarly to the Frames panel we discussed earlier, is used to select the rows or columns of a frameset. When you click on the tabs along the left or top frameset representation (in Figure 5-9 it is the area to the right of the RowCol Selection label), the appropriate row or column will be highlighted. Once selected, you can adjust the value and unit properties of the selected element.

- *Value and Units:* The value property is used to determine either column width or row height, depending on which is selected using the RowCol Selection area. The Value property is specified based on the option selected as the Units property. Later we will explore how to effectively use combined units to create good designs (that is, use pixels for one element and percentages for another). The following are the available options for the Units property.

  ○ *Pixels:* Selecting pixels will use the Value property as an exact pixel column width or row height. Columns and rows that use pixel units take the highest priority when space is allocated within the browser.

  ○ *Percentage:* This option is used to set the column or row to fill a percentage of the available space within the frameset. Rows and columns that use the percentage option are second in line when space is distributed within the browser.

  ○ *Relative:* This setting is used when you want the column or row to just take up whatever space is left. If the units are set to relative, the value property should be set to a value of 1.

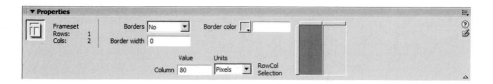

figure | 5-9 |

# Frame Properties

The frameset
Property Inspector.

There are a number of properties you can use to specify how an individual frame is displayed. Because each frame's properties can be set independently, it is important that the correct frame be selected. The following list details the available frame properties (shown in Figure 5-10) set using the Property Inspector.

- *Frame Name:* All frames should have a unique name. The name you specify here will be used later when creating hyperlinks. If you are using one of Dreamweaver's predetermined frameset layouts, the frames will be named for you by default. You may want to adjust the frame names based on the needs of your design.

- *Src (Source):* The source property determines the HTML page or frameset (if using nested frames) that will be displayed within the selected frame.

- *Borders and Border Color:* These settings are used precisely the same way that border attributes are set for the frameset. The difference here is that enabling the borders as a frame property will override whatever setting was made for borders within the frameset.

- *Scroll:* This setting is used to enable or disable scroll bars for the selected frame. Typically this will be set to No for no scroll bars or Auto, which will only use scroll bars if they are needed. The default setting allows the web browser to decide if scroll bars are used. Usually, web browsers use Auto as the default setting.

- *No Resize:* Enabling this option will prevent your users from being able to adjust the width or height of your frames.

- *Margin Width and Height:* These settings are used to specify a margin around the content within the frame. Using frame margins is similar to the cell padding you might add to a table.

NOTE: Using frame margins is very different from setting the margins using the Page Properties option discussed earlier in this book. If you are framing a page, realize that page margins will override the frame's margin width and margin height settings.

## Adding Content to Your Frames

figure | **5-10** |

Creating the frames is just the first step in the process to developing a page using frames. Once the frameset has been established, the next task is to add content to each of the frames. There are two basic ways that content can be added.

The frame Property Inspector.

The first method to add new content is by inserting an existing page into a frame. To do this, first place your cursor within the frame you want to add an existing page to. Next, select File I Open in Frame. This will summon the standard Open dialog box, where you can choose the correct page. Once the page has been selected, it will appear in the Document window within the frame you selected. You can also do this very same procedure by clicking on the appropriate frame using the Frames panel and then modifying the frame's *Src* property.

The other process for adding content is to simply develop directly within the frameset. When new frames are created, Dreamweaver will automatically add a new blank HTML page. Using this default blank page, content can be developed exactly the same way you would without the frames. If the page you are designing is slightly more complex, you may choose to develop the content outside the frameset, and then add it by opening it within the frameset. Doing it this way simply gives you a little more room to work as you are inserting content.

## Saving All Files

The process of saving a file is most likely second nature to you at this point. However, because developing with frames requires multiple files the process of saving takes a little extra care. If you were to just simply select File I Save, you would probably have a difficult time figuring out exactly which file you are saving.

At the beginning of this chapter, we took a look at the files that comprise a frames page. If you remember, in addition to the page that appears in each frame there is the frameset file that needs to be saved. For this reason there are three save options when working with a frames page.

● *Save Frame:* If your cursor is currently placed on a page within a frame, this save option is available by selecting File | Save Frame. Using this save option will only save the page that is currently within in the frame, not the frameset or any of the other frames.

● *Save Frameset:* If you have selected any of the frames or framesets using the Frames panel (or by other means), you can use this save option by selecting File | Save Frameset. Using the Save Frameset option will only save the frameset file and not the pages within each frame.

● *Save All:* This save option, as the name implies, will save the frameset and all pages in the frames. While this feature does simplify the process of saving frames, this is also where you need to be the most careful. To save the frameset and associated files, select File | Save All. This will open the standard Save As dialog box with one addition. If you look at the Document window behind the Save As dialog box in each part of Figure 5-11, you see that a dark outline has been added that surrounds the item being saved. Once you provide a file name and click on the Save button, a new Save As dialog box will appear for the next item to be saved. Figure 5-11 shows the steps in the save progression. Note that the frameset will be saved first.

figure | 5-11 |

The Save All option allows you to save each distinct file one after the other.

NOTE: The Save All option can be a little tricky to use. If you have multiple files open, in addition to your frames page, you will be prompted to save those pages as well. Just keep this in mind so that you don't inadvertently save the wrong file.

# FRAME NAVIGATION AND DESIGN

To this point we have been looking at the fundamentals of creating frames within the Dreamweaver workspace. Now comes the time to take a step back and examine how frames can be an effective tool for your designs. However, at the same time we should explore many of the reasons not to use frames.

## Navigation

The most significant advantage to using frames in web design is that you can build navigation schemes that go beyond the typical page-to-page style design. When a hyperlink is clicked inside a frame, as a designer you have a number of different options besides simply replacing the entire page within the browser.

By default, when the user clicks on a hyperlink within a frame the requested page will appear in that same frame. However, a hyperlink can also be designed to "target" an entirely different frame to display the page. Possibly the most common way to target a frame is by naming it. As we discussed earlier in this chapter, each frame within a frameset should be assigned a unique name. Using this name in conjunction with the hyperlink will allow you to click on a link in one frame and display the requested page in the targeted frame. The Property Inspector is used to assign a target to the hyperlink. Once a hyperlink is created, use the Target property to specify the name of the frame to display the requested page. If the frameset is currently open in the Document window, Dreamweaver will automatically add the names of all available frames to the Target menu. In addition to targeting a frame by its name, there are several targets that are available by default.

- _parent: Using the _parent target, a hyperlink will open the requested page, replacing the parent of the nested frameset.

- _self: Using the _self target, a hyperlink will open the requested page in the same frame that contains the hyperlink.

- _top: Using the _top target, a hyperlink will wipe out the entire frameset and open the referenced page to fill the web browser (replacing the frameset altogether).

**DON'T GO THERE**

Don't be tempted by the idea that you can open someone else's pages into a frame on your web site. This is technically possible, but it is an extremely poor practice. If your site uses frames, you should almost always use a _top or _blank target for links to pages that are not a part of your site. Using _blank as a target will open a new browser window for the link to be opened into.

## Sizing Frames Up

Designing a page that uses frames is not a process to be taken lightly. There are many decisions that need to be made before you can begin the construction of your frameset. One of the primary considerations is how much screen real estate should be allocated to each frame. Assigning space to the frames is a delicate process that requires balancing the nature of the content versus the available space within the browser.

Let's take a look at a specific example. A very common frameset design is to use a frame on the left for navigation and a frame on the right for content (see Figure 5-12). The end user would then click on a link in the navigation frame to open a new page in the content frame. Based on this scenario, it is easy to understand why the navigation frame on the left would take considerably less space than the content frame on the right.

Now comes the tough question: What should be the width of each frame? Due to the nature of the content that will appear in the navigation frame, we can assume that it will have a relatively predictable width. However, the information that appears in the content frame could potentially be of any shape, size, or amount. So the answer to this question is to fix the navigation frame to a specific pixel width; then set the other to expand and fill the remaining portion of the window. Setting the frame widths in this way, the content frame will adjust accordingly to the size of the end user's browser window.

No matter how you size the frames, there are two things you want to try to avoid when specifying frame widths. First, make sure the frames are wide enough so that the user is not expected to scroll horizontally. The second concept is that you shouldn't expect your end user to know that frames can be resized. Even if the user does know that the frame can be resized, chances are that they will not be compelled to actually do it.

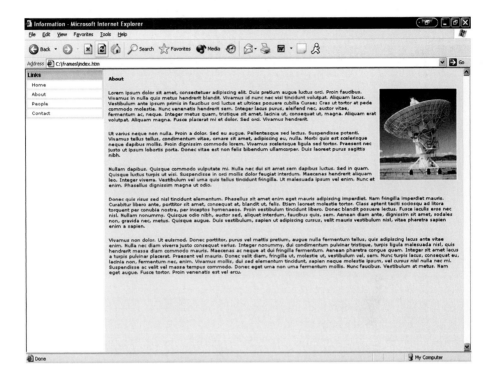

Setting proper widths for your frames will contribute directly to your site's usability.

## NoFrames Content

Some people choose to explore the Web using browsers that are either text only or don't support the use of frames (particularly as wireless handheld device use is increasing). While this presents a challenge when designing with frames, there is a way to work around it. When creating the frameset page, a special "NoFrames" section can be added. The "NoFrames" content can be edited by selecting Modify | Frameset | Edit NoFrames Content. This will change the Document window to the NoFrames Content mode, shown in Figure 5-13. As a visual clue, a banner has been added to the top of the Document window. You can return to the normal design view by once again selecting Modify | Frameset | Edit NoFrames Content.

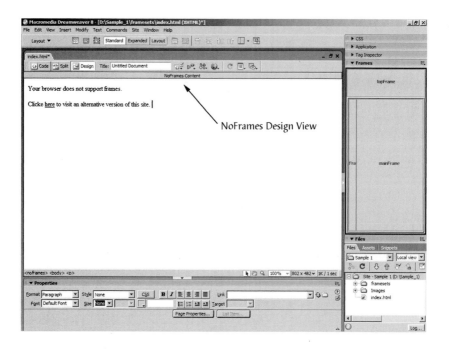

NoFrames Design View

figure | 5-13 |

NoFrames content
will be displayed
for browsers that
do not support
frames.

# Drawbacks

At the outset of this chapter I cautioned you on using frames as a part of your web designs. While there are a number of positive aspects to using frames, the following are a few of the biggest reasons to consider other solutions or approaches.

● *Frames can interfere with normal web browser functionality.* People who use the Web have come to expect a certain level of functionality when using a web browser. Unfortunately, frames pages can alter the behavior of the browser's back button and bookmarking capabilities. In particular, interference with bookmarking stems from another potential issue—confusing URLs. When viewing a frames page, the frameset URL will be displayed in the address bar at the top of the browser. Because the frameset will not likely change as you browse a site, neither will the URL. Thus, a bookmark established to a page within a frames site will point to the starting setup for the frames site, rather than to the actual page the user intended to bookmark.

● *Using frames may require greater site maintenance time.* When working with a frames site you must maintain a greater number of files than you might with a more conventional design. For example, if your frame design calls for three frames the site will require that at least four pages be maintained (one for the frameset, one for each frame) for just one screen of content. In addition, frame sites will also require you to maintain hyperlinks differently. As we discussed earlier, using links with frames will sometimes require adding target information for each link—yet another thing that needs to be managed and maintained.

● *Frames can cause problems when using search engines.* Search engines work by "spidering" the Web, indexing pages, and retaining the location of those pages it encounters. Of the pages that are found, it can be nearly impossible to tell those pages that are standalone from those that belong within a frameset. This can be problematic when the general public locates a page via the search engine's results. A piece of content on your site may be orphaned without the benefit of the surrounding frames.

● *Frames make supporting accessibility much more difficult.* Even though the largest percentage of web users use mainstream browsers, there are also a significant number of people who use alternative web browsers or adaptive software. Sometimes these browsers are used out of preference, while others are used out of necessity. For example, a visually impaired individual may use a screen reader to browse the Web, or a more seasoned web user may choose to use a browser that is text only to improve speed. No matter what the reason for using them, alternative browsers may have difficulty rendering frames properly, if at all. In addition, remember that display devices are getting smaller. How will your page be viewed on a PDA or tablet PC?

# SUMMARY

In this chapter we have explored how you can develop a site using frames. The key concepts you should take away are how frames work, how to construct pages using frames, and methods for creating hyperlinks that take advantage of frames. You should now also have an understanding of the drawbacks to using frames, so that you can try to avoid potential design pitfalls. As you gain more experience with web development, you will quickly discover how to build a balance between technology and design on your way to the ultimate goal of creating an exemplary experience for the intended audience.

## in review

1. What is the difference between a frame and a frameset?

2. What is a nested frame?

3. What are the possible ways to add frames?

4. What units are available to specify column width and row height?

5. What methods are used for adding content to a frame?

6. Why are hyperlink targets important when working with frames?

7. Why use NoFrames content?

## ↗ EXPLORING ON YOUR OWN

1. Now that you understand the process of creating pages with frames, plan out and develop a new page that uses two or more frames. Also, try developing a navigation scheme that calls for linking to pages within a specific frame. Experiment with different techniques for development.

2. Try building a new page using one of Dreamweaver's predefined templates. Work with the template by adjusting the frame and frameset properties. Also, try opening existing pages into each of the frames.

**notes**

_____

_____

_____

_____

_____

_____

_____

_____

_____

_____

_____

_____

_____

_____

_____

_____

_____

_____

_____

_____

_____

_____

_____

_____

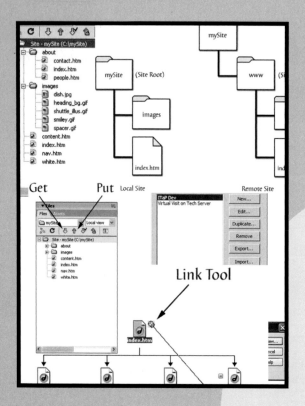

| Site Management |

*charting your course*

To this point we have been focusing on the fundamentals of physically building the pages that can make up your web sites. Now comes the time that we begin to grapple with the issues that arise from pulling the pages and images together to create an entire online presence. Our first step is to discover how such a monster can be managed.

Earlier in this book we discussed how a web site is not a single file. In reality, a site is an entire collection of files that have been intertwined and linked together to establish a complete presentation. The number of files needed will be different from site to site. Even a moderately sized web site can easily contain hundreds of individual files. Without a clear strategy to handle these files, the task of managing a web site can quickly become a chaotic process. In this chapter we are going to explore the tools Dreamweaver provides so that you can effectively manage your site no matter how many files it may contain.

 *goals*

- **Learn the fundamentals of managing web site files**
- **Explore the available options for configuring a new site**
- **Learn how the Files panel is used to work with files**
- **Discover how Dreamweaver can support collaborative development**

# WEB SITE MANAGEMENT

No matter what the size of your site may be, the use of Dreamweaver's site-building tools can simplify many different procedures. To take advantage of these features, you must first configure a new site within Dreamweaver.

## Local Versus Remote Locations

Dreamweaver's site-building tools are based on the simple model of maintaining a local and remote site. The local site is intended as a place where you can design and build all of your pages without releasing them for public viewing. Typically a local site will use a folder on your workstation, but it can also be on a separate web server from where your site is hosted. Using the local site, you can test to make sure that new or modified pages function correctly. The golden rule of working with your local site is that it should be an exact mirror of what is on your remote web server. This way, whenever a page is tested on the local site you can be assured that it will function properly on the web server.

The remote site is simply the server or network location from which your files are served to the world at large. The type, location, and access to your remote site will vary based on your web host. A little later we will take a look at the features Dreamweaver provides for you to access the remote site.

For the local and remote sites to work together properly, they must use the exact same directory names and structure. A critical aspect of this relationship is that your local and remote sites must specify the site's root (lowest-level directory or folder) as the same position in the directory hierarchy. For example, Figure 6-1 shows how the root of your remote site may be positioned deeper in a directory structure than the local site. Taking the time to synchronize the local and remote sites will allow Dreamweaver to help you maintain hyperlinks and file paths. Doing this manually with a small site is not too bad of a task, but could you imagine checking all the hyperlinks for hundreds pages? Needless to say, having Dreamweaver take care of this for you can save you considerable time.

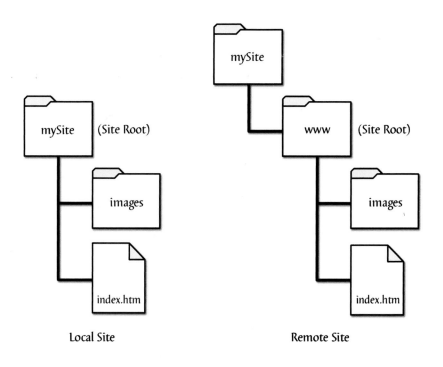

figure | 6-1 |

The position of the root directory may differ between the local and remote sites.

## Establish a Local Site

To take full advantage of Dreamweaver's site-building tools, you must first establish a new local site. Setting up a local site should be the first step in any web design project. By working with your local site at the onset of a project, you can begin to centralize all of the files needed to build your site. Begin the process of establishing a new Dreamweaver site by creating a new directory (or locate an existing directory) on your workstation. This new directory will serve as the root of your new web site. You should treat this folder exactly the same way you would treat the root of your web site on the web server.

Once a new folder is created, we need to let Dreamweaver know about it. Perform the following steps to summon the Site Definition dialog box so that you can configure a new local site within Dreamweaver.

1. Select Site | Manage Sites. Selecting this menu option will open the Manage Site dialog box, where all of your Dreamweaver sites are listed. Figure 6-2 shows this dialog box, and you can see that some web sites are already defined in the center of the dialog box. If you don't have any sites already established, you will be taken directly to the Site Definition dialog box. If this is the case, skip to step 3.

figure | 6-2 |

Manage Sites
dialog box.

2. Click on button marked New, and then select Site from the resulting pop-up menu. This will open the Site Definition dialog box.

3. If it is not already, select the Advanced tab at the top of the window (see Figure 6-3). Using either tab will essentially do the same thing. However, the Basic tab uses a wizard-style approach to establish a new site.

The Site Definition dialog box is used to define many different parameters for your web site. Note that there is a listing of categories along the left-hand side of this dialog box. Each of these categories is used to specify a different aspect of Dreamweaver's site management features. In this case, we are going to establish a new local site by using the local info category. The following detail the available options for a new local site.

● *Site name:* This field is used to specify a name for the site you are working with. This is the name that will appear in the Manage Sites dialog box.

● *Local root folder:* This field is used to specify the location of the folder on your workstation that is to be used as the local site.

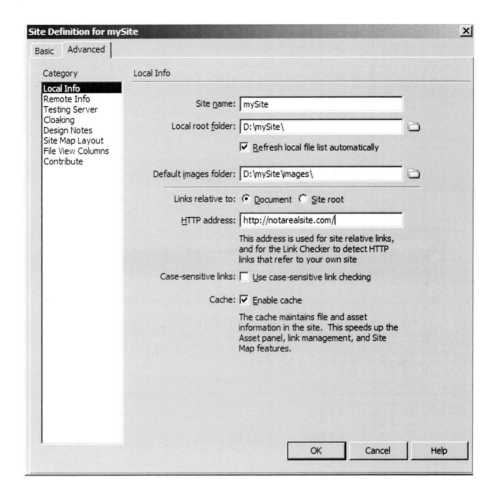

figure | 6-3 |

Site Definition dialog box with the Advanced tab selected.

Dreamweaver will use this directory to help determine file paths, so make sure you get this one right.

● *Refresh local file list automatically:* This option is offered so that you can stop Dreamweaver from refreshing the Files panel each time a new file is added. Only disable this feature if copying files into your local site seems sluggish.

● *Default images directory:* This field is used to specify a location for the folder where your images are stored within your site. If you try to insert an image located outside your local site,

Dreamweaver will automatically try to copy the image file to the default images directory.

- *HTTP:// address:* This field is used to specify the URL for your completed web site. While this feature is optional, providing this information will allow Dreamweaver to help you check absolute URLs used within your site.

- *Cache:* This option is used to determine if caching will be used to help with site management operations. Leaving this option enabled will improve the performance of Dreamweaver's site-building features.

## TRY THIS

Now that you have the knowledge, go ahead and create a local site on your computer. Use this local site for all of your test pages as you work your way through the rest of this book. In subsequent chapters, we will discuss several features of Dreamweaver that require the use of a local site. Setting up your local site now will put you ahead of the game.

## Establish a Remote Site

Now that the local site has been established, the next step is to specify the remote site. As I mentioned earlier, how you access the remote site will vary based on your web hosting service. For specifics on connecting to your web server, contact the systems administrator.

Setting up a remote site is done using the Site Definition dialog box, just like the process used with the local site. Once you have the Site Definition window open in Advanced mode, click on the Remote Info category option on the left. When this category is first displayed there is only one option that can be selected (see Figure 6-4). This is because the remote info options will differ based on the access model that has been selected. By default, the Access model will be set to None. If you click on the Access drop-down menu, you will notice that there are a number of different options for connecting to your remote site. For this book, I am going to cover the two most common access models: FTP and Local/Network.

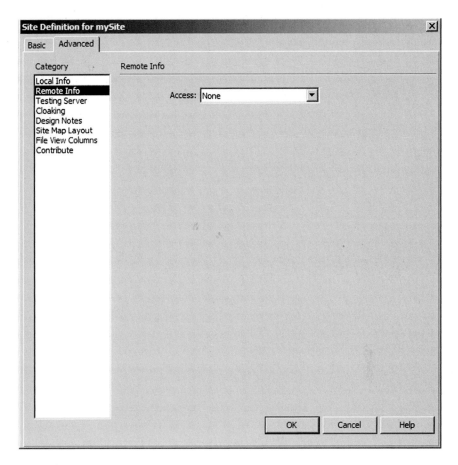

figure | 6-4 |

Manage Sites dialog box.

## FTP Access

FTP, or File Transfer Protocol, is probably the most common method for connecting to a remote web server. If you work with a hosting service for your web site, chances are that your files will be moved out to the web server using an FTP connection. The following list details the options (shown in Figure 6-5) that may be set to define your FTP access.

NOTE: The information needed to define FTP access for your remote site should be supplied by your systems administrator.

● *FTP host:* This field is used to set the name of the FTP server. For example, this may be something like *www.yoursite.com* or *ftp.yoursite.com.*

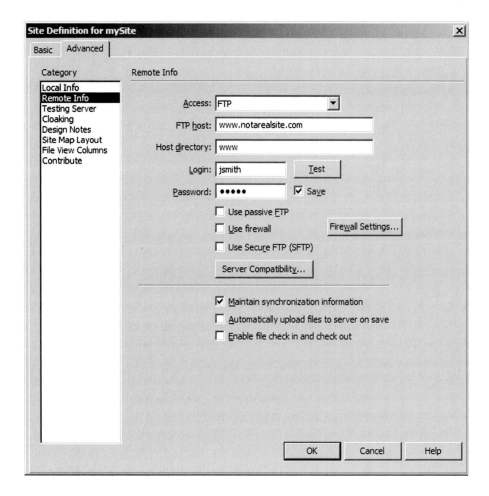

figure | 6-5 |

Setting up a
remote site with
FTP access.

- *Host directory:* The host directory is the folder where your publicly viewable pages will be placed. If your system administrator did not provide you with host directory information, try leaving this field blank.

- *Login and Password:* These fields are used to provide authentication (log-in and password) information to the web server. If you choose to enable the Save checkbox, this will store your password so that you will not have to enter the password each time you upload your files to your site. However, keep in mind that someone else could potentially use your computer to access the files on your web site.

- *Use passive FTP or Use Secure FTP:* By default these two options are not enabled. Only enable these options if advised to do so by your systems administrator.

- *Use firewall and Firewall Settings:* These options are needed only if you connect to your remote web server from behind a firewall.

- *Automatically upload files to server on save:* Enabling this option will automatically upload files to the remote site when they are saved within the local site. By default, this option is not enabled.

- *Enable file check in and check out:* The final four settings are used to enable Dreamweaver's collaborative development features (note that only one of the four options is visible if *Enable file check-in and check-out* is unchecked). We will cover these with greater depth later in this chapter.

## Local/Network Access

If you administer your own web server, or possibly work for a company that provides its own central web servers, you may need to use the Local/Network option. Using this option, you can copy files to the designated web space on a local or networked computer. The following list details the options (shown in Figure 6-6) that may be set to define your local/network access.

NOTE: The information needed to define network access for your remote site should be supplied by your systems administrator.

- *Remote folder:* This field is used to specify a path to the local or networked space that has been allocated for your web site. Just like selecting a folder to use as a local site, don't just select the drive – make certain you select the root directory or folder here as well.

- *Refresh remote file list automatically:* Disabling this option will prevent Dreamweaver from updating the remote file list when you upload new files from the local site. If the process of uploading new files seems to take longer than expected, you may wish to disable this option.

- *Automatically upload files to server on save:* Enabling this option will automatically copy files to the remote site when they are saved within the local site. By default, this option is not enabled.

- *Enable file check in and check out:* Just like with FTP access, the final four settings are used to enable Dreamweaver's collaborative development features, which are covered in detail later in this chapter.

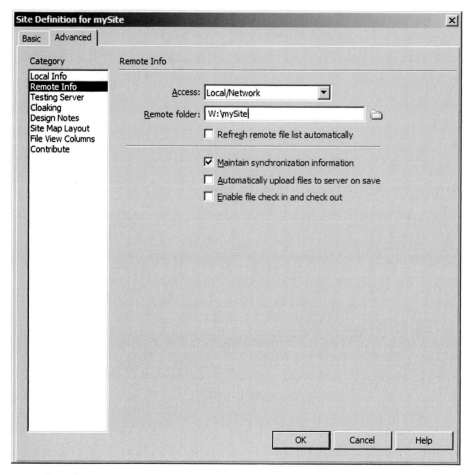

figure | 6-6 |

Setting up a remote site with Local/Network access.

## Working Without a Net

Nothing says that you absolutely must specify a site to be able to design and develop pages with Dreamweaver. If your site only requires you to work with a handful of files, or possibly you are web design purist that has no interest in taking advantage of the site management features, it is still possible to use Dreamweaver to develop with even though you don't set up a site. Using an FTP or RDS connection you can transfer files directly to and from the web server without using Dreamweaver. Follow these steps to set up a direct FTP or RDS connection:

1. Select Site | Manage Sites. This will open the Manage Site dialog box, where all of your Dreamweaver sites are listed.

2. Click on the button marked New, and then select FTP & RDS Server from the resulting pop-up menu. This will open the Configure Server dialog box, shown in Figure 6-7.

3. Provide the necessary information to establish an FTP connection with a remote site. For information on the available options, refer to the section on FTP access earlier in this chapter.

figure | **6-7** |

Configure Server dialog box.

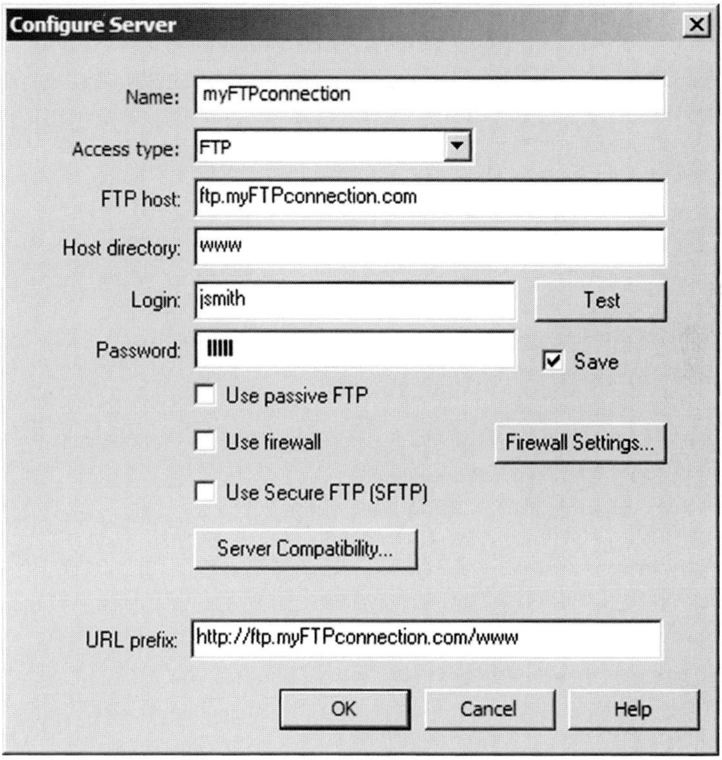

NOTE: What is RDS? RDS, or Remote Development Services, is a method of accessing web servers that uses Macromedia ColdFusion.

# MANAGING SITE FILES

With local and remote sites established, we are well on our way to effectively managing web site files. Now comes the time to reap the rewards of spending the time to plan ahead. The primary mechanism Dreamweaver provides for managing your site is the Files panel, which can be accessed by selecting Window | Files. This panel is broken into four separate views: local, remote, testing server, and sitemap. The views can be switched on the fly by using the menu at the top right of the Files panel (see Figure 6-8). I should acknowledge that while the testing server is an available view within the Files panel we will not be discussing it in this chapter. We will cover the testing server concept with greater detail in later chapters.

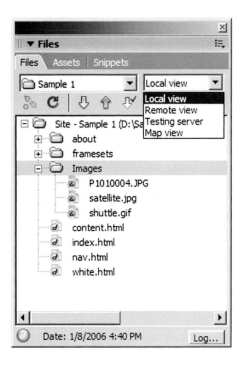

figure | 6-8 |

The Files panel can be modified to display different views.

## Local View

The view you will use most often is the local view, shown in Figure 6-9. The local view displays and provides access to the files and folders present within the local site. Using this view, you can perform common file tasks such as deleting, moving, copying, renaming, and so on by accessing the Options menu in the upper right-hand corner of the panel. In addition, if you double click on any of the pages shown in the local view it will instantly open the page within the Dreamweaver Document window. Once the changes are made, all you have to do is save and close. If there are several pages requiring changes, this type of direct access can make it a little quicker and easier to browse through and open files.

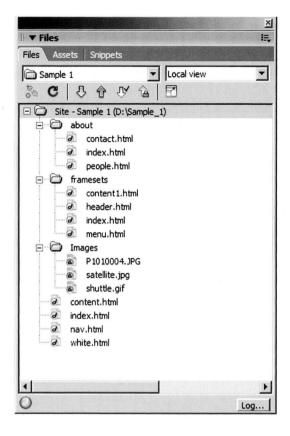

figure | 6-9 |

The local view of the Files panel.

## Remote View

Obviously, if there is a local view there should be a remote view. The remote view displays all of the files and folders currently on the web server. However, before seeing anything you may need to connect to the remote site, especially if your access is through FTP. To connect to a remote site, click on the *Connect to remote host* button at the top of the Files panel. Once connected, all of the files of your remote site will become visible. The thing to remember about the remote view is that all of the files you are seeing are "live." This means that any of these files could currently be in use by one of your visitors. So, remember to use extreme caution when working with files in the remote view. If you rearrange or delete files in this view, they affect your user's experience.

## Map View

The easiest way to think of the map view is that is provides a visual representation of the file structure for your web site. This view, also commonly called a site map, uses a series of icons and connectors to show the first two levels of your local site. As you can see in Figure 6-10, the site map can take a fair amount of space to be displayed entirely. For this reason, you should click on the Expand/Collapse button to maximize the Files panel whenever working within the map view.

figure | 6-10 |

The site map is a visual representation of your local site.

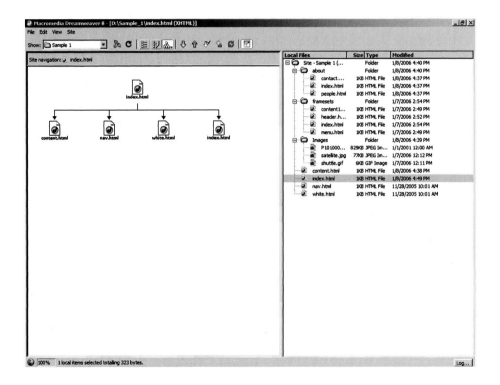

You can adjust how the site map appears in a number of different ways. The simplest method to adjust the site map is by hiding files of little consequence. To hide a file on the site map, click once on the File icon. Then select View | Show/Hide Link. To make the hidden file icons reappear, select View | Show Files Marked as Hidden.

In addition to showing and hiding files, you can make global modifications to the site map's appearance by using the Site Definition dialog box, discussed earlier. To access and modify the site map layout for the current local site, set the Files panel to Map view. Then click on the Files panel's options menu and select View | Layout.

This will open the Site Definition dialog box to the Site Map Layout category (see Figure 6-11). The following detail the available options for modifying the visual appearance of the site map.

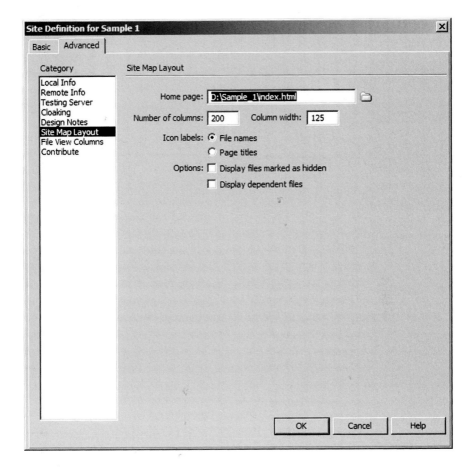

- *Home page:* This field specifies the home page for your local site. The home page is used as a starting point when Dreamweaver begins to construct the file tree.

- *Number of columns:* This field specifies how many page icons can appear for each row of the site map.

- *Column width:* This specifies the pixel width of each column.

- *Icon labels:* This option is used to determine if the document's file name or title information will appear under each icon on the site map.

figure | **6-11** |

Using the Site Definition dialog box, you can adjust the appearance of the site map.

*Options:*

- Enabling the *Display files marked as hidden* option will allow hidden files to appear as a part of the site map. To denote the hidden status of a page, the file's name will appear in italics.

- Enabling the *Display dependent files* option will display images and other types of media files as part of the site map.

NOTE: As you may have already found, many of the options available in the Site Definition dialog box are also available by clicking on the View menu of the expanded Files panel.

## Creating Links with the Site Map

In addition to providing a visual representation of your site, the map view can be used to create hyperlinks between files. This can be a handy tool when first starting your site. Some designers like to create an entire "wireframe" of a web site before going too far into development. This wireframe site is usually nothing more than the pages that will make up the site and links between the pages. This allows the designer to review the site structure and navigation model pretty quickly. The process of creating a hyperlink with the site map is simple. First, click on the file icon for the page you want to link from. Next, click and drag the Link tool (shown in Figure 6-12) to the file you want to link to. Dreamweaver will then add the appropriate hyperlink.

figure | 6-12 |

Using the Link tool, you can create hyperlinks in the map view of the Files panel.

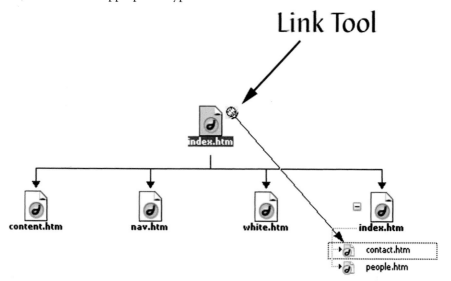

# Pushing Files Around

In addition to managing the local or remote site, the Files panel can be used to manage the migration of files from one site to another. As with most procedures within Dreamweaver, there is more than one way to accomplish this task. Something to keep in mind as you move files around is that they may not instantly appear within the Files panel. To force Dreamweaver to look for the changes in the site files, click on the Refresh button at the top of the Files panel.

## Drag and Drop

Using a drag-and-drop method, you can maintain complete control over what files are being moved and where exactly the files are placed on the other site. To facilitate this migration, you can expand the Files panel to display the local and remote sites at the same time (see Figure 6-13). First, click on the Expand/Collapse button. Then click on the Site Files button at the top of the maximized Files panel. As you will notice, the remote site is displayed on the left and the local files are shown on the right. To copy a file from one to the other, simply click and drag the file or folder from left to right, or vice versa. It is important to note that the files

figure | 6-13 |

Using the Files panel in expanded mode, you can move files between the local and remote sites.

Site Files

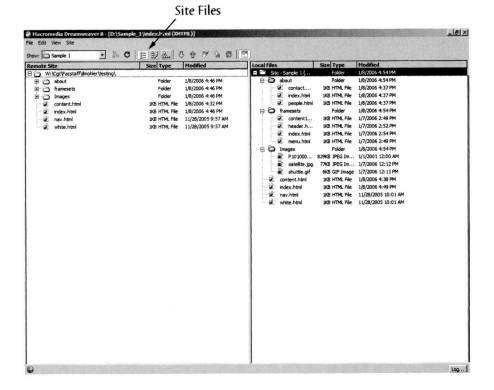

will be placed in any directory or subdirectory you may choose as the destination.

## Get and Put

The most exact way to move files (or directories) between sites is to use the "get and put" method. Simply stated, the *Get* method is used to copy selected files from the remote site to the local site. Conversely, the *put* method is used to copy selected files from the local site to the remote site. The key point to remember when using *get* and *put* is that this process will not only move the selected file but will create any directories that don't already exist in order to maintain a parallel directory structure. To get or put files, first select the files you wish to copy. Next, click on the Get or Put button, shown in Figure 6-14.

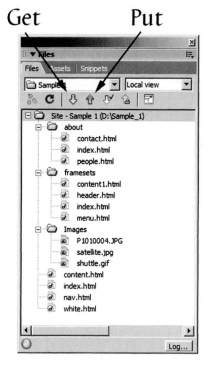

figure | 6-14 |

Using the Get and Put buttons, you can copy files between sites.

NOTE: Before copying the files using a *get* or *put* procedure, Dreamweaver may prompt you to also copy dependent files. By allowing this, Dreamweaver will also automatically copy files referenced within the pages to be copied. Examples of dependent files may include images or Cascading Style Sheets.

## Synchronizing

As I mentioned earlier, the golden rule when working in parallel development is that the local site should be an exact mirror of the remote site. However, sometimes things happen and everything can get all out of whack. To solve this problem you can use the synchronize feature. When you synchronize two sites, Dreamweaver will go through and examine each file of the local and remote sites, looking for any pages that may be different. To start the synchronization process, first right-click inside either the local or remote site areas within the Files panel. Next, select Synchronize from the resulting context menu. This will open the Synchronize Files dialog box, shown in Figure 6-15. This dialog box has four different options.

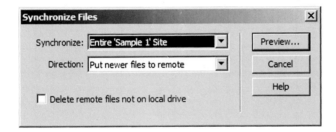

figure | 6-15 |

The Synchronize Files dialog box is used to specify the parameters for a synchronization between local and remote sites.

- *Synchronize:* This option determines what exactly is being synchronized. You can choose whether to sync the entire site or only selected files within the local or remote sites.

- *Direction:* This option determines if you are only going to put files from the local site or get files from the remote site. In addition, you can also use Get and Put to move files in both directions.

- *Delete remote files not on local drive:* Enabling this option will remove any files on the remote site that are not present within the local site. This feature may be useful if you have recently made a large number of changes to your site.

- *Preview:* When this button is clicked, Dreamweaver will open a window detailing any files that require action. Using the Preview button is a good way to check to make sure you are copying the intended files.

I cannot stress this enough: be extremely careful when using the synchronize feature. Make absolutely certain you are copying files in the intended direction. If you are going to synchronize your files, you may want to first consider backing up both the local and remote sites just in case something goes awry.

## COLLABORATIVE DEVELOPMENT

Now that you have a feel for how files are managed, let's take a look at some of the tools that can be used when working with a team of web developers. Developing a web presence is seldom a one-person job in the real world. In fact, a growing trend in web development is to make web design a collaborative process between several people with expertise in different areas. Anytime there is more than one person working on a project, you are bound to have conflicts. Especially with large web sites that contain many pages, it can be difficult to remember who was last working with what. To help keep things straight, Dreamweaver has three mechanisms that can be used to facilitate working with your team: check-in/check-out, cloaking, and design notes.

### Check In and Check Out

The worst thing that can happen when working on a team-based web project is that changes you make will overwrite and cancel out the changes made by another member of the development team. To keep this from happening, you can use the *Check in* and *Check out* features, to ensure that you aren't stepping on the toes of your fellow developers. Using a file check-out system, you can signal those files that are currently being worked with. When a file has been checked out, it will appear with a red mark if someone else has the file or a green mark if you currently have the file (see Figure 6-16). Once you are finished working with a file that has been checked out, you need to check it back in so that it will be available to the rest of the team. Once a file has been checked back in, the version of the file on your local site will become locked. Once locked, the only way you can edit the file is by checking out the file again.

**Checked Out**
(Someone else)

**Checked Out**
(You)

**Checked In**
(Locked)

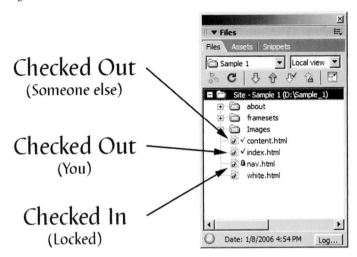

figure | 6-16 |

There are a number of visual cues that signal the check-in/check-out status of individual files.

### Enabling Check-in/Check-out

Once you agree with your teammates to use the check-in/check-out system, it can be independently enabled for any of your Dreamweaver sites. To get up and running with this system, you must have first defined a local and remote site. Next, following these steps will enable check-in/check-out for one of your sites.

1. Select Site | Manage Sites. This will summon the Manage Sites dialog box.

2. Click on the site you want to enable, and then click on the Edit button. This will summon the Site Definition dialog box, shown in Figure 6-17.

3. If it has not already been selected, click on the Advanced tab on the Site Definition dialog box, and then click on the Remote Info option from the category list on the left.

4. Click on the checkbox next to the *Enable file check in and check out* option. Once enabled, three additional options will appear.

5. Enter your name, handle, or designation into the *Check out name* field. This is the name that will appear next to the file you have checked out.

6. Enter your e-mail address in the *Email address* field. If you add an e-mail address, your name will appear as a mail link in the Files panel when a file is checked out.

7. Click on OK to finish the process.

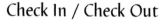

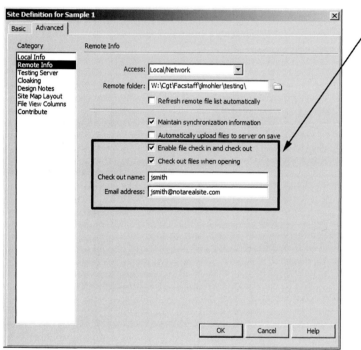

figure | 6-17 |

The check-in/check-out system is enabled using the Site Definition dialog box.

Effectively using the check-in/check-out system requires that everyone on the team use Dreamweaver as their page or site editor. If there are team members who use alternative tools to edit and upload files, they could unknowingly overwrite a file you are currently working with. There is one thing you can use to avoid this problem. When you check out a file, Dreamweaver will create a temporary file of the same name with an additional *.LCK* extension. While this file is not visible in the Dreamweaver Files panel, it will be displayed using another tool, such as an FTP client.

## Checking In and Checking Out

Now that you have everything turned on, there will be two new buttons available on the Files panel. The Check In and Check Out buttons, shown in Figure 6-18, work almost exactly like the Get and Put buttons we talked about earlier.

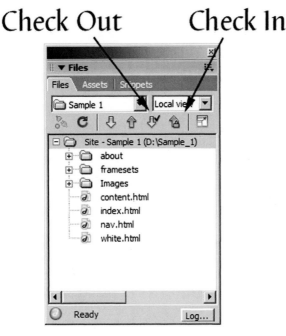

figure | 6-18 |

The Check In and Check Out buttons are used just like Get and Put.

Whenever you need to edit a file, the process begins by setting the Files panel to the remote view. Now you can highlight the file or files on the remote site you want to check out so that no one else can work with them at this time. Then, to check out the files click on (you guessed it) the Check Out Files button. At this point, a prompt may open asking if you want to include any dependent files. If you choose Yes, this will download the dependent files (along with the files you have already selected) to your local site.

NOTE: If you inadvertently check out the wrong file, or decide against making any changes, a check-out procedure can be reversed. To undo a check-out, open the file you wish to return and select Site | Undo Check Out. This will lock the local copy of the file. However, the remote version will remain unmodified.

When you are finished working with the checked-out files (or newly created files), they can be checked back in so that your fellow team members will be free to use them. To check in a file, high-light the files you wish to free and click on the Check In button on the Files panel. This will copy the selected files from your remote site to replace the same file that resides on the remote server. Remember that checking in a file will lock the copy on your local site so that it will be read-only.

## Cloaking

Every person works through the web design process differently. Some developers prefer to build wireframe sites, while others like to build visual mock-ups in Photoshop. However you choose to design your sites, there will always be additional files that are created but never intended to be part of the remote site. This is where cloaking can help. Cloaking is basically a method of restricting folders or specific file types to the local site, thus excluding them from the remote site where they could become available to your team or the world.

When a folder has been cloaked, you will be unable to perform the typical *put* or check-in procedures you may use for other elements on your local site. In reality, Dreamweaver will ignore cloaked folders and file types for nearly any site-wide operation. Examples of files you might cloak would include support documents that have helped in the design process but have nothing to do with the final implementation of the site, or possibly a new part of the site you are still working on and are not yet ready to move out to the remote site. You can also use cloaking for operational reasons, such as excluding a directory from synchronizing procedures.

### Enabling and Using Cloaking

Cloaking is like a light switch that can be turned off and on for each of your Dreamweaver sites. Because cloaking is managed as part of your local site, you can feel free to use cloaking whether the rest of the team decides to use the option or not. You can switch on cloaking for your local site by clicking on the Options menu button on the Files panel and then selecting Site | Cloaking | Enable Cloaking. Once it has been turned on, you can begin cloaking folders and types of files within the local site.

As I have alluded to, there are two ways cloaking can be used. You can cloak any individual folder by first selecting the folder in the

Files panel. Then click on the Options menu button on the Files panel, and then select Site | Cloaking | Cloak. As you can see in Figure 6-19, a cloaked folder (and its content) will appear with a red line through the corresponding icons. To uncloak a folder, once again start by selecting the folder in the Files panel. Next, click on the Options menu button on the Files panel and then select Site | Cloaking | Uncloak.

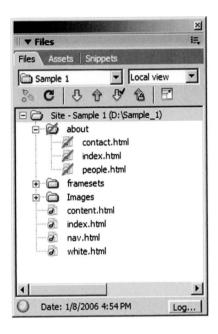

figure | 6-19 |

Cloaked files will appear with a red slash through the corresponding icon.

In addition to cloaking individual folders, you can cloak files of a particular type. For example, if there are a number of Photoshop source files you may choose to cloak all *.PSD* files. Start the process of cloaking a specific file type by clicking on the Options menu button on the Files panel and then selecting Site | Cloaking | Settings. This will open the Site Definition dialog box to the Cloaking category (see Figure 6-20). Now you can specify the file types by enabling the checkbox next to *Cloak files ending with* and entering the desired file extensions in the available field. Once you are finished, click on the OK button so that your changes can take effect. Once again, just like when cloaking a folder all files of the specified type now have a red slash though their file icon.

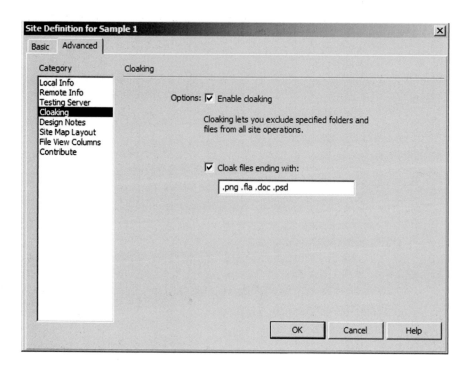

figure | 6-20 |

# Design Notes

Using the Site Definition dialog box, you can specify file types to cloak.

Whenever multiple people are working on the same file, there is often extra information about the file that needs to be communicated to others or stored as notes to jog your memory about something. All too often this information is passed along in the way of e-mails to the development team or as a comment within the document itself. To solve this problem, Dreamweaver provides a design notes feature. A good way to think of design notes is that it is like leaving a virtual sticky-note attached to a particular web page. Design notes are typically used to store information about a particular file you may not want to actually include in the file itself. The nature of information in a design note may include a rationale for why something was designed a particular way or possibly a list of items that still need to be done.

## Enabling Design Notes

There are two different models for using design notes with your files. First, you can enable design notes just to be used with your local site. In this scenario, the design notes will only be stored and displayed for your personal use. The other way to use design notes is to upload and store the information as part of the remote site.

Using this model, design notes can be shared with your fellow team members. Follow these steps to enable design notes for your site.

1. Select Site I Manage Sites. This will summon the Manage Sites dialog box.

2. Click on the site you want to enable, and then click on the Edit button. This will summon the Site Definition dialog box.

3. If it has not already been selected, click on the Advanced tab on the Site Definition dialog box, and then click on the Design Notes option from the category list on the left (shown in Figure 6-21).

4. Click on the checkbox next to the Maintain Design Notes option.

5. If you want to share design notes with your team, click on the checkbox next to the *Upload Design Notes for sharing* option.

6. Click on OK to finish the process.

figure | **6-21** |

Using the Site Definition dialog box, you can enable the design notes feature.

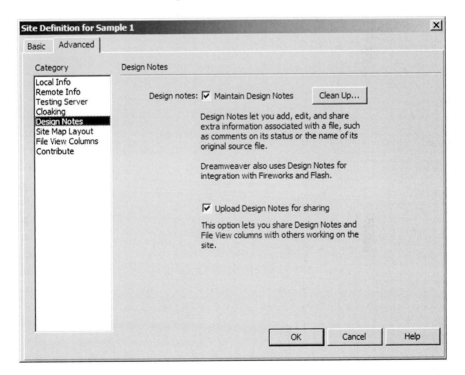

## Using Design Notes

You can create and attach design notes to virtually any file used with your site. To attach a design note to one of your pages, first open the file into the Document window. Then select File | Design Notes to summon the Design Notes dialog box, shown in Figure 6-22. Before moving on, make sure the Basic Info tab is currently selected. Using the following Basic Info options, you can create a new design note for this document.

- *Status:* Selecting an option for this menu will assign a status to this document.

- *Notes:* This field is used to add any commentary that should be attached to this page.

- *Date:* Using the Insert Date button, you can instantly add the current date to the Notes field.

- *Show when file is opened:* If this option is enabled, the design notes will appear when this file is next opened in Dreamweaver.

figure | 6-22 |

The Design Notes dialog box can be used to attach basic information to a page.

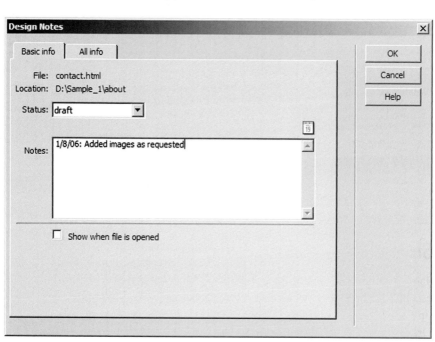

In addition to the Basic Info design note options, an All Info feature is available. The All Info options (other than being named in a peculiar way) are provided so that you can add structured information to your design notes. Rather than just providing a "Notes" box to type in whatever you want, the All Info tab uses a series of name and value pairs. So, for example, you can create an option named *client* to maintain specific information about who the client is for a particular page. You can create structured design notes by clicking on the All Info tab in the Design Notes dialog box (see Figure 6-23). Add a new name/value pair by clicking on the Add (+) button and then entering the name and value information into the fields of the same name.

NOTE: Adding an element named *status* will allow you to create a custom type for the Status menu under the Basic Info tab.

figure | 6-23 |

The Design Notes dialog box may also be used to add structured informa- tion for each page.

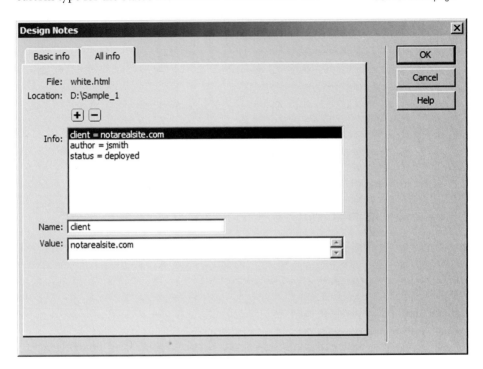

## SUMMARY

Taking charge of a new site is like caring for a new pet. Without establishing clear expectations early, you will find yourself cleaning up many messes later. In this chapter we have explored how Dreamweaver can be used to help manage and maintain your web presence. The core concepts to take from this chapter are an under- standing of local and remote sites, how to use these sites effective- ly, and the tools and features Dreamweaver supplies to make the management of your web site easier. Over the next two chapters we are going to focus on additional tools Dreamweaver provides so that you can efficiently manage reusable assets, in addition to exploring techniques to automate the development of pages with- in your site.

## in review

1. What are the advantages of creating a Dreamweaver site?

2. What is the difference between a local and remote site? Explain how each may be used.

3. What is the Files panel used for?

4. What is the site map, or map view, used for?

5. What is meant by "get and put"?

6. How is synchronization used?

7. How does check-in/check-out work?

8. What is cloaking? Explain a situation where it may be used.

9. What are design notes? Explain a situation where they could be used.

## ➚ EXPLORING ON YOUR OWN

1. Now that you understand Dreamweaver's site-building tools, create a new local site you can use for this book. Use this new site to collect all of the files you test out or play with as you work your way through the remaining chapters. Also, try enabling the cloaking and design notes features for your own personal use.

2. Just as an experiment, try defining a local and remote site for a fictional company. If you don't have access to an actual remote site, use the local/network access option for a folder on your local workstation. Once you have this site set up, try working with some of the synchronization and check-in/check-out features.

**notes**

# ADVENTURES IN DESIGN

## SITE MAINTENANCE WITH TEMPLATES

For many people the most enjoyable part of working with the Web is doing the design and development. This is a wonderful activity where we can really stretch our creative abilities. For a web designer, there are few things more satisfying than a perfectly designed and functioning web site. Unfortunately, not long after the euphoria has worn off we are faced with the obligatory task of maintaining the monster that was just built. I don't know about you, but as a web developer I am passionate about making the maintenance process as easy and painless as possible. Using templates in conjunction with your web design activities can provide you with some relief in this department.

## Project Example

I once had a freelance project that involved building a web site for a company that provided driver education for high school–aged students. This was a fairly small web site, so it wasn't going to take any real time to build. However, the problem was that because the courses were offered every month, the site was going to have to change on a regular basis. Because maintenance of the site was going to be a mindless activity, it really wasn't anything I wanted to commit to doing. So, as a result, I decided to design the site, but then at the same time design a series of Dreamweaver templates for each of the page types that existed. This way, I could provide the company with a set of templates, and they would be empowered to maintain the site themselves. This was a win-win scenario because it kept me from having to make changes on the site, and the company wouldn't have to pay me to make those changes. It worked out best for everyone.

To accomplish an arrangement such as this, more time was spent planning outside Dreamweaver than developing within it. To kick off the process I had to work with the client to develop an outline of content that would exist on the site. With an outline in hand, I could actually begin to build the site. The first goal was to develop a visual design that was conducive to adding many different types of content (see Figure A-1).

Once the overall design was complete, I converted it into a Dreamweaver template that all other templates would be embedded within. This way, a change to this one template would propagate across all pages on the site. Next, I used the master template to create several additional templates, one for each type of content. In this case, I created templates for course offerings, news items, customer testimonials, and driving

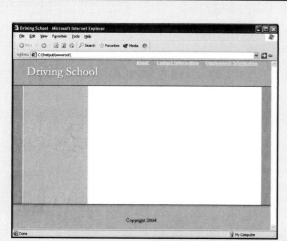

*LEFT:*
Figure A-1. Building a good template scheme is helped by establishing a flexible visual design.

*BELOW:*
Figure A-2. By thinking ahead, you can build templates that can meet many of your clients' needs.

instructor pages. After developing the templates, the site was ready to be built. Now all I had to do was fill in the blanks with content and the site was ready to roll (see Figure A-2).

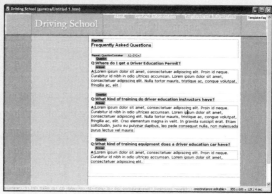

## Your Turn

Now it is your turn to be the architect. You can either select a fictitious site or create a new site of your own. Plan out what types of content will appear on the site. Think about the content at its most granular level. In my case, I wanted the company to maintain the site on their own. This means that I had to make the templates as fill-in-the-blank as possible. For example, a course offering had blanks for the title, location, time, description, and cost. Once you have this all in mind, it is time to build.

1. Determine the areas of content that will exist within the site. Are any of them so similar they might use the same template? Try to focus on those areas of content that are likely to change on a regular basis.

2. Plan and build a visual design that is extremely flexible. This will help accommodate the different types of templates.

3. Plan out the template objects that will be available for each type of content. Think about the content at its most fundamental level.

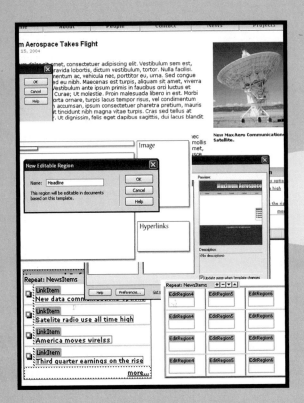

| Automating Web Development with Templates |

*charting your course*

A key success factor for any web developer is their ability to design, build, and deploy pages efficiently. Dreamweaver templates are a tool you can use to help speed along web development, maintain consistent design, and automate the process for making sweeping updates to your site.

Every site, but particularly larger ones, will have a number of design elements that are common to every page. For example, every page of your site may have the exact same banner and footer information. So, if your site contains a hundred files do you really want to go through and manually add these elements to all of the pages? Probably not. By using Dreamweaver templates, each new page built for the site will include all of the common elements the page should have. In addition to these elements, a template can also include fixed areas for adding content within an established layout. Adding these areas, or regions, will allow you to maintain design consistency, but at the same time you can delegate the addition of content to other members of your team without having to worry about anyone getting too creative on their own. The other major advantage to using Dreamweaver templates is that they can automate some site maintenance procedures. For example, what happens when something on a banner needs to change? Using Dreamweaver templates, you can modify one file and the change will cascade across your entire site. Needless to say, starting a new design process by establishing Dreamweaver templates can be a real time saver.

In this chapter we are going to take a close look at how you can build custom templates for your site. Dreamweaver offers a number of different mechanisms that can be used in combination to build templates that will meet your design needs. Knowing about these mechanisms and how to implement them is what will ultimately save you development time in the future.

 *goals*

- **Learn how Dreamweaver templates are created**
- **Explore the different elements that can be used to construct a template**
- **Discover how templates can be used to create new templates**
- **Learn how templates can be used to automate the production process**

# OVERVIEW

Typically when starting a new design project you will begin by sketching out the visual aspects of the design, such as banners, logos, and other images. While this is an important step in the design process, many people overlook the necessity of designing a consistent content architecture (or information architecture) for the entire site. You can think of content architecture as planning out what content is available on the site, in addition to how and where it will appear on each page.

For example, your design may call for a title, short description, and possibly an image to appear at the top of each page. Based on this design, you should have a plan for how each of these elements will appear once added. In fact, your planning should go so far as to define an instance where the items are not to be included at all, or where their use may be optional. Anytime you start a new design you should think about these types of issues, because establishing a clear content architecture can help you transition directly into using templates.

## Template Basics

The process of effectively using templates with your site all starts with the web designer. It is up to the designer to not only design and build all of the elements that will be common to most pages but to designate how future pages are designed. Using templates, you can establish a consistent look and feel yet still provide flexibility for your template users to create new pages by adding content within editable areas (though other areas might be locked).

To start learning how templates work, we will use a simple example that most people can understand: the news release. Our sample release, shown in Figure 7-1, includes many of the elements you would expect to find for a news release on the Web: headline, date, story, image, and hyperlinks for related information. If you think about the nature of each of these content areas, you can begin to identify different areas of information. In Figure 7-2, you can see how this news release example can be divided into regions that can be translated to a new template.

figure | 7-1 |

A news release is a good example of content that can easily be structured with a template.

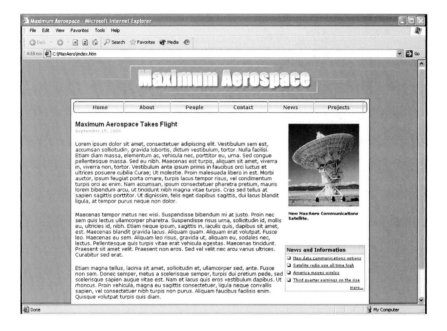

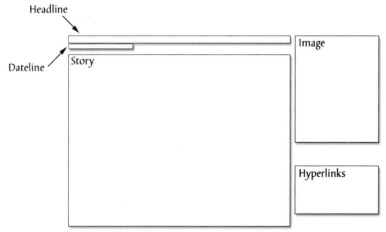

figure | 7-2 |

## Nuts and Bolts of Dreamweaver Templates

The majority of this chapter is going to be spent examining all of the options you have when designing and building templates. But before we get too deep in the process, we should first discuss what technically makes a template a template. Simply put, a template is nothing more than an HTML (or ASP, JSP, ColdFusion, and so on) file that has a series of embedded HTML comment tags used to define the content areas (see Figure 7-3). HTML comment tags are used because they can be embedded in the pages that are created from templates, and your audience will never really know (unless they tip-toe through your source code). It is important to keep these tags in your pages, because they will associate the page with the template and template regions that were used to create it. Maintaining this relationship will facilitate making any global changes that may be needed later.

figure | 7-3 |

HTML source code with the Dreamweaver template markup.

```
1  <!DOCTYPE HTML PUBLIC "-//W3C//DTD HTML 4.01 Transitional//EN"
2  "http://www.w3.org/TR/html4/loose.dtd">
3  <html>
4  <head>
5  <!-- TemplateBeginEditable name="doctitle" -->
6  <title>Untitled Document</title>
7  <!-- TemplateEndEditable -->
8  <meta http-equiv="Content-Type" content="text/html; charset=iso-8859-1">
9  <!-- TemplateBeginEditable name="head" -->
10 <!-- TemplateEndEditable -->
11 </head>
12
13 <body>
14 <p>
15     <!-- TemplateBeginEditable name="Headline" --><!-- TemplateEndEditable --><br>
16     <!-- TemplateBeginEditable name="Dateline" --><!-- TemplateEndEditable -->
17 </p>
18     <!-- TemplateBeginEditable name="NewsStory" -->
19     <p></p>
20     <!-- TemplateEndEditable -->
21 </body>
22 </html>
```

When a new template file is created, it is saved with the .*DWT* extension. In addition, the .*DWT* files are stored within the *Templates* directory at the root of your local site. All of the templates used with the site should be stored within this same directory. Because the local site may be on your personal workstation, you can share Dreamweaver templates by simply giving a copy of the *Templates* directory to co-workers to place at the root of their local site. Dreamweaver will automatically search this directory first when a user creates a new page from a template.

## Creating New Pages from Templates

To understand the template development process, it is important to know how templates are used once created. After you have designed, built, and saved your template, it can then be used to generate new web pages. To create a new page based on a template, select File | New, which will open the New Documents dialog box. At the top of this window, click on the tab labeled Templates (see Figure 7-4). From the left-hand column select the site that contains the template you wish to work with. Once you select the site, a list of all available templates will appear in the right-hand column. As you select each of the available templates, a visual depiction will appear in the preview window. When you have the appropriate template selected, click on the Create button. This will open into the Document window a new file based on the template. Now you can add content to each of the editable fields and then save the file in the desired format.

figure | 7-4 |

New Documents dialog box.

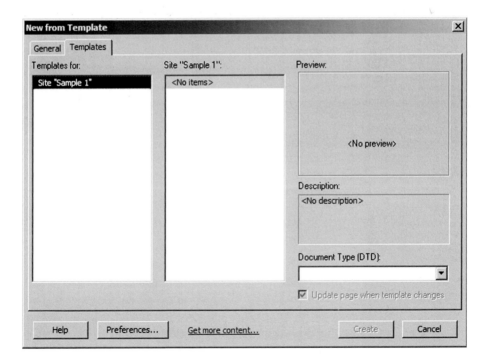

## BUILDING TEMPLATES

Now that you have a feel for the concepts, let's press on into the process of building templates. As we progress through this section, you will begin to notice that templates are really comprised of three different types of regions. No matter how complex the template, it all boils down to using the editable, repeating, and optional regions in combination to establish a content architecture for your site. But before you begin to establish these regions, let's first take a look at how to kick off template construction.

## Starting a New Template

There are two basic methods for creating a Dreamweaver template. You can take an existing HTML page and convert it to a template or you can start from scratch. "Templatizing" an existing page is more common, but either technique can get the job done. No matter what method you use for starting the template, once the template has been established you can begin to add regions for housing content.

figure | 7-5 |

New Document dialog box.

Creating a new template from scratch is very similar to creating a new page. First, select File | New to open the New Document dialog box, shown in Figure 7-5. Then click on the General tab and select the Template page category from the left. Note that there are

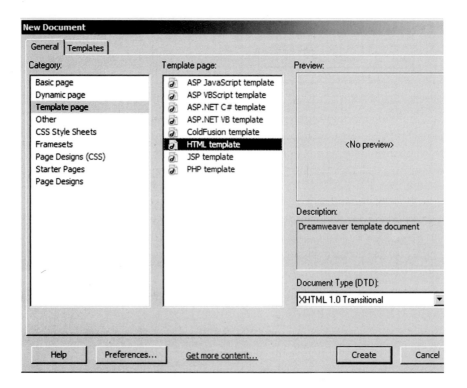

a number of template types available. Using Dreamweaver, you can template not only HTML but pages that use different dynamic server technologies. For this chapter, I am going to use the HTML template option. In reality, selecting a different template page type will not really affect how users interact with the template.

The process of creating a template from an existing page is equally simple. First, select File | Open to open the page you want to use as the basis for the new template. Now all you have to do is save the page out as a new template. I should note that the process of saving a template is exactly the same whether you begin with a new template or convert an existing document. To create the template page, select File | Save as Template. This will open the Save as Template dialog box, shown in Figure 7-6. Using this dialog, specify the site this template should belong to and then assign it a unique name in the *Save as* field. Once the Save button has been clicked, a new *.DWT* file will be saved in the *Templates* directory. If this directory does not already exist within the local site, Dreamweaver will create one for you. You should always save your template file before adding elements.

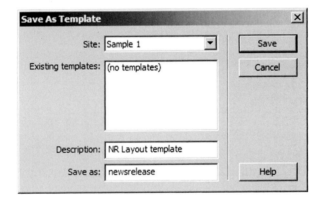

figure | 7-6 |

Save As Template dialog box.

## Nested Templates

Once you have established a new template, it is possible to create what is referred to as a nested template. A nested template, simply put, is a template made from another template. This type of design is typically used when you have a series of templates that are basically the same. However, there are some variations between templates. The advantage of nesting templates, rather than just creating many separate templates, is that you can make sweeping changes to your pages from editing a single base template file.

The process of developing a nested template begins with creating and saving a standard template to use as the base. Now create a new page from the base template. With the new page open in the Document window, select Insert | Template Objects | Make Nested Template. This will open the Save as Template dialog box, where you can save your new nested template. Now you can divide editable regions from the base template into new regions for the nested template. Keep in mind that any editable regions in the base template will automatically be passed on to the nested template. In addition, any changes made to the base template will now be carried through to any pages created from the nested template.

## Editable Regions

Now that you have established a new template, the next step is to add the desired template regions. The most fundamental of template elements is the editable region. Editable regions, as the name suggests, are those areas where you allow the user to add content of their own. For the news release example we looked at earlier, the headline, date, and story are all examples of editable regions. How you add editable regions to your template will determine the level of flexibility users will have when populating pages with content.

The process of creating a template can be started in two different ways. If the editable region includes additional elements such as tables or images, you can start the region by selecting these elements. Otherwise, you can simply place your cursor on the page where you want the region to be added. Once you determine placement, select Insert | Template Objects | Editable Region. This will open the New Editable Region dialog box, shown in Figure 7-7. Using this dialog, add a name that will be displayed for this editable region. It is critical that each editable region within your template have a unique name. Once you click on OK, the edible region name and outline will appear in the Document window (Figure 7-8). If

figure | 7-7 |

The editable region is designated by name and a colored outline.

**New Editable Region**

Name: | Headline |

This region will be editable in documents based on this template.

OK

Cancel

Help

you mistakenly add an editable region, it can be removed by clicking on the region's name and then selecting Insert I Template Objects I Remove Template Markup.

figure | 7-8 |

Headline

NOTE: Anytime you start a new template, Dreamweaver will automatically add two editable regions: doctitle and head. As you will notice, these regions are not visible in the Document window like the editable regions you inserted. This is because they actually reside outside the body of the page. These two regions are inserted so that template users can use the doctitle region to modify the page title and use the head region to insert common elements that are placed within the head area of a document such as JavaScript or CSS.

## Repeating Regions

Sometimes just providing your user with a single editable region is not enough. On occasion your design will call for the template user to redefine the template regions on the fly. This is where repeating regions come into play. Using a repeating region, template users can duplicate a portion of the template as many times as needed. Figure 7-9 shows how the repeating region will appear to the template user. By clicking on the Plus (+) or Minus (-) button, additional regions can be added or removed from the template. In addition, using the up and down arrows the repeated item can be moved up or down within the list of repeated items.

Repeat: NewsItems  +|-|▼|▲|
Item
Repeating Item 1
Item
Repeating Item 2
Item
Repeating Item 3
Item
Repeating Item 4

figure | 7-9 |

The important thing to know about repeating regions is that by default the repeated content is in no way editable. To provide this level of functionality, repeating regions are commonly used in conjunction with editable regions. Referring again to our news release example, a repeating region can be used to provide the mechanism necessary for enabling a list of hyperlinks for related information (see Figure 7-10). In this example we want the template user to add several hyperlinks, but we don't know how many links that will be. By using a repeating region in combination with an editable region, you can enable the user to add as many or as few options that may be needed for any particular story.

figure | 7-10 |

Our news release example makes use of the repeating region.

There are two techniques for inserting a repeating region into your template. One technique is to select the element you want to repeat and then add the repeating region by selecting Insert | Template Objects | Repeating Region. This will open the New Repeating Region dialog box, where you can provide a unique name for this repeating region. Typically this technique is used when you want to duplicate already-established design elements. The other method for insertion is to go ahead and add the repeating region, as previously discussed, and then insert the elements to repeat.

NOTE: It is possible to nest a repeating region within a repeating region (and so on). Using repeating regions in this way will allow you to replicate a series of replicated regions. As you can imagine, this can get fairly complicated. However, nested repeating regions may be a helpful technique if your design calls for a hierarchical set of navigation options.

## Repeating Tables

A common implementation of the repeating region is its use in conjunction with table rows, as in the news release example. Using a repeating region in this way, a table row can be duplicated over and over, thus maintaining the physical layout. Because this technique is so common, Dreamweaver provides the repeating table feature. To add a repeating table to your template, select Insert | Template Objects | Repeating Table, which will open the Insert Repeating Table dialog box, shown in Figure 7-11. Using the options in the top portion of the dialog box you can define the layout of the repeat table. For more information on how to edit table properties, see Chapter 3. Using the *Starting row* and *Ending row* fields, you can define the row or series of rows that will be duplicated using the repeating region. The *Region name* field is used to specify a unique name for this repeating region. Once you have clicked on OK, a new table with associated repeating region will be added to your document (see Figure 7-12). Also, note that editable regions have been added to each of the table cells within the repeating region. You may need to use the Property Inspector to rename each of the editable fields, because Dreamweaver will automatically add a sequential name for each of the editable regions.

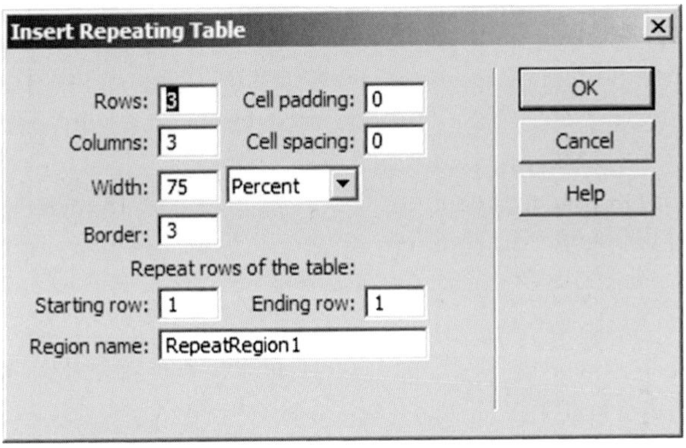

figure | 7-11 |

Insert Repeating
Table dialog box.

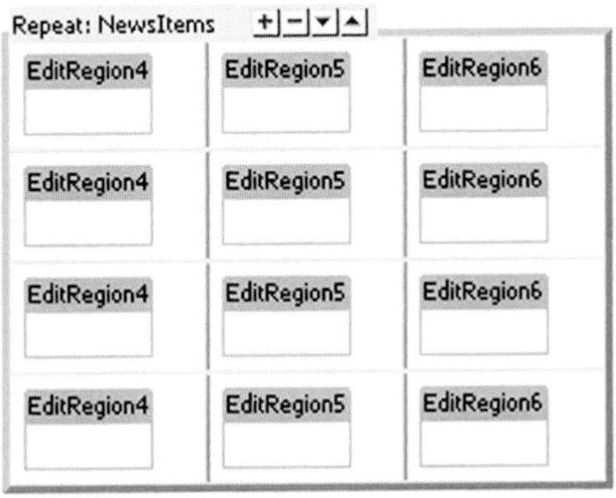

figure | 7-12 |

When you add a
repeating table,
editable regions will
be added to each
cell for you.

## Optional Regions

You may find a situation where you want to let the template user make the decision to turn on or off a particular portion of a template. This can be handy if you have defined a particular element that may not always be present in pages based on this template. The optional region works somewhat like the repeating region in that by itself it is not editable. However, Dreamweaver also provides an Editable Optional Region feature that will create a typical optional region with an additional editable region. For example, the news release template would have an area where an image can be associated with the story. However, the addition of an image will not always be available, so in reality this particular feature would be optional. The advantage to this element is that you can empower the template user to include the element and at the same time as designer maintain control over how the element is used.

Once again, there are two techniques for inserting an optional region into your template. One technique is to select the element you want to make voluntary and then add the optional region. Typically this technique is used when you want to make an already-established design element optional. Start this element by selecting Insert I Template Objects I Optional Region. This will open the New Optional Region dialog box (see Figure 7-13), where you can provide a unique name for this region. In addition, by enabling the *Show by default* checkbox the optional region will be displayed when a new page is started with this template. The additional method for insertion is to first add the region and then insert the page elements. Also, as I mentioned earlier, the optional region comes in a secondary flavor called the Editable Optional Region.

figure | 7-13 |

New Optional
Region dialog box.

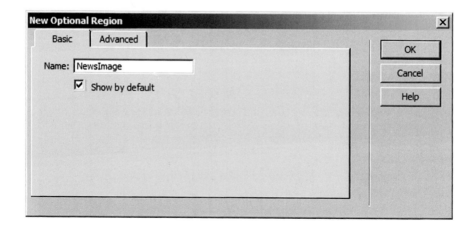

This type of region can be added by selecting Insert I Template Objects I Editable Optional Region.

So now that I have added an optional element, how can the template user turn it on and off? Template users can show or hide an optional region by selecting the Modify I Template Properties menu option. This will summon the Template Properties dialog box, shown in Figure 7-14. From the name list, select the element that corresponds with the name of the optional element. Once selected, the options for this item are displayed at the bottom of the window. By selecting the Show checkbox, the optional region will appear in the Document window. If you are planning on making this page a new nested template, checking the *Allow nested templates to control this* option will pass the show/hide option on to new pages started from the nested template.

figure | **7-14**

Template Properties dialog box.

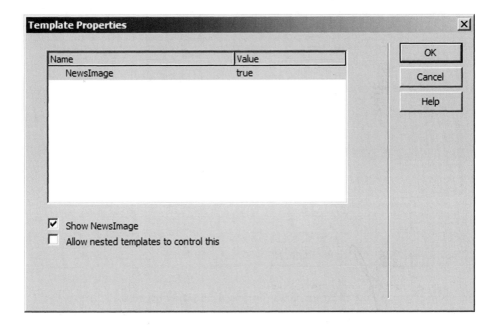

As you may have noticed, the New Optional Region dialog box contains an additional tab labeled Advanced. The Advanced tab allows you to add custom parameters and expressions to your template. Using template expressions you can actually calculate values or use conditional statements that can control what information is inserted into your new page. It is beyond the scope of this book to go into the specifics of programming template expressions.

If you are interested in more information, consult the Dreamweaver help by selecting Help | Using Dreamweaver; or visit the Macromedia web site at *www.macromedia.com.*

## Editable Tag Attributes

A situation may arise where you want to lock down a particular design element, but at the same time want to allow the user to change a particular attribute of that element. For example, possibly your design includes a hyperlink labeled *Home.* You could put that entire hyperlink inside an editable region and allow the template user to modify all of the available attributes (size, style, color, and so on). However, you may not want the template user to have this level of control. An alternative to using an editable region is to use an editable tag attribute. This template feature is only used on those elements that fall outside editable regions, and works by allowing the user to only modify the attributes you define. In this example you may only want the link information of this hyperlink to be modified. The following steps outline how you can add an editable tag attribute.

1. Select the item in your template to which you want to add an editable tag attribute. In this example, I am going to select a hyperlink.

2. Select Modify | Templates | Make Attribute Editable. This will summon the Editable Tag Attributes dialog box, shown in Figure 7-15.

3. Using the Attribute menu, select the attribute you want to make editable.

4. Click on the *Make attribute editable* checkbox. This will enable the remaining options within the dialog box.

5. Enter a name for this attribute into the Label field. This label is what the template user will use as a reference for this attribute.

6. Select a type for this attribute. The selected type will determine the nature of the values that can be entered for this attribute. For this example, the type is set to URL.

7. Enter the initial value of this attribute into the Default field.

8. Click on the OK button.

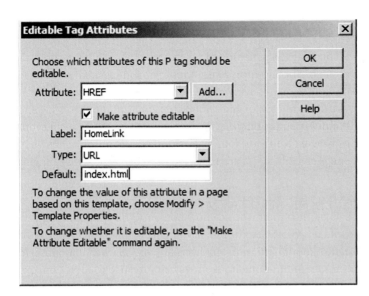

figure | **7-15**

Edit Tag Attributes
dialog box.

figure | **7-16**

Once an editable tag attribute has been added, users can modify the value via the Template Properties dialog box (see Figure 7-16) by selecting Modify | Template Properties. This dialog box will list all of the available properties for this template. For this example, selecting the *HomeLink* property will allow you to enter or select a new file.

The Template Properties dialog box allows you to adjust predetermined template properties.

> ### TRY THIS
>
> Now that we have gone through all of the possible template regions, take a few minutes to get yourself acquainted with how they work. Start a new template, and then try adding a few different template regions. Also, don't forget to try to create new pages from this template to gain the template user's perspective.

# WORKING WITH TEMPLATES

Now that you have put together a template, there are a number of options for how it can be used to automate the web development process. In addition, there are many different options you can use to develop several different types of content you may not have expected.

## Applying Template Changes

As I mentioned earlier, one of the big advantages to using Dreamweaver templates is that they can facilitate making large sweeping changes to your entire web site. By making a change, whether small or large, templates can be applied to all pages that were generated from the same template.

The process of modifying a template starts with opening the *.DWT* file that exists in the *Templates* directory at the root of your site. For the change to cascade across your entire site, it is important to open the *.DWT* file and not a page that was saved from the template. Once you have the file open in the Document window, you can make all of your desired changes. After you have finished making changes, select File | Save.

At this point, Dreamweaver will summon the Update Template Files dialog box, shown in Figure 7-17. This dialog box contains a listing of all pages that were saved from the template you are currently working with. Clicking on the Update button will trigger Dreamweaver to run through all pages on this list and make the same changes you made to the original template. Conversely, if you want to manually update your pages clicking on the Don't Update button will cause Dreamweaver to skip the update process entirely. We will look at how to update pages manually a little later on.

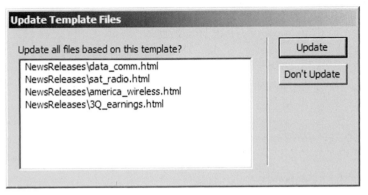

figure | 7-17 |

The Update Template Files dialog box lists all files attached to the current template.

Once all of your pages have been modified, Dreamweaver will display the Update Pages dialog box, shown in Figure 7-18. For this operation, the primary information to take from this dialog box is found in the log area at the bottom. This log information primarily explains what files were updated, the numbers of files examined, those updated, and those that could not be updated. Make sure the number of files that could not be updated equals zero. If there were any, this means that there was a reason Dreamweaver was unable to make the change and you might want to investigate the problem further.

figure | 7-18 |

Update Pages dialog box.

## Jump-starting the Update Process

Sometimes you want to jump-start the process of updating pages across your site that are based on templates. This process works almost exactly the same way as editing and saving a template. To start the update process, select Modify | Templates | Update Pages, which will open the Update Pages dialog box, shown in Figure 7-19. Using this dialog box, you have two options for how the pages will be updated. First, by selecting Entire Site from the *Look in* menu you can update all pages within the specified site to use their attached template. The other option is to update only those pages that use a specified template. To do this, select the Files That Use option from the *Look in* menu. Then select the corresponding template you want Dreamweaver to search for.

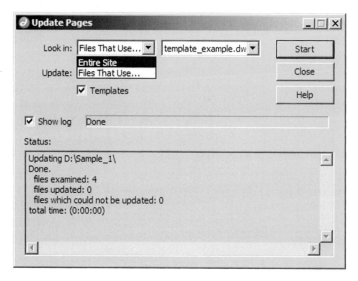

figure | 7-19

Update Pages
dialog box.

### Manually Updating Templates

On occasion you will want to make a change to your template file, yet only selectively update certain pages that use that template. To make this happen, open, edit, and save your template as already discussed. However, make certain you tell Dreamweaver not to update the files that use the edited template. Now that the template has been edited and saved, open the page to which you want to apply the edited template. Then select Modify | Templates | Update Current Page, which will apply the template changes to this page. You can repeat this process for additional pages that require updating.

## Applying Templates

If you are anything like me, you probably started building your new web site the second you picked up this book. So now that a few pages have been built, how can you go back and take advantage of templates? Well, there is no one silver bullet you can use to convert your static free-form pages and convert them into full-on structured content that uses templates. However, you can take one of your pages and apply a template to it. While not perfect, it does give you a good start.

This process starts by opening the page you want to apply a template to. Once open in the Document window, select Modify | Templates | Apply Template to Page. This will open the Select Template dialog box, shown in Figure 7-20. Using this dialog, first select the site that houses the template you want to apply. Then select the template name from the Templates list. Next, click on the button marked Select to move on to the Inconsistent Region Names dialog box, shown in Figure 7-21. This dialog box is used so that you can move existing content on your page to one of the regions within your template. Most likely, unless you are applying a template to a page where a template had once been there are only two items that need to be resolved: the head and body. If you had preexisting regions in your documents, the process is the exact same to move content from one structure to the other. When you select *Document body*, for example, the *Move content to new region* menu will become available. By default, the value will show as *<Not resolved>*, but Dreamweaver will not accept this as a solution. You must assign each unresolved region to a new template region. Using this menu, you can assign the content to any of the editable regions within the documents, in addition to three other options that almost always exist.

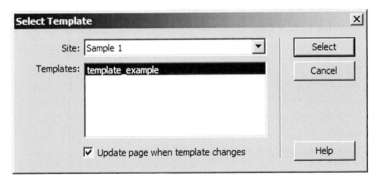

figure | **7-20**

Select Template dialog box.

- *Nowhere:* Selecting this option will remove the selected content from the page.

- *Doctitle:* Unless it has been deleted, selecting this option will assign content to the default doctitle region of the template.

- *Head:* Once again, selecting this option (unless deleted) will assign content to the default head region of the template.

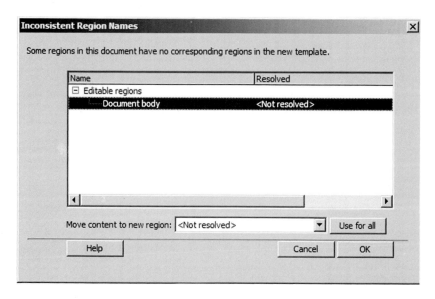

figure | 7-21 |

Using the
Inconsistent Region
Names dialog box,
you can assign
existing content to
specific template
regions.

Once you have made your selections, click on the OK button. Your content will now appear in the template regions you have assigned. This process doesn't get you all the way home, but now it is just a matter of rearranging the content.

## Detaching Pages from Templates

Sometimes you build pages based on a template and then change your mind and decide that the page would be better off without a template entirely. This can happen for a number of reasons. Possibly a part of the page that needs to be edited is locked down, or maybe you got a little overly zealous when designing the template and the design no longer meets your needs. Whatever your reason, a template can be completely detached from a page. To perform this task, select Modify | Templates | Detach from Template. This will strip all of the code that once tied this page to a template. Keep in mind that any changes to the template documents will no longer be applied to this page.

**DON'T GO THERE**

Make sure that detaching a page from its template is something you really want to do. Once the template has been detached, there is no easy way to go back. In reality, the only way to re-add the template is to apply the template as discussed earlier. Before choosing to detach, you might want to consider if there is a way to modify the template file such that it meets your needs.

# Export Options

Whenever you create a new page from a template, the obvious thing to do is to save the file in your desired format; for example, as HTML. However, by going through the trouble of building and applying a template to your pages you now have some new options. Using these special export options will allow you to either streamline your HTML code or leverage template content in ways you might not have thought about.

## Export Pages Without the Template Markup

As we talked about earlier, pages based on a Dreamweaver template will have a series of HTML comment tags embedded. These tags, while completely invisible when rendered within the browser, are still present within the HTML code. It may not seem like a big deal, but these comment tags do increase the file size (a very small amount, but it can add up). Leaving in the comment tags is really just wasting the end user's bandwidth. Removing the tags is by no mean critical, but it can streamline your HTML code. For this reason, Dreamweaver provides a mechanism that can strip all template markup from your entire site.

In addition to lightening your code, this feature is also helpful if you want to completely start over with the templates. Over the course of your design career, you may inherit an existing site that was designed and built by someone else. Stripping out all the template tags gives you a method for beginning again and not worrying about someone else's template strategy.

With a page from the site open, the process of exporting your site without the template markup starts by selecting Modify | Templates | Export Without Markup. This will open the Export Site Without Template Markup dialog box, shown in Figure 7-22. The following explain the options available.

- *Folder:* This option is used to specify the folder where the site, once sanitized, will be exported to. This folder location must not be located within the current local site.

- *Keep template data files:* Enabling this option will save an XML version of the page in addition to the page minus the template markup. We will talk about uses for these XML documents in the next section.

**Export Site Without Template Markup**

Choose a folder to export the site into.

OK

Cancel

Folder: [                              ] Browse...

Help

☑ Keep template data files

☑ Extract only changed files

figure | 7-22

Using the Export Site Without Template Markup dialog box, you can strip all template information from your pages.

• *Extract only changed files:* Enabling this option will only export those pages that have been changed since the last time the site was exported. You can think of this like synchronization between the copy of your site with template markup and that without.

## Saving as XML

An interesting feature Dreamweaver offers is the ability to save your template's content as XML. It is well beyond the scope of this book to explore the particulars of XML, but let me give you the basic explanation of what this means when using a template. Exporting your page as XML, such as that shown in Figure 7-23, will save only the content within the template regions, and none of the stuff around them on the page. There are many different reasons you may want to export template content as XML. For example, you might want to move your content from template to template, or from site to site. Another common use is so that you can move web content from an HTML page to some other structured form such as a database. No matter what the reason, exporting content to XML increases the versatility of the pages you build with templates.

figure | 7-23

This XML code is an example of the file created when exporting data from a Dreamweaver template.

```
1  <?xml version="1.0"?>
2  <templateItems template="/Templates/newsRelease_blank.dwt" codeOutsideHTMLIsLocked="false">
3     <item name="NewsStory"><![CDATA[
4        <p>The news story area. </p>
5        ]]></item>
6     <item name="Dateline"><![CDATA[September 15, 2004 ]]></item>
7     <item name="head"><![CDATA[
8  ]]></item>
9     <item name="doctitle"><![CDATA[
10 <title>Untitled Document</title>
11 ]]></item>
12    <item name="Headline"><![CDATA[the headline area ]]></item>
13 </templateItems>
```

To begin the process of exporting your template content as XML, select File | Export | Template Data as XML. This will summon the Export Template Data as XML dialog box (see Figure 7-24), which allows you to select between using standard and editable region names as the XML tags. As a general rule of thumb, use the standard tags if your template contains any repeating regions. Otherwise, the choice is yours. Once you click on the OK button, select a location to save the XML file. Now Dreamweaver will create a new XML document based on the regions defined within the page template.

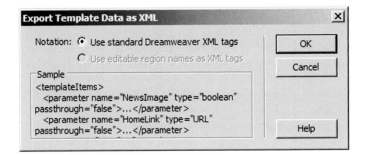

figure | 7-24 |

The Export Template Data as XML dialog box allows you to specify the tags that will be used in the XML file Dreamweaver creates.

Once the data has been saved into an XML format, it can be imported and regenerated into a new HTML file with the associated template regions. To create a new page, you use the File | Import | Import XML into Template menu option. The new page will now appear in the Documents window with the appropriate template regions populated with content from the XML file.

# SUMMARY

In this chapter we have covered how templates are built and leveraged within Dreamweaver. While building templates is not the most exciting topic, the time that can be saved by using templates will free you up to work on other aspects of your site. As we move on, think about how you can design your sites to fit within a template structure. Also, take note of ways you can use templates to automate the development of new pages. Remember that the ability to efficiently build and maintain a web presence is what makes an effective web designer.

**in review**

1. What is a Dreamweaver template?

2. What are the primary advantages to using templates?

3. How are template regions defined within the HTML code?

4. What file extension is given to Dreamweaver templates?

5. What is the advantage of creating nested templates?

6. What is an editable region used for? Provide an example.

7. What is a repeating region used for? Provide an example.

8. What is an optional region used for? Provide an example.

9. Why might you export your site without template markup?

# ↗ EXPLORING ON YOUR OWN

1. Now that you have an understanding of how templates work, plan out and build a template for simple page text, such as a news release or job posting. Experiment with the various template region types available.

2. Take an existing page design and build a new template to reproduce the design. Try building several templates by nesting your regions within one base template.

**notes**

_____
_____
_____
_____
_____
_____
_____
_____
_____
_____
_____
_____
_____
_____
_____
_____
_____
_____
_____
_____
_____
_____

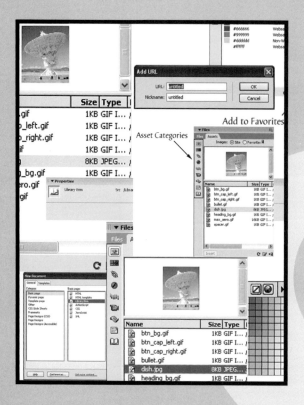

Managing Assets and Building Libraries

*charting your course*

Through the process of designing and building a site you will accumulate an enormous number of assets. In Chapter 6 we discussed how you can manage the files that comprise your web site. But how do you keep control of other pieces and parts that are either used in a supporting role only or as component parts of pages?

In this chapter we are going to explore how Dreamweaver can help manage your site's assets. In using the Assets panel, you can track, sort, locate, and preview several predefined categories of assets. Assets come in many different flavors. Some assets (such as images or Flash movies) can help you build your pages more quickly, while other assets can enable you to efficiently maintain your site. A little later in this chapter we are going to take a closer look at a key supporting asset— the library item. This asset is used to help facilitate building and maintaining reusable chunks of pages. Working with assets and libraries has little to do with the visual design process, but spending time learning these management techniques can free you up to spend more time working on that exciting design.

 *goals*

- **Discover how the Assets panel can be used to manage web site elements**

- **Explore the types of assets that can be managed with Dreamweaver**

- **Learn how to add assets to your page designs**

- **Discover how library items can be used for reusable site elements**

# ASSETS

As your web site continues to grow, so will your reliance on the assets that appear in your pages. If you are working with a larger site, a great amount of time can be spent sifting through all of your files, looking for just the right image. You will also begin to accumulate a number of assets that really don't appear as a part of your site, but are completely supporting documents such as templates or library items. Then, there are those things such as colors and URLs that aren't really embodied by any particular file. So how do you manage those? In Dreamweaver, the answer is simple: the Assets panel. Using this panel, shown in Figure 8-1, you can centralize the management of those elements you use to help build content that will appear on any page. It also provides a mechanism where you can view the asset before it is inserted or applied to your page.

figure 8-1

The Assets panel will aid you in managing many elements of your web design.

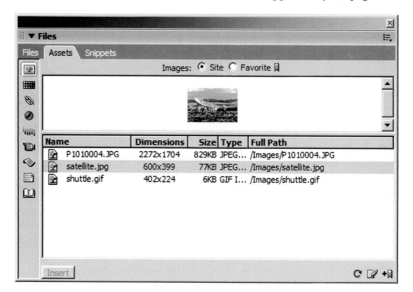

## What Is an Asset?

At this point you are probably asking what exactly can be considered an asset? I have already mentioned a few common elements (such as images, colors, and URLs), but there are still more possibilities. The Dreamweaver Assets panel organizes elements based on the following categories.

● *Images:* This category of asset would be any *.GIF*, *.JPG*, or *.PNG* file stored within your site.

- *Colors:* This category of asset is any color whose hexadecimal value has been defined within a page on your site. The color asset is something that isn't often considered, but using this asset you can manage all colors applied to visual elements, ranging from backgrounds to text.

- *URLs:* This category of asset is any absolute URLs used within a page on your site. This would include links that begin with the following protocols: *http, https, ftp, mailto,* and *file.*

- *Flash Movies:* This category of asset is for any Flash file using the *.SWF* extension on your site. I should note that *.FLA,* or flash source files, will not be displayed within the Assets panel.

- *Shockwave Movies:* This category of asset is for any Shockwave file that is a part of your site. These files will use the *.DCR* extension.

- *Movies:* This category of asset is for any QuickTime or MPEG movies stored within your site. These files will typically use the *.MOV* and *.MPG* extensions.

- *Scripts:* This category of asset is for any external JavaScript or VBscript files stored within your site. These files will typically use the *.JS* or *.VBS* extension.

- *Templates:* This category of asset is for any Dreamweaver Template files used with your site. These files will use the *.DWT* extension.

- *Library:* This category of asset is for any Dreamweaver library files used with your site. These files will use the *.LBI* extension.

## Using the Assets Panel

To make it easier to locate and leverage common site assets, Dreamweaver includes the Assets panel. This panel scours the pages of your local site looking for references to elements you may want to reuse. It also provides a central point to access your site's assets (the sort based on the categories we just explored) and directly add these elements to your pages.

By default, the Assets panel can be found within the Files panel group, or it can be summoned via the Window I Assets menu option. As you can see in Figure 8-2, the Assets panel has a series of icons lining the left-hand side. These icons represent each of the categories of assets discussed earlier. If it isn't completely obvious what a particular icon represents, you can place your cursor over top of the button and a tool tip will appear. By clicking on any of these buttons, you can sort the items to show a listing of all assets belonging to particular category. If you click on the name of a particular asset, a visual preview will appear in the top portion of the panel. In the case of the multimedia elements, such as Flash assets, you can actually preview the movie by selecting the Play button in the upper right corner of the preview area (see Figure 8-3).

Asset Categories

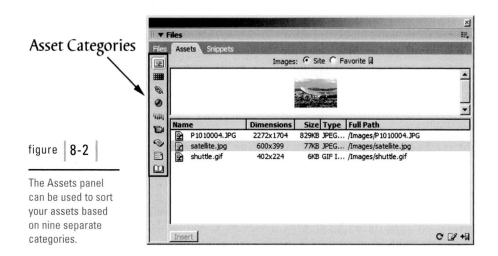

figure | 8-2 |

The Assets panel can be used to sort your assets based on nine separate categories.

Play Button

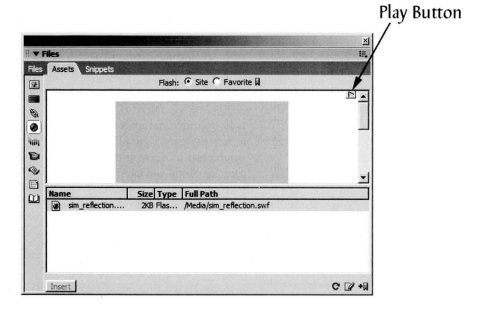

figure | 8-3 |

Using the Assets panel, you can preview multimedia-based assets such as Flash movies.

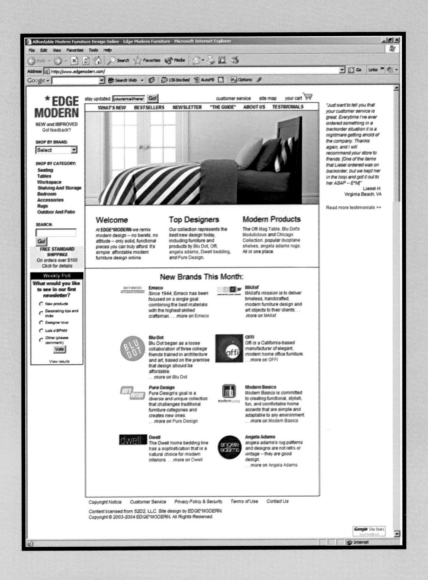

EDGE*MODERN (http://www.edgemodern.com/).
The EDGE*MODERN site succinctly provides a
design that makes it easy to find out more information about their products and services. Courtesy of
Edge*Modern.

| figure 2 |

Royal Roads University *(http://www.royalroads.ca/ Channels/)*. Royal Roads University shows a good example of using drop-down menus and CSS integrated throughout the site. Courtesy of Royal Roads University.

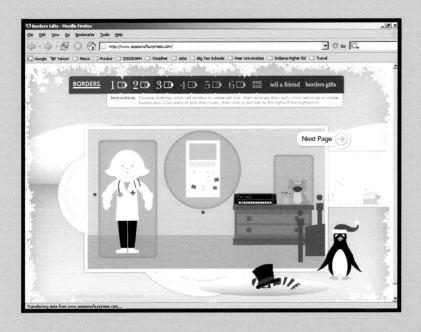

Border's holiday site *(http://seasonofsurprises.com/)*
provides a unique method of navigation and information
gathering, gleaning personal tastes and interests through
interactive graphics, rather than through simple written
questions.

| figure 4 |

Blue Ribbon Flies *(http://www.blueribbonflies.com/).* Blue
Ribbon Flies provides an aptly styled site that provides an
entire range of cataloged items related to fly fishing.
Courtesy of Blue Ribbon Flies.

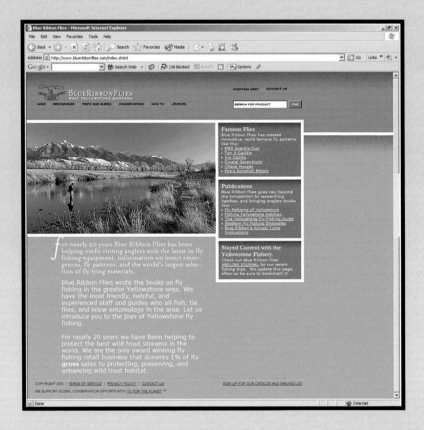

**figure 5**

OMNOVA Solutions Inc. *(http://www.omnova.com/)* used Dreamweaver to set up the initial page templates, making loading information easy.

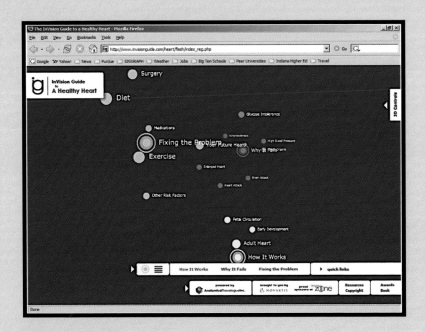

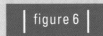

The Guide to a Healthy Heart *(http://www.invisionguide.com/heart)* provides unique navigation and superb graphics.

| figure 7 |

Brevard County Board of County Commissioners (*http://brevardcounty.us/bcc/*). The Brevard County Board of County Commissioners provides a portal-like interface to their web site. The site also provides a scalable approach to their interface. Courtesy of Brevard County Board of County Commissioners.

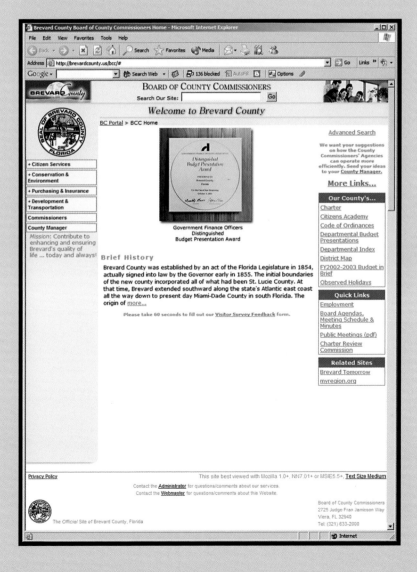

| figure 8 |

National Remote Controls *(http://www.nationalremotecontrols. com/)*. The National Remote Controls web site uses a straight-forward approach to viewing their products. Courtesy of National Remote Controls.

**figure 9**

Girls & Boys Town (http://www.boystownpediatrics.
org/). The Omaha Boys Town Pediatrics presents an
inviting design to their ASP-based web site.
Courtesy of Girls & Boys Town.

| figure 10 |

Kidport *(http://www.kidport.com/)* provides an engaging web site that provides a range of learning activities for children using Shockwave for Director. Courtesy of Kidport.

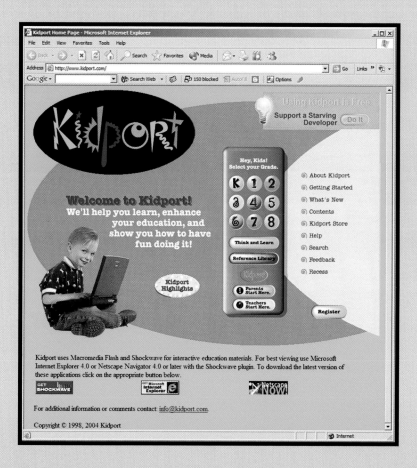

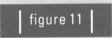

## figure 11

This site *(http://www.graphicvisioninc.com/holiday/)*
allows the user to create his or her own holiday
card.

| figure 12 |

The University of Rochester Medical Center
*(http://www.stronghealth.com/)*. The University of
Rochester Medical Center site provides a very
effective design with a nice balance between
photographs and graphical elements. Courtesy of
the University of Rochester Medical Center.

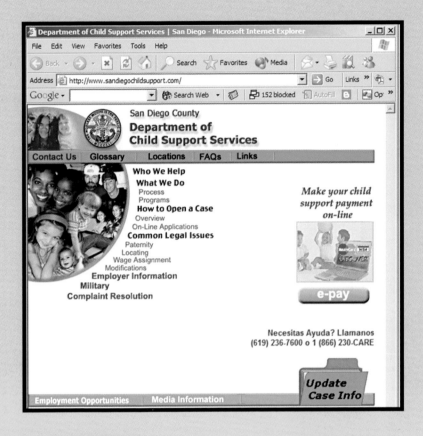

| figure 14 |

JPL Multimedia *(http://www.jpl.nasa.gov/multimedia/2005images/)* presents an interface for viewing images and other data.

## | figure 15 |

PrimeLearning.com *(http://www.primelearning.com)*. With a massive amount of information to convey, the Prime Learning web site presents an easy to navigate design. Courtesy of PrimeLearning.com.

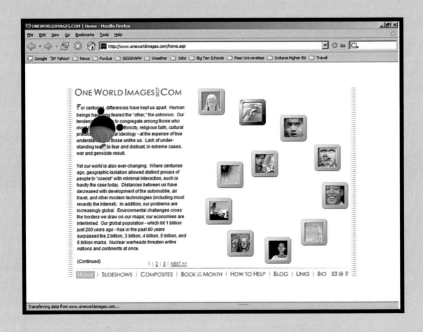

| figure 16 |

The One World Images site *(http://www.oneworldimages. com/home.asp)* provides an interesting look at various cultures. Courtesy of ONEWORLDIMAGES.COM.

## figure 17

Gulfstream Aerospace Company *(http://www.gulfstream.com/).* From navigation to the thoughtful placement of images, this web site demonstrates true design excellence. Courtesy of Gulfstream Aerospace.

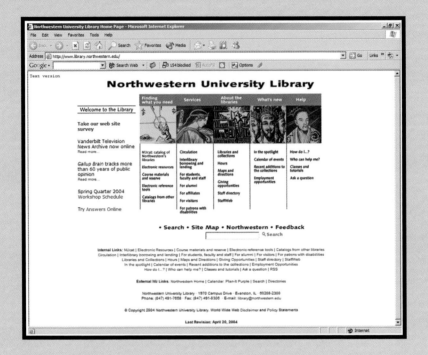

Northwestern University Library *(http://www.library.northwestern. edu)*. Northwestern University's library web site uses a navigation menu that doubles as a site map of sorts. Courtesy of Northwestern University Library.

| figure 19 |

Alphablox Corporation *(http://alphablox.com)*. The
Alphablox web site uses a fixed-width design, providing
some solidness to how it is laid out on various browsers
and screen sizes. Courtesy of Alphablox Corporation.

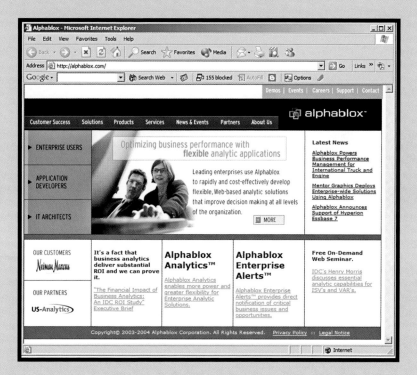

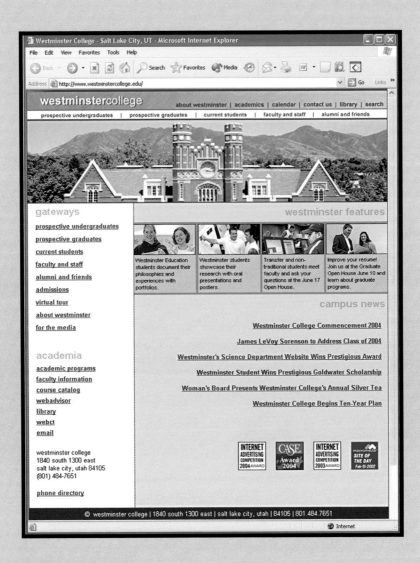

Westminster College *(http://www.westminstercollege. edu)*. With their award-winning site, Westminster College provides a quick overview of the primary areas of information. Courtesy of Westminster College of Salt Lake City, Utah.

## figure 21

Sallie Mae *(http://www.salliemae.com)*. The Sallie Mae web site is part information site, part application site, and provides an integrated design for both. Courtesy of Sallie Mae.

**| figure 22 |**

Memphis Cancer Center *(http://www.memphiscancercenter. com)*. From the flowing pop-out menus to content organization, the Memphis Cancer Center web site provides a truly refreshing design. Courtesy of Memphis Cancer Center.

**figure 23**

Crayola *(http://www.crayola.com/)*. Crayola.com is an attractive web site for kids of all ages. Courtesy of Binney & Smith.

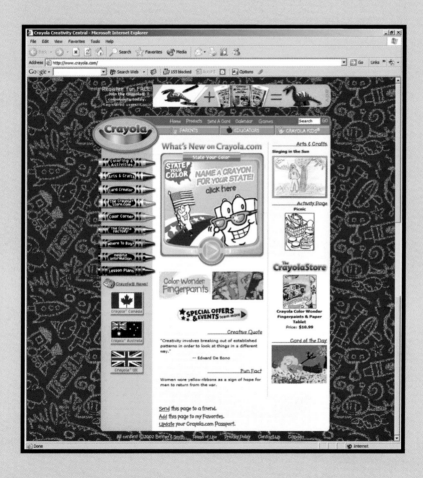

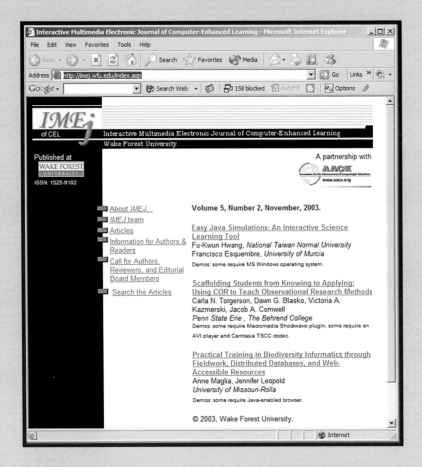

| figure 24 |

Journal of Computer Enhanced Learning *(http://imej.wfu.edu/index.asp)*. This site demonstrates a utilitarian approach—that of an academic journal. Courtesy of IMEJ, Wake Forest University.

Adding assets to your site is a continual process. For this reason, keep in mind that not everything will immediately appear within the Assets panel. This will commonly happen if you add site assets from outside Dreamweaver. For example, you may export a new movie from Flash, or create and add a new graphic from within Macromedia Fireworks. When this happens, you will need to manually refresh the list of items in the Assets panel. You can do this by clicking on the Refresh Site List button (see Figure 8-4) at the bottom of the panel. Keep in mind that if you have a fairly large site the process of building the list of assets may take a few moments.

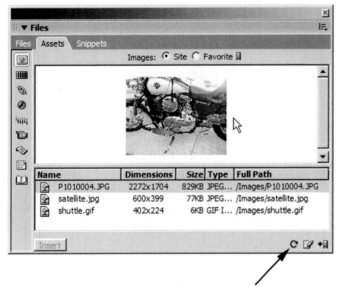

**Refresh Button**

figure | 8-4 |

You may need to refresh the Assets panel if you have recently added items from outside Dreamweaver.

In addition to sorting and managing, the Assets panel can help you find a particular element within the structure of your site. This feature only works with those assets (such as images, Shockwave files, or Flash movies) embodied by a particular file. To locate an asset, you can click on the element within the Assets panel and then click on the Locate in Site option from the panel's menu. This will automatically summon the Files panel, where the selected asset is highlighted.

## Inserting Assets into Your Page

One of the big advantages to using the Assets panel is that you can use it as a mechanism to directly add content to your pages. This is a very convenient way to add these elements without having to sift through all of the files that are a part of your site. There are two ways you can insert an asset into your page. The first method is to use the Insert button on the Assets panel (see Figure 8-5). To do this, place your cursor on the page where you want to drop in the element. Now select the item within the Assets panel, and then click on the Insert button. Dreamweaver will add the element with any associated HTML code. The other way to insert an asset is to use a drag-and-drop technique. Simply click on the item within the Assets panel, and then drag to the desired location in the Document window.

figure | 8-5 |

You can use the Insert button to add assets to your pages.

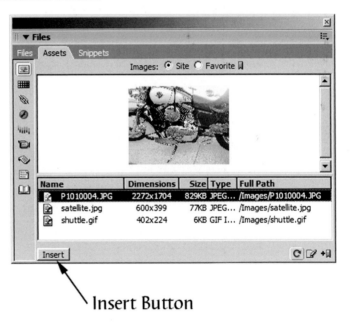

**Insert Button**

### Applying Color or URL Assets

Another asset you don't always think about when designing your web page is color. Typically when designing a site, you will decide on a palette of colors that will be used for elements such as text, links, and backgrounds. Once you establish this color palette, it can be difficult to remember details: "What was the hex number for that blue color I was using?" Using the Assets panel, you can track, manage, and apply color to objects within your pages.

In addition to applying color, you can attach a URL to text and images on your page. The Assets panel can be handy if you have a URL that is commonly used throughout your site. It also provides a way to manage external links, ensure that they are always the same when applied, and simply save you the time of typing each one in by hand.

To attach a new color or URL, start by highlighting the object on stage that will inherit the asset. Next, using the Assets panel (see Figure 8-6) click on the icon for either the color or URL category. Now you can select the item you wish to apply, and then click on Apply. The object should now exhibit traits of the asset.

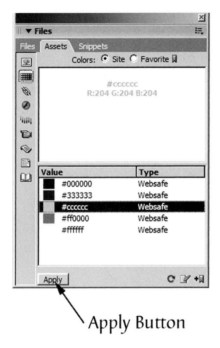

Apply Button

figure | 8-6 |

You can use the Apply button to attach colors or URLs to elements on your page.

It is possible to drag and drop colors and URLs just like with any other type of asset. However, when using this technique sometimes the asset will be applied to a part of the page you may not have intended.

**DON'T GO THERE !**

## Favorites

By default, Dreamweaver will display the Assets panel in the Site view. This view will list all assets for the entire site. If you have a large site, this can get to be a fairly lengthy list. To solve this problem, you can use the Favorites feature of the Assets panel. The Favorites view allows you to designate those assets that are particularly important, or frequently used. To enable this view, click on

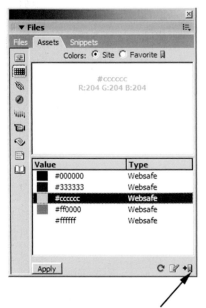

## Add to Favorites

figure | 8-7 |

You can use the Assets panel to help mange your "favorite" assets.

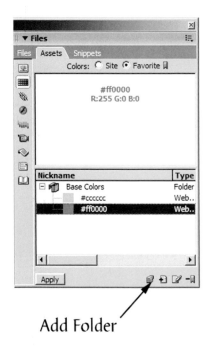

## Add Folder

the Favorites button at the top of the Assets panel. Once selected, only your "favorite" assets will appear.

So now you are probably wondering "How do I make something a favorite?" The process is simple. First select the asset in the Site view, and then click on the Add to Favorites button in the lower right of the panel (see Figure 8-7). If you enable the Favorites view now, this element will now appear. Now that the asset is a favorite, you can give it a nickname. You can think of an asset's nickname as a more friendly way of referring to an asset. For example, you might change a color asset to go from *#5f768b* to *Headline Color*. To make this change, select the item, and then select the Edit Nickname option from the Asset panel menu. You can now add whatever name makes sense to you.

When working in the Favorites view, you can further group assets by using folders. For example, if there is a series of colors that are only used with a particular part of your site you may want to separate these assets by dropping them into folders. To create a folder, click on the New Favorites Folder button (see Figure 8-8) at the bottom of the Assets panel, and then provide a name. Once created, you can drag and drop assets into this folder.

### Creating New Favorite Assets

When working with favorite colors and URLs, you can actually create new assets that will only appear in the Favorites panel. These are the only elements that can show

figure | 8-8 |

You can add folders to the Assets panel to further organize your assets.

up in your Assets panel without being used anywhere on the site. The process of creating a new color or URL asset is basically the same. First select either the color or URL category button on the Assets panel. Now click on the New Color (or New URL) button at the bottom of the panel. In the case of a new color, the standard color picker will appear (see Figure 8-9). Simply select your color to have it added to the list of assets. In the case of a new URL, the Add URL dialog box will be summoned (see Figure 8-10). Using this dialog box, you can define both a URL and nickname for the new asset. Once you click on OK, the item will be added to the list.

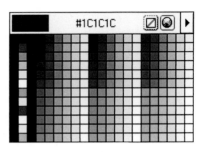

figure | 8-9 |

You can add new colors to the Favorites view of the Assets panel.

figure | 8-10 |

You can add new colors to the Favorites view of the Assets panel.

# ALL ABOUT LIBRARIES

A challenge many web designers face is how to manage modular elements that may appear across an entire site. Because these elements may appear on every page, it is important that they appear consistently throughout the site. For example, many web pages include copyright information at the bottom of each page. Because this element appears on every page, it is important that it always appear the exact same way. To solve this problem, Dreamweaver offers the Library feature. Using Library items, you can create an element once and then repeat it across your entire web site.

## How Libraries Work

Libraries, somewhat like templates, are Dreamweaver-specific files that contain a piece of code that can be inserted into a web page. There are many advantages to building library items out of your reusable elements. First, library items can be used to replicate any item that may appear in the body of a web page. It makes little difference whether that item is as simple as copyright information or as important as a menu bar. In the case of elements such as images or movies, the library will only store a link to the included asset. In addition, library items can be portable. This means that you can develop library items and share them with several web sites. Probably the best reason to use library items is because you can help automate the maintenance of your web pages. If you think about the copyright information example I used earlier, what happens if you want to update the year of the copyright without editing each page individually? Using a library item, you can simply update a single file and then cascade the change across your entire site.

## The Nuts and Bolts of Library Items

Before we get too deep in the process of building library items, we should first discuss what exactly it is made of. Simply put, a library item is nothing more than a chunk of HTML (or ASP, JSP, ColdFusion, and so on) code. When a library item is embedded into a document, HTML comment tags are used to designate the library item and to denote what library file it is attached to (see Figure 8-11). Your audience will never really know (unless they go looking) that the element has been treated any differently. It is important to keep these tags in your pages because it will associate the item with the file used to define it. Maintaining this relationship will facilitate making any global changes that may be needed later.

figure | 8-11 |

Dreamweaver will use special markup to designate library items that have been embedded into your pages.

Library Item

```
1  <!DOCTYPE HTML PUBLIC "-//W3C//DTD HTML 4.01 Transitional//EN"
2  "http://www.w3.org/TR/html4/loose.dtd">
3  <html>
4  <head>
5  <title>Untitled Document</title>
6  <meta http-equiv="Content-Type" content="text/html; charset=iso-8859-1">
7  <link href="maxaerostyle.css" rel="stylesheet" type="text/css">
8  </head>
9
10 <body>
11 <!-- #BeginLibraryItem "/Library/menuBar.lbi" -->
12 <table width="100%" border="0" align="center" cellpadding="0" cellspacing="0">
13   <tr>
14     <td width="10"><img src="images/menubar/btn_cap_left.gif" width="10" height="28"></td>
15     <td width="227" align="center" class="menuBar">Home</td>
16     <td width="227" align="center" class="menuBar">About</td>
17     <td width="227" align="center" class="menuBar">People</td>
18     <td width="227" align="center" class="menuBar">Contact</td>
19     <td width="227" align="center" class="menuBar">News</td>
20     <td width="217" align="center" class="menuBar">Projects</td>
21     <td width="10"><img src="images/menubar/btn_cap_right.gif" width="10" height="28"></td>
22   </tr>
23 </table>
24 <!-- #EndLibraryItem -->
25 </body>
26 </html>
```

Each library item will be saved as an individual file with an *.LBI* file extension. In addition, the *.LBI* files are stored within the *Library* directory at the root of your local site. All of the library items used with the site should all be stored within this same directory. If this directory does not already exist, Dreamweaver will create it for you when the first library item is saved (see Figure 8-12).

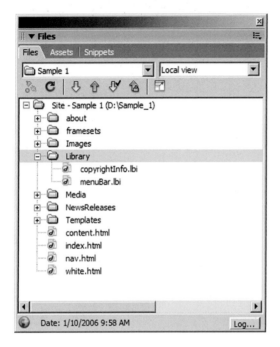

figure | 8-12 |

All library items are stored within the Library directory at the root of your local site.

## Building Library Items

Once you've decided that a library item is the way to go, how do you put one together? There are two different ways you can build a library item. If the element doesn't already exist, you can start a library item from scratch. Or, if you already have an existing design you can select a portion of the page to convert to a library item. Let's take a look at the former first.

Building a library item from a blank slate is exactly like working with a standard HTML page. To start the process, select the File | New menu option to open the New Document dialog box, shown in Figure 8-13. From the Category list on the left, select the Basic Page Option; then click on the *Library item* option from the right. Once you click on Create, a new library item file will open within the Document window. You can now use the standard editing tools to add any elements your library item requires. After you have finished, save your file to the *Library* directory we discussed earlier.

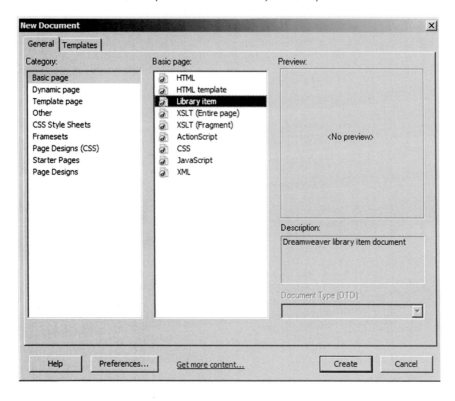

figure | 8-13 |

You can start a new library item much the same way you would create a new HTML page.

NOTE: You can also start a library item by using the Assets panel. All you need to do is select the Library button from the left-hand side of the panel, and then click on the New Library Item button, shown in Figure 8-14. Once created, you can use the Edit button to open the file for modification in the Document window.

To build a library item, you can start with a blank HTML page and build the element or you can open an existing page that already contains the element. Start the process by selecting the object within the Document window that is to be converted into the library item. Once selected, select Modify I Library I Add Object to Library. If it is not already open, this will summon the Assets panel. At this point the item has been added to the Assets panel, but still needs a name. Using this panel, add the name that will be used to reference this item. This same name will also be assigned to the *.LBI* file within the *Library* directory.

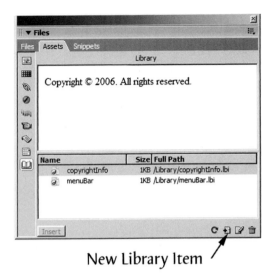

New Library Item

figure | 8-14 |

You can use the
Assets panel to start
a new library item.

Once you build a library item that includes images, or other linked elements, it is important that these items never change in name or location. Because the library item only stores a reference to these assets, altering the path information would cause the library item to not work correctly. If you do need to rename or move a linked asset, make certain the library item is also updated to reflect the change.

# Inserting Library Items

Now that you have developed a library item, it can now be inserted into a page within your site. The first step is to place your cursor at the point in the Document window where you want to insert the library item. Now, if it is not open already summon the Assets panel by selecting Window | Assets. In this panel, click on the library item you wish to add, and then click on the Insert button. All of the objects within the library item will now appear in the Document window. Note that once inserted they will appear with a light yellow highlight. This is a visual cue that we are working with one contiguous library item. Also, the entire item will appear selected if you click or highlight anywhere within this element (see Figure 8-15). This way, you can move, copy, or delete a library item as one complete element.

figure | 8-15 |

Once you have
added a library item
to your page,
Dreamweaver will
treat it as one com-
plete object.

| HOME | ABOUT | PEOPLE | CONTACT | NEWS | PROJECTS |

## Modifying Library Items

As I mentioned earlier, one of the big advantages to using library items is that they can facilitate making changes across an entire web site. By adjusting a library item, the change can be applied to all pages that have a reference to that library file.

The process of modifying a library item starts with opening the *.LBI* file that exists in the *Library* directory at the root of your site. A library file can be opened by double clicking on the item's name within the Assets panel. Once you have the file open in the Document window, you can make all of your desired changes as you would normally work within Dreamweaver. After you have finished making changes, select File | Save.

At this point, Dreamweaver will summon the Update Library Items dialog box, shown in Figure 8-16. This dialog box contains a listing of all pages that were saved with a reference to the library item you are currently working with. Clicking on the Update button will trigger Dreamweaver to run through all pages on this list and make the same changes you made to the original library item. Conversely, if you want to manually update your pages clicking on the Don't Update button will cause Dreamweaver to skip the update process entirely.

figure | 8-16 |

The Update Library Items dialog box lists all pages that will be modified to reflect any new changes.

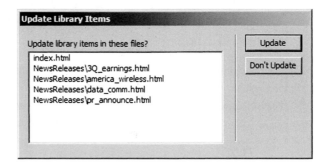

Once all of your pages have been modified, Dreamweaver will display the Update Pages dialog box, shown in Figure 8-17. For this procedure, the information to take from this dialog box is found in the log area at the bottom. This log information explains what files were updated, the numbers of files examined and updated, and those files that could not be updated.

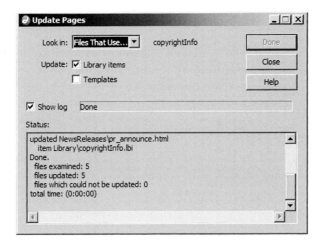

figure | 8-17|

Update Pages
dialog box.

## Working with Item Properties

After a library item has been inserted into a page, you can open, detach, or recreate the item using the Property Inspector (see Figure 8-18). To take advantage of these features, first select the item and then click on the appropriate button in the Property Inspector. The following describe the options available.

figure | 8-18|

Using the Property
Inspector, you can
work with a library
item.

- ● *Open:* Clicking on this button will open the library item in the Document window. Using this feature will allow you to make updates to the library item as you are working with other documents. If you make a change, and choose to update all the files within your site, the change will also be applied to the document you are currently working on.

- ● *Detach from original:* Clicking on this button will remove the relationship to the library file. In fact, the item will no longer be considered a library item at all. This can be useful if you need to make a one-time change to a library item.

- ● *Recreate:* When a library file is deleted from the site, references to that file will still exit in those pages where it had been embedded. So, if you ever accidentally deleted a library item that has already been inserted into a page this option can be used to regenerate the library file.

# SUMMARY

In this chapter we explored how you can manage your site's reusable assets and the process for building library items. As you continue to design and build pages of your own, every second of work you can save will count. Using the Assets panel can save you time when attempting to locate design elements, and help you maintain consistency. Also, by building and implementing library items as site assets you can streamline the production process. As you move on through the remainder of this book, begin to think about techniques you can use.

## in review

1. What types of elements can be managed using the Assets panel?

2. What is the difference between Site and Favorites in the library?

3. How do you create colors and URLs in the Favorites view of the Assets panel?

4. What is a library item used for?

5. What are the advantages to using library items? Discuss an example where using a library item would facilitate development.

6. How do you create a library item?

7. Once created, how can you modify a library item and apply the change to your entire site?

## ↗ EXPLORING ON YOUR OWN

1. Use the Assets panel to explore the objects used with your current local site. If you already have a site within Dreamweaver, try setting up a few of the more common elements in the Favorites view.

2. Develop library items from the key components of your own web designs. These components are typically items such as banners, footer information, or menus. Once you have a library item created, try making a modification and apply that change to your site.

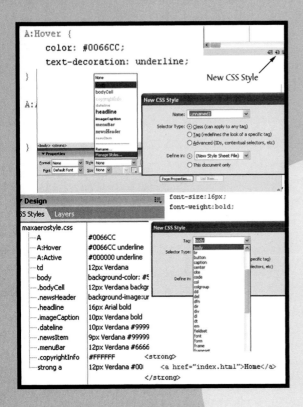

Formatting Text with CSS

*charting your course*

A growing trend in web design is to use techniques that reinforce the hard line that should exist between the content of a page and that page's appearance. For example, the message portrayed by a blurb of text is very much different than how that text may appear. This is an important point to make because the style or design applied to the content of your site is highly volatile. By the time you finish one design, it will be time to move onto the next. For that reason, making the separation between design and content can help facilitate keeping your site in a fluid state. By effectively implementing Cascading Style Sheets (CSS) you can maintain design control over the content on your page, and keep the segregation between design and content in ways not afforded to you with standard HTML. If there is one design tool the modern web designer must master it is CSS.

Through this chapter and the next we will explore the two fundamental ways designers typically use CSS. In this chapter, we are going to take a look at how you can develop style sheets, and then apply those styles to the text on your page. I should also preface this by saying that this chapter is by no means an exhaustive review of everything you can do with CSS, but it should be a good start. Next, in Chapter 10, we will dive into how CSS can be used to set your page's physical layout.

 *goals*

- **Learn about the pieces and parts that comprise a style**

- **Learn how styles can be used to design your site**

- **Explore the Dreamweaver tools that can be used to build styles**

# ABOUT CSS

In a nutshell, CSS is a tool that allows you to apply specific style rules to the content of your pages at several different levels. For example, some styles may be applied to an entire page, while others may only apply to just one sentence, word, or letter. In addition, you can also treat some HTML elements, such as hyperlinks or form elements, differently than anything else. Almost any element that appears on your page can have a style applied to it. Let's take a look at some of the general concepts behind developing with CSS.

## Why Use CSS?

Using CSS with your web designs has several distinct advantages. First is that it reduces that amount of time or code needed to maintain the visual appearance of the elements on a page. By editing one style, you can change the appearance of all elements on your site that use that same style. This can also be helpful in enforcing a consistent appearance with common elements across your site. For example, by applying a style to the headline of your news releases you can be assured that all of your headlines will have the exact same formatting.

Another major advantage to CSS is that it provides you with greater formatting options than HTML alone. For example, with HTML all hyperlinks on your page will look exactly alike. Using CSS, you can apply styles to hyperlinks that will make some appear differently than others, and completely at your discretion. In the next chapter, we will take a look at how we can use some of these unique formatting options to establish tighter control over page layouts.

## Anatomy of a Style Sheet

CSS are all built with the same basic parts, shown in Figure 9-1. Generally speaking, a style sheet is comprised of a collection of CSS rules. If it is easier, you can think of this as each rule defines an individual style that can be applied to your page. A rule, or style, is further broken down into two component parts: the selector and the definition. The selector, simply put, is the name of the style. This is the name used within your HTML page to reference this particular style. There are special considerations to make when

```
.headline {
    font-family: Arial, Helvetica, sans-serif;
    font-size:16px;
    font-weight:bold;
}
```

figure | 9-1 |

The basic parts that comprise a CSS rule.

choosing the name to use as the selector. Dependent on how a selector is defined, a style may be applied completely differently. In the following section, "Selecting Selectors," I will go over what you need to know to choose the right name.

The aforementioned CSS declaration establishes the attributes of a style. Once you have applied a style to an element within your page, the declaration determines how this object will appear. The declaration does this by using two additional parts: the property and the value. For example, you might have a property of "font weight" and a value of "bold" that would be applied to text. There is a fairly lengthy list of the possible properties you can use within a declaration. In addition, each type of property may require that values be defined in different ways.

At this point you are probably asking, "If I am working in Dreamweaver why is this all important?" Although Dreamweaver provides a number of tools to help you specify styles, it is still important to understand the vocabulary. It also helps to know that when you make text bold, blue, and twelve pixels tall what this actually means behind the scenes. Understanding the holistic picture of CSS will help you be more efficient when working with styles within Dreamweaver.

## Selecting Selectors

As I mentioned earlier, what you use as a selector may impact how a style is applied. In addition to being able to create your own custom styles, called classes, you can leverage existing HTML tags to help you apply styles within your document. There is also a third method you can use to apply styles only under certain conditions. Let's take a look at each of these a little further.

### Redefining a Tag

The easiest and quickest way to establish and apply a style is by redefining an existing HTML tag. This means that any content that

```
<a href="index.html">Home</a>
```

figure | 9-2 |

The typical HTML code used to create a hyperlink.

```
A {
    color: #0066CC;
}
```

figure | 9-3 |

This CSS will redefine the appearance of any hyperlink that appears on a page using this style.

```
A:Hover {
    color: #0066CC;
    text-decoration: underline;
}

A:Active {
    color: #000000;
    text-decoration: underline;
}
```

figure | 9-4 |

These sample pseudo-classes define how hyperlinks will behave when the user interacts with them.

appears between two HTML tags will now present the visual properties defined within the style sheet. For example, a very common use of style sheets is to define the color of hyperlinks. If you look at the sample HTML in Figure 9-2 you can see that hyperlinks are denoted using the <a> tag. By using CSS and redefining the <a> tag, to use our style rather than the default appearance we can establish the visual attributes of every hyperlink that has this style sheet attached. In case you are curious, Figure 9-3 shows an example of a style rule that redefines the <a> HTML tag.

## Pseudo-classes

Typically when you specify a new selector you are tying it to a specific tag or reference within the HTML document. However, sometimes a web design includes more than just the content of a page. Pseudo-classes offer you a mechanism to attach a style to an event that may occur when your page is displayed within the browser. This allows your web design to interact with external information from the user. Probably the most common pseudo-classes are those used with hyperlinks. Because the user interacts with hyperlinks, they can have several different states. For example, a hyperlink can be clicked on or visited by the end user. But there are other interesting effects you may not instantly think about. CSS offers something called the hover pseudo-class, which is used to define what a hyperlink looks like when the user's cursor is placed over the link. Figure 9-4 shows several example CSS rules that use pseudo-classes. Effectively using pseudo-classes, such as those mentioned here, can create a slightly more interactive experience for the visitors of your site.

## Contextual Selectors

Sometimes you may want to define a style by using an HTML tag, but you don't want to apply it to every instance within your page. Using a contextual selector, you can apply a style based on the presence of a series of HTML tags. You can think of the contextual selector as specifying an "exception to the rule." Building on our last example, you may want to define a hyperlink to appear in a different color, but only if this hyperlink appears within the bold (or <strong>) HTML tags. Figure 9-5 shows an example CSS rule that uses the contextual selector of *strong a*. This style will only appear with elements that are within the <strong> and <a> tags (see Figure 9-6). It is important to mention that the contextual selector is sensitive to the order in which the tags appear. If the tags are reversed, the style will not be applied.

figure | **9-5**

This CSS rule will only apply to elements within the <strong> and <a> tags.

```
strong a {
    font-family: Verdana, Arial, Helvetica, sans-serif;
    font-size: 12px;
    font-weight: bold;
    color: #000033;
}
```

```
<strong>
    <a href="index.html">Home</a>
</strong>
```

figure | **9-6**

This HTML will inherit the style defined in Figure 9-5.

## Adding Class

Probably the most common way to establish a style is by defining a new class. This type of CSS element is used when you want a custom style that can be applied to anything on the page. Usually you will create a new class to accompany a particular area of content within your design. For example, if your web site includes a number of news releases, you may want to create a new class just to define what the headline for each release will look like. By creating this style and then applying it to your news releases you can maintain control over how all of your headlines will appear. If you ever change the declaration of this style, any page elements that use this style will be instantly updated. Figure 9-7 presents a CSS rule that uses a custom class called *headline*.

A little later in this chapter, we will cover how you can apply your classes to areas of content using Dreamweaver. However, keep in mind that behind the scenes there are multiple ways this style is applied. Figure 9-8 shows two different methods by which this type of style may be embedded into your HTML code.

figure | 9-7 |

```
.headline {
        font-family: Arial, Helvetica, sans-serif;
        font-size:16px;
        font-weight:bold;
}
```

This CSS style rule is used to define a class called head-line.

figure | 9-8 |

```
<span class="headline">
        Maximum Aerospace Takes Flight
</span>

<p class="headline">
        Maximum Aerospace Takes Flight
</p>
```

Two samples of how a CSS can be imple-mented.

## Implementing CSS

Although CSS formatting rules are generally consistent in how they are written, there are actually three different ways they can be implemented. The first and most common method is to establish a linked style sheet, which is a separate document with a *.CSS* extension. In practice, this is the most effective way of using style sheets because it allows you to share styles across your entire site. When using this model, each of your HTML pages will include a refer-ence, or link, to the external style sheet within the *<head>* area. This way, you could actually change the entire visual appearance of your site by editing just one file. It is also important to note that you can reference more than one style sheet with any page. Using multiple CSS files will provide you with a little extra flexibility when developing styles that may be used across your entire site, or just on a few pages.

Another method for defining styles is to embed the CSS within the *<head>* area of a document. This method defines styles in the exact same manner as the external file. The primary difference is that embedded CSS will only be available to that one page. In reality, using this technique negates some of the advantages to using style sheets at all.

The last technique for establishing styles is by using what is called an inline style. This method defines a style directly within the HTML code where it is used. For example, you could define a style within a paragraph tag to affect the appearance of just that one paragraph. Defining styles in this way has many drawbacks, and thus it should probably never be used unless you have a pretty good reason.

# WORKING WITH CSS

Now that you understand some of the general concepts, let's roll up our sleeves and take a look at how Dreamweaver can help you build, maintain, and apply CSS rules. The emphasis of the opening pages of this chapter was on how CSS works despite any tool you may use. Now it is time to see where the rubber hits the road. Through the remainder of this chapter we will be exploring how the information from introductory pages of this chapter can be implemented using CSS within Dreamweaver. So, if you were a little confused by this chapter at first never fear. By the time we are finished, you will be defining classes and applying styles with ease.

figure | 9-9 |

The CSS Styles panel is used to view and manage available styles.

## The Styles Panel

The central operations point for using styles within Dreamweaver is the CSS Styles panel. This panel, shown in Figure 9-9, can be summoned via the Window | CSS Styles menu option. Once opened, it may be used to view, create, edit, and delete styles for your web design. The CSS Styles panel can also be used to attach preexisting style sheets to your current document. If you take a look at this panel, you will notice that it is

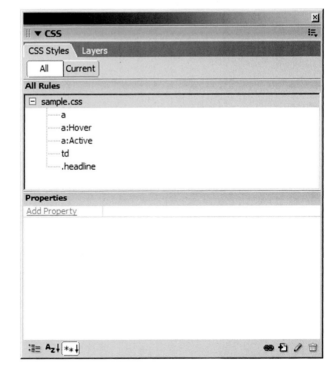

broken into two columns. On the left you will see the selector for each CSS rule, whereas the right-hand column displays a portion of the declaration. From this you can already begin to see how understanding the basics of CSS can help you work with styles within Dreamweaver. Let's get started by building a new style.

## Creating Styles

As we discussed earlier in this chapter, there are several ways you can implement styles within your web designs. No matter how you may choose to create the styles, in Dreamweaver it all begins with one button, the New CSS Style button (shown in Figure 9-10). When you click on this button, the New CSS Style window will be summoned. At first glance you will notice some of the terminology we talked about earlier in this chapter. Using this dialog box, shown in Figure 9-11, you can specify three critical aspects of any CSS rule.

figure | 9-10 |

Use the New CSS Style button to start a new style.

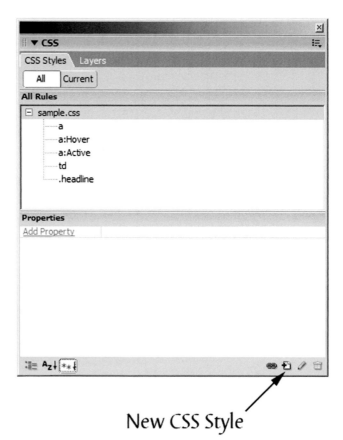

New CSS Style

figure | 9-11 |

The New CSS Style dialog box is used to establish where and how your new style will be implemented.

**NOTE:** There are multiple ways you can begin the process of creating a new style within Dreamweaver. Another common method is to start a new CSS rule via the Text | CSS Styles | New menu option.

The first thing you need to decide about for your new CSS rule is what type of selector this style will use. The selector is specified by choosing the appropriate item from the Selector Type list. If you don't exactly recall what each of these types does, see the "Selecting Selectors" section from earlier. What you choose as the selector type will directly affect how you specify the selector's name. The following detail the implications of using each of these options.

● *Class:* Using this selector type will allow you to specify a custom class that can be applied to nearly any object on your page. Once you select the radio button corresponding to this option, you can specify a name at the top of the New CSS Style dialog box. In reality, a class name can be any combination of numbers or letters. However, keep in mind that the class name must always begin with a period. This period is what lets the browser know that we are dealing with a custom CSS class and not a redefined HTML tag.

● *Tag:* Using this selector type will allow you to specify a single HTML tag whose appearance will be redefined. Once you choose the radio button corresponding to this option, you can use the Tag pull-down list (see Figure 9-12) to specify the HTML tag. For example, if you wanted to redefine the hyperlink tag you would select an option from this menu.

● *Advanced:* Using this selector type will allow you to specify an alternative type of style, such as a contextual selector or pseudo-classes. By default, once you select the radio button corresponding to this option the Selector pull-down menu (see Figure 9-13) will automatically be populated with several common pseudo-classes. If you are using the advanced selector

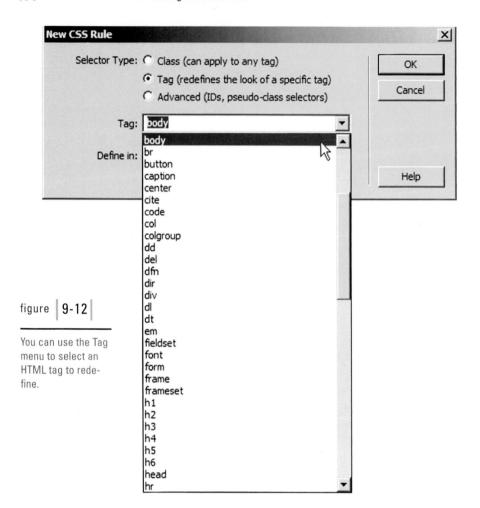

figure | 9-12 |

You can use the Tag menu to select an HTML tag to redefine.

figure | 9-13 |

When the advanced option is enabled, the Name menu will have several pseudo-classes available by default.

type to define something other than a pseudo-class, such as a contextual selector, simply type in the names of the tags you wish to use.

After choosing the appropriate selector you can specify where this new style should be implemented. In practice, Dreamweaver provides two of the options we discussed earlier. You can either add the style to an external *.CSS* file or drop the style within the *<head>* area of the current document. If you do want to add the style to the current document, you can select the *This document only* option. Otherwise, you can use an external file (which you probably should do most of the time) by choosing to start a new *.CSS* file or by adding the style to an existing one. Using the *Define in* menu you can select which scenario you prefer. By selecting the New Style Sheet File option, you will be asked to provide a name and location for the new *.CSS* file as the next step in this process. When creating a new file in this way, it will automatically be attached to the current document.

figure | **9-14** |

Once you have finished making the decisions as to how to implement your new style, click on the OK button to open the CSS Style Definition dialog box, shown in Figure 9-14. As you can see, this dialog box has been divided into eight separate categories. Because this chapter is focused on applying CSS to the text within your page, we

The CSS Style Definition dialog box is used to specify the parameters of the new style.

**CSS Rule Definition for .ImageCaption in sample.css**                    ✕

Category                    Type

Type
Background          Font:
Block
Box                Size:          pixels    Weight:
Border
List               Style:                   Variant:
Positioning
Extensions         Line height:        pixels    Case:

                   Decoration:  ☐ underline              Color:
                                ☐ overline
                                ☐ line-through
                                ☐ blink
                                ☐ none

                   OK          Cancel          Apply          Help

are only going to talk about the Type and List categories. In Chapter 10 we will take a closer look at the others, which deal with visual design and layout.

The Type category, shown in Figure 9-14, is used to specify the typical text formatting options, such as font, size, or color. You can use these properties in combination to specify how your text will appear when rendered within the web browser. The other text-focused CSS style option is the List category, shown in Figure 9-15. Using this category, you can specify properties that will determine how HTML lists appear. A common use for this style is to define a different, or custom, bullet to use with an unordered list.

figure | 9-15 |

You can use the List category to adjust the physical appearance of an HTML list.

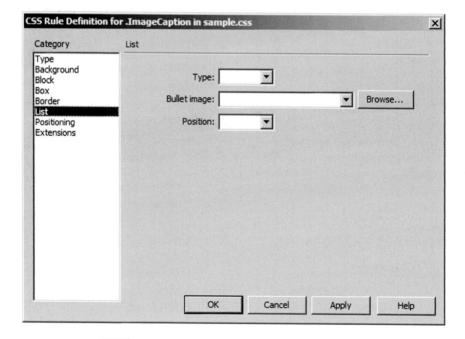

**NOTE:** It is beyond the scope of this book to go into the particulars of what each of the properties within these two categories will do when applied. If you are interested in more information, see the Dreamweaver help file available via the Help | Using Dreamweaver menu option or visit the W3C web site at *www.w3.org*.

Once you have completed specifying values for your desired properties, click on the OK button. This will add the CSS style rule to the external file, or internally within the *<head>* area of the current document. If you take a look at the CSS Styles panel, you will see the new style you just created.

## TRY THIS

Now that we have gone through the process of building styles, take a few minutes to specify a few of your own. Try creating a style using each of the different selector types we discussed earlier. You will probably want to save these styles in an external style sheet so that you have something to use when we get to the part of this chapter that deals with applying your styles to content within a page.

### Edit a Style

Now that you have created a new style, you may need to continue to tweak the settings to achieve your desired effect. To edit an existing style, select its entry within the CSS Styles panel; then click on the Edit Style button (see Figure 9-16) to open the CSS Style Definition dialog box we used to create a style earlier. Now all you have to do is make your adjustments and click on the OK button. If you are using a linked style sheet, any reference to the edited style will now inherit the new settings when displayed. In Chapter 10, we will explore the CSS Properties area of the Tag Inspector. Using this tool, you can gain direct access to edit properties within a CSS style.

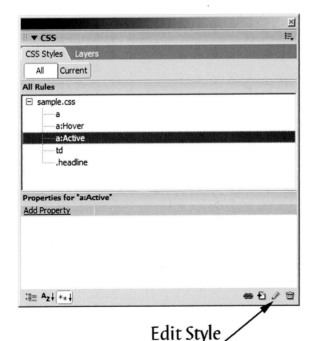

Edit Style

figure | 9-16 |

By clicking on the Edit Style button, you can adjust a preexisting style.

## Exporting a Style Sheet

Sometimes when I am working on a new design, I like to insert all of my CSS styles within the same document I am working on. This way, everything I need is in one file, so I don't have to flip back and forth between several files. Although, when I am ready to move past the design phase of a project keeping styles within the <head> of a document is not a very elegant way of using CSS. For this reason, Dreamweaver provides the Export CSS option. By selecting File | Export | CSS Styles, you can copy all the style rules from your document and then save them as an external file. It is important to mention that exporting the CSS only gets you part of the way to relying on an external style sheet. You must delete the CSS code that still exists within the head of your document, in addition to linking to the new .CSS file. To do this, read on.

## Deleting a Style

You may find yourself in a situation where you may no longer need a particular style, or a reference to a collection of styles. When this happens, you can use the CSS Styles panel to remove references to the CSS. To do this, first click on the name of the style within the CSS Styles panel, and then click on the Delete CSS Style button, shown in Figure 9-17. If you wish to remove a link to a style sheet, repeat this same process but click on the name of the file that is shown in the CSS Styles panel. Keep in mind that this will only remove the reference to the style sheet, and not delete the .CSS file itself. You can also permanently remove any CSS code contained within the current document by selecting the CSS Style panel's <style> element as the item to delete.

## Attaching a Style Sheet

If you are starting a new page and want to leverage the styles from an existing style sheet, you can use the CSS Styles panel's Attach Style Sheet option, shown in Figure 9-18. Once you have clicked on this button, the Attach External Style Sheet dialog box will appear. Using this dialog box, shown in Figure 9-19, you can use the File/URL field to specify the .CSS file to reference within this page. After selecting a file, you must also choose weather to Link or Import this style sheet. Typically you will choose to link to the file because it is supported by the widest number of web browsers. However, you also have the option to import the .CSS file. Using this option will add an import element within CSS code that is

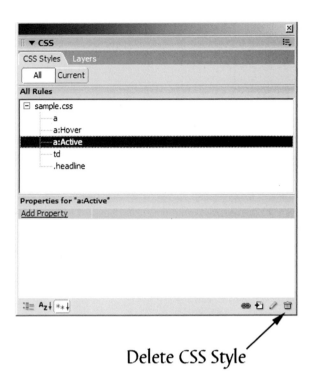

Delete CSS Style

figure | **9-17** |

You can use the CSS Style panel to delete styles, or references to style sheets.

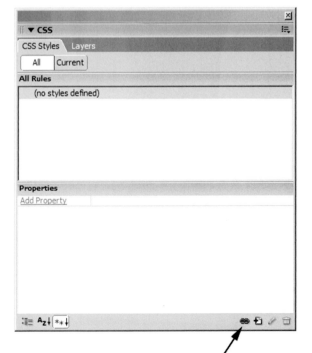

Attach Style Sheet

figure | **9-18** |

You can use the CSS Styles panel to attach an existing *.CSS* file.

embedded in the current HTML document. By importing rather than linking, you will be creating a nested style sheet, whereas the CSS in the external file is treated similarly to styles embedded within the HTML. This relationship comes into play when considering what happens when there are conflicting styles. We will be covering conflicting styles a little later in this chapter.

figure | 9-19 |

You can either link to or import an existing style sheet.

## Applying a Style

When designing with CSS a majority of your time will be spent defining all the styles that will be used throughout your site. Once all of the styles have been established, only those that are custom classes will need to be applied to elements within your page. The other selector types will automatically be applied to the HTML tags they have redefined.

The process of applying a style is as easy as any other type of formatting you may have applied in the past. It all starts by selecting the text that will inherit the new appearance defined within your CSS. Next, use the Style menu within the Property Inspector (see Figure 9-20) to select the style you want to apply. This menu should display all of the possible options per the style sheets currently referenced within the current document. Once you have clicked on the desired style's name, the text element will appear with this style within the Document window. Now that the style has been applied, any edits you make to the style itself will appear with any text that has referenced that style. I should also note that if you have inadvertently applied a style to the wrong text element you can remove it by selecting the None option from the Style menu on the Property Inspector.

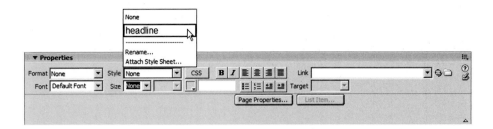

figure | 9-20 |

## Conflicting Styles

With so many ways of implementing CSS rules, in addition to all of the possible elements that may have a style applied, what happens when styles conflict? For example, you may have a text element that has two or more styles that are currently affecting how it is being displayed. In one instance, you may have redefined the paragraph tag to display all text using the font Verdana. Somewhere in the middle of a paragraph you may have applied a custom class that specified text as being blue. In this case, since there is no direct conflict the text will combine the two applied styles and display the text as Verdana and blue. However, if your custom class were to specify that this text use a Courier font now we have a conflict. The conflict rests in that portions of the same paragraph of text have two styles that define the font as something different; so which does it use? The general rule is that the style with priority is that which is closest to the element. So, in this case the text would appear in the Courier font as defined by the class. A key thing to remember is that styles defined as a class will override styles that are the redefinition of an HTML tag.

You can use the Property Inspector to apply CSS classes to your text.

# SUMMARY

In this chapter we have explored many of the basics related to Cascading Style Sheets (CSS). The key concepts you should have picked up are how CSS works, the pieces and parts that are used to define a CSS rule, and how to construct and apply styles within Dreamweaver. In the next chapter we focus on how you can use CSS to establish visual layouts on your pages without having to use images of tables for spacing. Although this functionality has been around since the conception of CSS, it is just now beginning to be a hot topic among web designers.

## in review

1. What are the advantages to using CSS with your web designs?

2. What are the three ways CSS may be defined?

3. What is the selector within a CSS rule?

4. What is the declaration within a CSS rule?

5. How do pseudo-classes differ from other types of CSS selectors?

6. What are the two parts that make up a declaration? Give an example of each.

7. What are the three types of selectors that can be used?

8. How are styles established within Dreamweaver?

9. How can you apply CSS to text elements within your pages?

10. How are conflicts between CSS styles resolved?

## ↗ EXPLORING ON YOUR OWN

1. Create a series of CSS styles you can use for future projects. Export and/or save these styles to an external *.CSS* file. Try to use several of the available selector types.

2. Begin planning a style sheet for a new project you would like to take on once you have completed this book. Think about the different types of content you may use with this site, and how they may visually appear on the page.

3. Building on what you learned in Chapter 7, try taking one of your Dreamweaver templates and attaching an existing style sheet to it. Once attached, apply the changes to the template across several pages within your site. Now you can adjust the properties within the style sheet to see the effects on your templated content.

**notes**

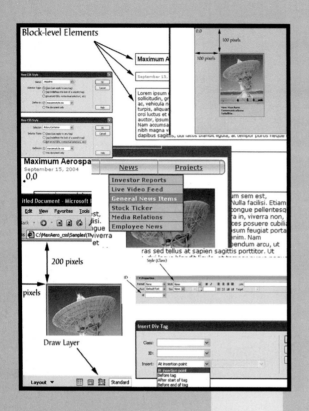

Developing Layouts with CSS

*charting your course*

For a number of years developers have been using HTML tables as the primary tool to create layouts for their web designs. This method has been thoroughly battle tested, and is supported by several generations of popular web browsers. Despite the fact that designing with tables is now more a science than art, this method is still far from perfect. HTML tables were never designed to be used for visual layout. Web designers have managed to contort the use of tables well beyond their intended purpose—containing tabular data. So if tables were not meant as design tools, what is the alternative?

This question is the basis for one of the most recent debates within the web design community. Cascading Style Sheets (CSS) offer designers an alternative to using tables for layout. This technique of using CSS is commonly referred to as creating "tableless" layouts. By using CSS, designers have a level of control over their designs that was never afforded with tables. Although using CSS is not necessarily a new idea, only recent developments in web browsers and design tools, such as Dreamweaver, supported this concept.

In this chapter we are going to explore how CSS can be used to build and maintain tight control over your web designs. For those of you that aren't quite ready to make the jump to tableless design, CSS can still be used to grant you greater control over how tables are rendered. Some of the same styling techniques used with tableless layouts can be carried over into other types of layouts.

 *goals*

- **Discover the advantages to using CSS for layout**

- **Learn terminology associated with CSS-P**

- **Explore the Dreamweaver tools that can be used to create CSS-based layouts**

- **Learn what CSS elements are available to develop and maintain your designs**

# CSS POSITIONING

The first implementation of CSS primarily dealt with text formatting, in addition to control over margins and padding. There was really no tight control over how elements could be positioned on the page. So, in its next release positioning features were added. These features are commonly referred to as CSS Positioning, or CSS-P. In reality, CSS-P is just a small portion of CSS level 2 (the second version of CSS).

Building on its predecessor, CSS-P uses a model where content is contained within rectangular boxes. These boxes can then have a number of properties that can be controlled. Primarily these properties will establish how the content of that box, or possibly the box itself, appears visually. By using CSS-P, you can also define where a box will appear on the page. Using this type of positioning for all elements within your design can lead to a completely tableless layout while still providing control over layouts across browsers and platforms.

If you have ever built a web design layout using tables (like those we explored in Chapter 3) you have experienced a process that is relatively simple, but not all that elegant nor providing tight control. Using tables as a design layout tool has several significant drawbacks. First, tables don't provide you with the same level of positioning accuracy as CSS. For an element to exist in a very specific position on a page, you will need to get creative about using clear image spacers and row heights to hit your mark. Another major challenge to tables is that they increase the amount of maintenance needed. If your design ever changes (and we all know that never happens) you would literally have to edit the table, in some way, on each page. Last, tables are just so darn clunky. Using a table for layout will introduce all sorts of HTML tags to the source of your document. If you use many tables within your design, the addition of these tags can have an inflating effect on the overall file size of your page. Like I said, there are many reasons not to use tables for web design. But these are just a few of the issues to using tables that are addressed by using CSS.

In this section I am going to give you a little background and vocabulary on CSS positioning. As you read though this section, the importance may not seem immediately apparent. In all honesty, learning how best to position elements can be tricky. It may take a little trial and error to figure things out—especially the first time. But understanding some of the terminology and available options can help you weather the storm.

## DIV and SPAN

When working with CSS there are two HTML elements you will need to be familiar with: DIV and SPAN. These tags are used to add a basic structure to the content within your HTML document. Unlike the many of the other HTML elements we have explored to this point, the DIV and SPAN tags are not represented visually when a page is rendered within a browser. For these tags to affect the presentation of a page, you will need to apply CSS to the DIV or SPAN tags (something we will do a little later on).

Although they both are generally similar, the DIV and SPAN tags are used in two completely different scenarios. The DIV element is used for what is referred to as "block-level" content. Paragraphs, headings, or tables are all objects that would be considered block-level content. For example, if you had an HTML page that is a news story, the headline and story may be two separate block-level elements, as shown in Figure 10-1. When designing your HTML page to use CSS for layout, the DIV tags will be used to define the content areas before they are given positioning or style.

In contrast, the SPAN element is used for "inline" content. This type of content is typically a portion of a block-level element. For example, in the news story page we just looked at you may want to bold only the first line of the news story. Because the entire story is a block-level element, just the first line would be an inline element.

**Block-level Elements**

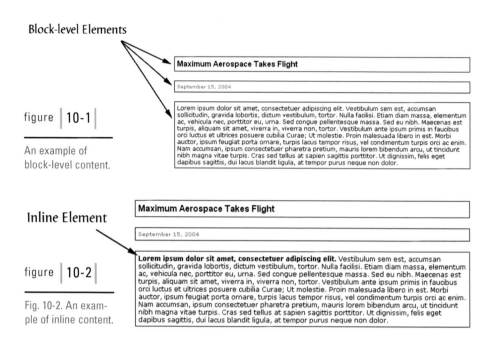

figure | 10-1 |

An example of
block-level content.

**Inline Element**

figure | 10-2 |

Fig. 10-2. An exam-
ple of inline content.

Therefore, in this case you would use a SPAN as opposed to a DIV. Figure 10-2 shows an example of how this might work.

## Positioning Elements

Now that you have a feel for the DIV grouping elements, we can begin to explore how we can use them to define layout on a page. Once an area of content has been designated using a DIV tag, you have three options for providing positioning information: static, absolute, and fixed. These positioning options are one of the biggest advantages to using CSS for layout. Using tables to get positioning is a little cumbersome, but using CSS you can achieve pinpoint precision. In addition to positioning elements, there are also several properties that directly affect how (or sometimes if) an element is displayed. This is by no mean an exhaustive list of properties, but it should give you a good start. Let's take a look at the positioning options.

### Static Positioning

Static positioning is the default type for any DIV element that has been added to an HTML page. The name "static" may imply that the position of this element is fixed, but that is hardly the case. A statically positioned DIV element does not have a specific location on the page, and in fact static DIV elements cannot be positioned in any way. These elements will simply go with the flow of the other items that make up the page. So, as an HTML page is displayed in the browser it will be rendered from the top to bottom. This means that the static element will be placed wherever the preceding element stops. For example, if you have a static element as the very last item on your HTML page when the page is presented in the browser the element will appear at the very bottom. It is also important to note that a statically positioned element may also be placed within additional elements, such as tables or other DIV tags.

## Absolute Positioning

The real power of CSS-P is using absolute positioning. As the name suggests, elements with absolute positioning have a location (defined by X and Y coordinates) on the page that has been specifically defined. Any absolute-positioned element will appear completely autonomously of the other areas of content on the page.

Unlike an element with static positioning, absolute positioning will render an item outside the normal flow of the page—even if it means layering the DIV area on top of other content. A little later we will talk about the z-index, which is a way to control the stacking order for these elements.

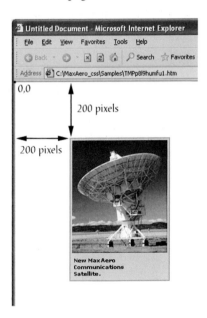

The location for an absolutely positioned element is defined by using a system of coordinates. The origin (0, 0) for these coordinates is in the upper left-hand corner of the browser window, assuming the element is not placed within another DIV tag. The position is defined as the number of pixels the upper left-hand corner of the DIV element is from the top and left-hand sides of the page. This relationship is illustrated in Figure 10-3. If the absolutely positioned element is within another parent DIV element, the coordinate system is adjusted. In this scenario, the upper left-hand corner of the parent DIV element is used as the origin. This child and parent relationship is illustrated in Figure 10-4.

figure | 10-3 |

This illustrates how a staticly positioned element can be positioned relative to the upper left-hand corner of the page.

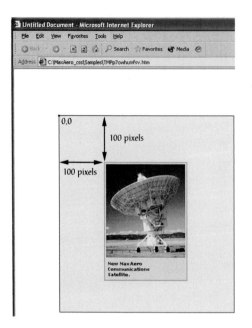

**NOTE:** When using CSS to position page elements, there is actually a fourth possible option, referred to as fixed. Fixed positioning is really just a derivative of the absolute positioning option. The only real difference is that an object with fixed positioning will not move when a page is scrolled. This is because it will always display itself in reference to the edges of the browser window, and not to any parent element. This is an interesting effect, but proceed with caution: some popular browsers do not support this type of positioning.

## Relative Positioning

Relative positioning may be one of the more confusing types of positioning to work with. An easy way to think about it is that it is a combination of static and absolute positioning. So how is that possible? Relative positioning works by placing the element in an absolute position, relative to where its static position would be. For example, take a look at Figure 10-5. Here we have a static-positioned element. If we make this a relative-positioned element and add a top and left value of 20 pixels, the element would be displayed like that shown in Figure 10-6. Also, in addition to its positioning properties a relatively positioned element may have a z-index value that allows you to control how this element may overlap other elements on screen.

figure | 10-4 |

This illustrates how the parent/child relationship can change the placement of an element with absolute positioning.

figure | 10-5 |

An element with static positioning.

## Maximum Aerospace Takes Flight
September 15, 2004

0,0

Lorem ipsum dolor sit amet, consectetuer adipiscing elit. Vestibulum sem est, accumsan sollicitudin, gravida lobortis, dictum vestibulum, tortor. Nulla facilisi. Etiam diam massa, elementum ac, vehicula nec, porttitor eu, urna. Sed congue pellentesque massa. Sed eu nibh. Maecenas est turpis, aliquam sit amet, viverra in, viverra non, tortor. Vestibulum ante ipsum primis in faucibus orci luctus et ultrices posuere cubilia Curae; Ut molestie. Proin malesuada libero in est. Morbi auctor, ipsum feugiat porta ornare, turpis lacus tempor risus, vel condimentum turpis orci ac enim. Nam accumsan, ipsum consectetuer pharetra pretium, mauris lorem bibendum arcu, ut tincidunt nibh magna vitae turpis. Cras sed tellus at sapien sagittis porttitor. Ut dignissim, felis eget dapibus sagittis, dui lacus blandit ligula, at tempor purus neque non dolor.

**Maximum Aerospace Takes Flight**

September 15, 2004

.*0,0*

Lorem ipsum dolor sit amet, consectetuer adipiscing elit. Vestibulum sem est, accumsan sollicitudin, gravida lobortis, dictum vestibulum, tortor. Nulla facilisi. Etiam diam massa, elementum ac, vehicula nec, porttitor eu, urna. Sed congue pellentesque massa. Sed eu nibh. Maecenas est turpis, aliquam sit amet, viverra in, viverra non, tortor. Vestibulum ante ipsum primis in faucibus orci luctus et ultrices posuere cubilia Curae; Ut molestie. Proin malesuada libero in est. Morbi auctor, ipsum feugiat porta ornare, turpis lacus tempor risus, vel condimentum turpis orci ac enim. Nam accumsan, ipsum consectetuer pharetra pretium, mauris lorem bibendum arcu, ut tincidunt nibh magna vitae turpis. Cras sed tellus at sapien sagittis porttitor. Ut dignissim, felis eget dapibus sagittis, dui lacus blandit ligula, at tempor purus neque non dolor.

figure | 10-6|

An element with relative positioning that has been offset 20 pixels from the top and left.

Throughout this chapter I will discuss distances in terms of the number of pixels. While it is possible to specify distances in units other than pixels, this will rarely be done. Pixels are the universal standard for measurement when displaying elements on screen.

## Z-index

As we discussed earlier, it is possible to position DIV elements in very specific positions within your HTML page. Many times, this type of positioning means that you are possibly displaying the element on top of a page's content (see Figure 10-7). In addition, it is also possible to overlap two or more DIV elements. When this happens, the z-index is used to determine the order in which elements are displayed. Z-ordering is normally specified from back to front.

**Maximum Aerospace Takes Flight**

September 15, 2004

Lorem ipsum dolor sit amet, consectetuer adipiscing elit. Vestibulum sollicitudin, gravida lobortis, dictum vestibulum, tortor. Nulla facilisi elementum ac, vehicula nec, porttitor eu, urna. Sed congue pellente nibh. Maecenas est turpis, aliquam sit amet, viverra in, viverra non, ipsum primis in faucibus orci luctus et ultrices posuere cubilia Curae malesuada libero in est. Morbi auctor, ipsum feugiat porta ornare, t risus, vel condimentum turpis orci ac enim. Nam accumsan, ipsum ( pretium, mauris lorem bibendum arcu, ut tincidunt nibh magna vitae turpis. Cras sed tellus at sapien sagittis porttitor. Ut dignissim, felis eget dapibus sagittis, dui lacus blandit ligula, at tempor purus neque non dolor

**New MaxAero Communications Satellite.**

figure | 10-7|

An element with absolute positioning can be displayed on top of a page's content.

For example, an element with a z-index of 1 will display behind and element with a z-index of 2 (and so on). Figure 10-8 shows a simple example of this relationship. The text has an index of 1, the satellite image has an index of 2, and the news and information box has an index of 3.

figure | 10-8 |

Using the z-index, you can adjust which layers appear on top.

**Maximum Aerospace Takes Flight**
September 15, 2004

Lorem ipsum dolor sit amet, consectetuer adipiscing elit. Vestibulu sollicitudin, gravida lobortis, dictum vestibulum, tortor. Nulla facilis elementum ac, vehicula nec, porttitor nibh. Maecenas est turpis, aliquam sit ipsum primis in faucibus orci luctus et malesuada libero in est. Morbi auctor risus, vel condimentum turpis orci ac pretium, mauris lorem bibendum arcu at sapien sagittis porttitor. Ut dignissim, felis eget dapibus sagittis, dui lacus blandit ligula, at tempor purus neque non dolor.

News and Information

☐ New data communications options
☐ Satelite radio use all time high
☐ America moves wirelss
☐ Third quarter earnings on the rise

more...

## Floating

Sometimes you may want ultimate flexibility in your design. For this reason, a particular element may be set to "float" to the left or right. You can think of this somewhat like the *ALIGN* attribute that can be applied to an image, in that it can be aligned to the left or right and text will flow around it. Figure 10-9 shows an example of an element that has been set to float to the right. Note that all of the text (or other elements) simply flow around the floated element.

figure | 10-9 |

Elements that "float" will cause adjacent content to flow around.

**Maximum Aerospace Takes Flight**
September 15, 2004

Lorem ipsum dolor sit amet, consectetuer adipiscing elit. Vestibulum sem est, accumsan sollicitudin, gravida lobortis, dictum vestibulum, tortor. Nulla facilisi. Etiam diam massa, elementum ac, vehicula nec, porttitor eu, urna. Sed congue pellentesque massa. Sed eu nibh. Maecenas est turpis, aliquam sit amet, viverra in, viverra non, tortor. Vestibulum ante ipsum primis in faucibus orci luctus et ultrices posuere cubilia Curae; Ut molestie. Proin malesuada libero in est. Morbi auctor, ipsum feugiat porta ornare, turpis lacus tempor risus, vel condimentum turpis orci ac enim. Nam accumsan, ipsum consectetuer pharetra pretium, mauris lorem bibendum arcu, ut tincidunt nibh magna vitae turpis. Cras sed tellus at sapien sagittis porttitor. Ut dignissim, felis eget dapibus sagittis, dui lacus blandit ligula, at tempor purus neque non dolor.

News and Information

☐ New data communications options
☐ Satelite radio use all time high
☐ America moves wirelss
☐ Third quarter earnings on the rise

more...

## Visibility

Just like a light switch, the visibility of DIV elements can be turned on or off. By default, an
element will be visible. There are a number of
uses for this type of functionality. The most
common use is to create drop-down navigational menus like that shown in Figure 10-10.
This interaction is created by using a scripting
language such as JavaScript to turn the visibility of an element on or off depending on the
interaction of the end user's mouse pointer. In
Chapter 11, we will explore how you can use
Dreamweaver's behaviors to create this type of
interactivity.

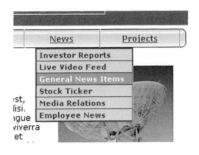

figure | 10-10 |

Visibility is a common way to create
drop-down menus that show or hide
based on the user's interaction.

# BUILDING CSS LAYOUTS

Now that we have discussed some of the options for using CSS to
develop layouts, it would be a good time to jump in and explore the
tools Dreamweaver offers to accomplish this task. There are two
ways you can build CSS layouts. The first method is to use a tool
called Layers. Layers are a great way to get up and going with CSS
positioning elements fairly quickly. However, using the Layers
capability is not necessarily the best practice. The problem with
layers is that all of the CSS information used for positioning is
embedded within the HTML. If you remember back to the last
chapter, I cautioned you on using this type of inline CSS. To build
a layout with regard for maintenance and reusability, the DIV tag
option should be used. Using this option allows you to visually create your page elements but at the same time manage the CSS code
from a separate file. For this chapter we are going to explore both
options for developing CSS-based web design layouts.

## About Dreamweaver Layers

Layers are one of the mechanisms Dreamweaver provides for
developing visual layouts. In reality, layers are just a "Dream-
weaver-ism" that is used to describe DIV elements that use absolute
or relative positioning. The term *layer* is merely a warm and fuzzy
name given to the rectangular chunks of structured content within an HTML page. What you do with them after that is completely
up to you.

Layers are designed to hold any content that may be needed. Be it text, images, navigational components, or even another layer, layers are a tool that allows you to structure your documents and maintain consistent styling.

## Creating Layers

There are two ways you can add layers to your design. The first method is to "draw" the layer onto the page. This technique is helpful if the layer's size and position is determined by adjusting design elements. To draw a layer, start by making sure the Insert bar is set to Layout mode, as shown in Figure 10-11. On this bar you will find the Draw Layer button. Once you click on this button and move the cursor to the document's window, the mouse pointer will appear as a crosshair. Now you can click in the position where the layer should be positioned and drag it to the desired size. This will place a layer within the Document window, like that shown in Figure 10-12.

figure | 10-11 |

The Draw Layer button is located on the Insert bar.

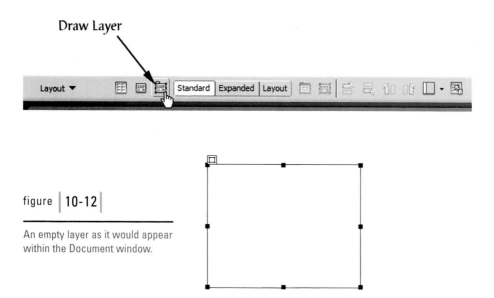

figure | 10-12 |

An empty layer as it would appear within the Document window.

The other technique for adding a layer is to add the layer into your document on the same line as your insertion point. Start by placing your cursor on the page where you want the layer to appear. Now use the Insert | layout Object | Layer menu option. This will add a layer to your document at a default size of 200 pixels by 115 pixels.

## Nesting Layers

Previously we discussed how DIV elements can be created with a child/parent relationship. This is simply where one DIV tag has been nested within another. Layers are no exception. You can nest one layer inside another by pressing the Alt key (or Option key on the Mac) while drawing your layer. This way, if you have an existing layer within the Document window you can use this technique to draw layers directly inside one another (see Figure 10-13).

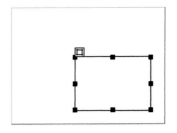

figure | 10-13 |

You can nest one layer inside another.

When creating a nested layer, make certain you are holding down the Alt (or Option) key. Otherwise, the layer you draw may look like it is nested but in reality it is not. A little later we will explore the Layers panel, where you can confirm a layer's nested status.

## Adjusting Layers

More than likely the first time you create a layer it isn't the size or position you had in mind. For this reason, once a layer has been added there are a number of options for how it may be adjusted within the Document window. To freely resize a layer, simply click and drag one of the layer's resize handles (see Figure 10-14) to the desired width or height. Or, if there is another layer that has the exact same height or width that you are looking for the align feature can be used. To resize your layers in this way, select two or more layers by holding down the Shift key while clicking on the layer's borders. Keep in mind that the last layer selected will be the layer used to determine the dimensions. Now use the Modify I Align I Make Same Width (or Make Same Height) menu option. This will resize all selected layers to the same width or height.

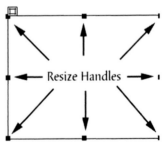

figure | 10-14 |

The layer's resize handles.

Just like you can adjust a layer's size, you can change its position. To move a layer, simply click on the border and while holding down the mouse button drag it to a new position on screen. Or, if the layer is just slightly out of position you can nudge it in one direction or another by using the arrow keys on your keyboard. This will move the layer one pixel in any direction. Another positioning option, similar to resizing, is to use the align feature. This way, you can place layers that are aligned within one another. To do this, select the layers you wish to align. Once again, keep in mind that the last layer will be used as the reference point. Then use the Modify | Align | Left (Right, Top, or Bottom) menu option. This will place all of the selected layers in alignment.

NOTE: If you need a little help determining size or positioning on your page, Dreamweaver offers rulers and grids that can help. Rulers can be turned on by selecting View | Rulers | Show. In addition, the grid can be turned on by selecting the View | Grid | Show Grid menu option.

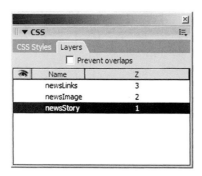

figure | 10-15 |

The Layers panel allows you to manage all of the layers within the page.

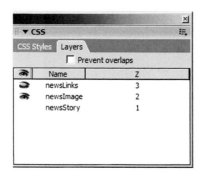

figure | 10-16 |

A layer can have three different types of visibility.

## Layers Panel

Now that you have created a few layers, we should explore how they are typically managed. The Layers panel is provided as a way to not only manage your layers but to adjust several key properties. Using the Layers panel, shown in Figure 10-15, is not that different from layers panels in other software packages such as Adobe Photoshop or Macromedia Fireworks. This panel works by listing out all of the layers, in order by z-index.

The first column of the Layers panel allows you to set the visibility of the layer. Clicking once in this space will display a closed eye, which indicates that the layer is hidden. If you click again, an open eye will appear, which means the layer is currently set to visible. Also, if you click one more time this will remove the visibility property completely. When no visibility is set, the layer will appear visible unless it is placed within another layer that is hidden. Figure 10-16 shows the different states a layer's visibility may have.

The second column displays the name of the layer. A layer's name also doubles as its ID value, which can be referenced by a style sheet. By default, Dreamweaver will sequentially name the layers. You can use the Layers panel to adjust the name of the layer to something a little more descriptive by double clicking on the layer's name.

If you created a nested layer somewhere, the Layers panel will indicate this by placing a Plus (+) button next to the layer's name (see Figure 10-17). This will allow you to expand or contract to show which layers are currently nested. You can also use the Layers panel to separate or nest additional layers. To separate nested layers, click on the layer's name and then drag to a position in the stack outside the parent layer. This will not change the physical location on the layer on the page, but it will break the parent/child relationship. To nest additional layers, hold down the Ctrl key (Command key on the Mac) and drag the layer to a position on top of the name of the desired parent layer.

figure | **10-17** |

You can use the Layers panel to manage nested layers as well.

The third column of the Layers panel indicates the z-index for the layer. As each new layer is inserted into this page, Dreamweaver will add it to the top of the list by default. If you remember back to the beginning of this chapter, the lower the z-index values the further to the back the element will appear. If you wish to reorder the layers (which you will probably want to do) you can do this in two different ways. First, by clicking on the z-index number next to the layer name, you can directly type in the exact value you want to use. Or, you can click on the layer's name and then drag the layer up or down. As you drag, note that an insertion line is created to indicate the point where the layer will be placed in the stack.

The last major function of the Layers panel is to enable or disable the *Prevent overlaps* option. As the name suggests, when this feature is enabled Dreamweaver will keep you from overlapping one layer on top of another. If you already have overlapping layers on your page, enabling this feature will not separate them. In this case, you will need to manually separate any preexisting overlapping layers.

## TRY THIS

Now that we have explored layers, take some time to experiment. Start by opening a new document and draw in several layers. Get familiar with the layers by resizing, positioning, or nesting them. Also, don't forget to take the Layers panel out for a spin. Using this panel you can show and hide layers, or adjust their stacking order.

## About Content Blocks

As I mentioned at the outset of this section, Dreamweaver offers two methods for using CSS positioning within your page. We have already explored how layers can be used, so next we will take a look at how the DIV tag can be used to build what is commonly referred to as a content block. This technique is not quite as warm and fuzzy as is creating layers, but using DIV tags can get your design off on the correct foot. Unlike the layers feature, using DIV tags for your content blocks will help you establish consistent, reusable styles that can be maintained from one central location—the style sheet.

## Planning and Developing Content Blocks Using DIV Tags

When building a layout from the ground up using CSS, many web designers prefer to create all of their elements and then address the positioning. This is exactly how we are going to approach the topic of developing content blocks using DIV tags. However, before we get started defining areas of content a plan must first be created. It is always helpful to take the time and sketch out what you are trying to build on paper first. This will save you some development time. Your sketch should outline the major areas of content and the names of the styles that would be associated with each content area. For example, Figure 10-18 illustrates this concept with a common left-hand navigation-style layout. As you can see, all of the major portions have been delineated and the areas are assigned a style name.

### Adding the DIV Tag

Once all of your planning is out of the way, it is then time to create the DIV tag. Unlike working with layers, building content blocks using DIV tags takes a little bit of knowledge of

#Banner

#NavigationBar

#BodyContainer

#Footer

figure | 10-18 |

Planning out your page first can save you development time later.

what is happening behind the scenes (or in the HTML code). To insert a DIV tag, start by making sure the Insert bar has been set to the layout category. Then place your cursor on a spot of the page where you want to add the DIV element. Next, click the Insert Div Tag button (see Figure 10-19) on the Insert bar. This will summon the Insert Div Tag dialog box, shown in Figure 10-20.

figure | 10-19 |

The Insert Div Tag button is located on the Insert bar.

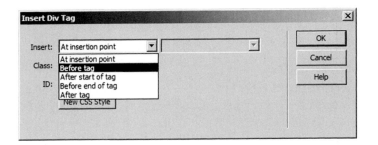

figure | 10-20 |

The Insert Div Tag dialog box allows you to specify three key pieces of information about the DIV element.

When defining a new DIV tag, you will need to associate either a custom class or an ID to this element. You already know about the class CSS selector type from Chapter 9, but IDs are probably a new concept. An ID is really not that much different from a class. In looking at them within the style sheet, the only visual difference is that a class name begins with a period (.) and an ID begins with a pound sign (#), as shown in Figure 10-21. Beyond that, what makes them different is how they are used. IDs are typically used with

```
.headline {
        font-family: Arial, Helvetica, sans-serif;
        font-size: 16px;
        font-weight: bold;
}

#headline {
        font-family: Arial, Helvetica, sans-serif;
        font-size: 16px;
        font-weight: bold;
}
```

figure | 10-21 |

Two example CSS style rules that show both a class and an ID.

major areas of unique content on the page. For example, you might associate an ID with a DIV element that is used for the banner, the left-hand navigation bar, or the footer. The general rule of thumb is that one ID should only be associated with one element on the same page. Conversely, for elements you may use multiple times across a page a class should be used.

In looking at the Insert Div Tag dialog box, you will notice that there are corresponding options for both IDs and classes. This is a good example of why planning ahead can help you save some time. Using the areas available, go ahead and type in either the ID or class names you decided on with your sketch. Make certain you only enter the name of the style and not the corresponding period (.) or pound sign (#). Also, if you are working with an existing style sheet these two options are both pull-down menus that are pre-populated with any styles (IDs and classes) already associated with this page. So, if you have already defined a style for this element it can be selected from the appropriate menu.

The last item that needs to be set is where that DIV element should be inserted. This menu has several different options you can use to determine placement. Effectively using this takes at least a cursory knowledge of how the tags are arranged within your HTML page. The following detail the available options and what they mean.

- *At insertion point:* This option will add the DIV element at the point where your cursor is located on the page. If your cursor is currently within another DIV element, the new DIV element will become nested.

- *Wrap around selection:* This option is only available if you select a portion of your page's content before clicking on the Insert DIV Tag button. This allows you to add a DIV tag that will encompass the selected objects.

- *After start of tag / After end of tag:* This option allows you to specify the position of an element within another content block. Once either of these options is enabled, the menu on the right will become available. This secondary menu is used to specify which existing content block will contain the new element. By selecting the *After start of tag* option, the new DIV element will appear as the very first item within the existing content block. Selecting the *After end of tag* option will do the exact opposite: the new DIV tag will be the very last thing in the existing content block.

● *Before tag / After tag:* This option is only available when there are preexisting DIV elements. Once this option has been selected, the menu on the right will become available. This menu allows you to specify which DIV element you would like to insert the new element either before or after.

Once you have made all of the proper selections, click on the OK button to add the DIV tag to your document. When a new DIV tag is added, it will contain some default text to let you know that it is there. In addition, if you move your mouse pointer over the edges of each DIV area a red outline will appear (see Figure 10-22). By default, the new DIV element will stretch horizontally to fill any available space (unless you have attached a style to indicate otherwise). Now that you have added the DIV element, we can begin to adjust the CSS to control that element to achieve the design you are looking for.

figure | 10-22 |

A red line will appear if your mouse is over the edge of a DIV element. This line is only for development purposes. It will not appear in the final web page.

### Maximum Aerospace Takes Flight
September 15, 2004

Lorem ipsum dolor sit amet, consectetuer adipiscing elit. Vestibulum sem est, accumsan sollicitudin, gravida lobortis, dictum vestibulum, tortor. Nulla facilisi. Etiam diam massa, elementum ac, vehicula nec, porttitor eu, urna. Sed congue pellentesque massa. Sed eu nibh. Maecenas est turpis, aliquam sit amet, viverra in, viverra non, tortor. Vestibulum ante ipsum primis in faucibus orci luctus et ultrices posuere cubilia Curae; Ut molestie. Proin malesuada libero in est. Morbi auctor, ipsum feugiat porta ornare, turpis lacus tempor risus, vel condimentum turpis orci ac enim. Nam accumsan, ipsum consectetuer pharetra pretium, mauris lorem bibendum arcu, ut tincidunt nibh magna vitae turpis. Cras sed tellus at sapien sagittis porttitor. Ut dignissim, felis eget dapibus sagittis, dui lacus blandit ligula, at tempor purus neque non dolor.

NOTE: Can you have both a class and an ID? Sure, this can be a handy way to reuse your styles. However, if the ID and the class both specify the same style, the ID will take precedence. For example, if the ID defines the color as green and the class defines it as blue, the DIV element will appear green.

## The Box Model

Before we actually begin to build styles that have been applied to DIV elements, we should first explore some of the fundamental CSS concepts. To make the most of CSS positioning, it is important to have a familiarity with what is referred to as the box model. As we talked about earlier, DIV elements are rectangular-shaped areas of content. When styling your DIV elements, you can think of each of them as an individual box. Each box has the following areas (see Figure 10-23).

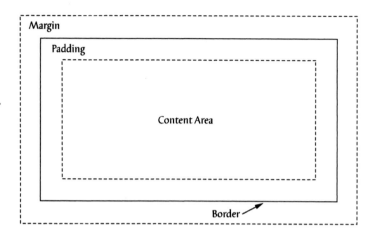

figure | 10-23 |

This diagram illustrates the areas of the box model.

- *Content area:* This is the real meat of your DIV element. The content area, as the name suggests, is simply where the content of your element resides. This would include any text or images that may exist within the element.

- *Padding:* This area is very similar to the table padding we discussed earlier in the book. Padding is the distance between whatever is in the content area and the edge of the box. Using CSS, padding can be set to a specific pixel dimension on the top, left, bottom, and/or right of the content area.

- *Border:* This area defines the edge of the box. Using CSS, the border is not only set to a specific pixel width but may also accept a defined color or line type. Also, just like the padding area the border can be set on the top, left, bottom, and/or right of the box.

- *Margin:* This defines the area between the edge of the box (or the border) to any surrounding elements. You can think of this sort of like a padding area that completely surrounds the box. Using CSS, the margin can be set to a specific pixel dimension on the top, left, bottom, and/or right of the box.

## Building Styles for Your Elements

Even though we are building styles that will be used for positioning, the process is the same as was explored in Chapter 9. The process all starts with the CSS Styles panel, which can be opened via the Window | CSS Styles menu option. Once open, click on the New CSS Style button at the bottom of the panel (see Figure 10-24). This will open the New CSS Style dialog box. If you remember back to when you inserted the DIV tags, you had to choose whether to assign a class or ID to each element. If a class was assigned to a DIV element, you need to make sure the Class option is selected within this dialog box. If an ID was used, the Advanced Selector Type option should be enabled. Also, remember that when you name each of these that you should use a period (.) before the class name or a pound sign (#) before an ID name (see Figure 10-25). Last, to get the most out of your CSS you should choose to define the style in a new style sheet (unless you already have an external style sheet linked to the current document).

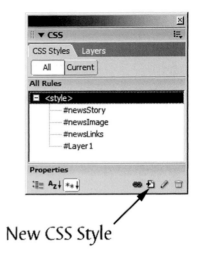

New CSS Style

figure | 10-24 |

To create a new style use the New CSS Style button of the CSS Styles panel.

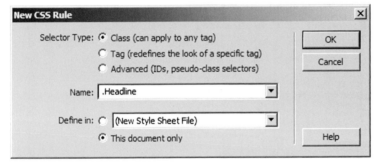

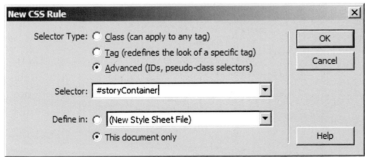

figure | 10-25 |

When specifying a name, remember to use a period (.) for classes and a pound sign (#) for IDs.

Remember that if you need to create a new style sheet once you click on the OK button you will need to assign this style sheet a name and location.

Once you have approved the name and selector type for this style (and possibly saved a new .CSS file), the CSS Style Definition dialog box will appear. When designing with CSS to develop a layout, the primary CSS style categories you will work with are Box and Positioning. However, the Background, Block, and Border categories all affect how the content area will appear within the browser. While in this chapter we are focusing on using CSS for positioning, many of these options also apply to other types of elements. Let's take a closer look at the available categories of the CSS Style Definition dialog box. As you look through these options, also keep in mind that you can use many of these same styles with tables in addition to DIV elements. I am not going to cover every possible style, but I will touch on those more commonly used.

figure | 10-26 |

The Background category of the CSS Style Definition dialog box.

## Background

The Background category of the CSS Style Definition dialog box, shown in Figure 10-26, is used to adjust what appears within the background of any block-level content, such as a DIV element. The following define some of the available options.

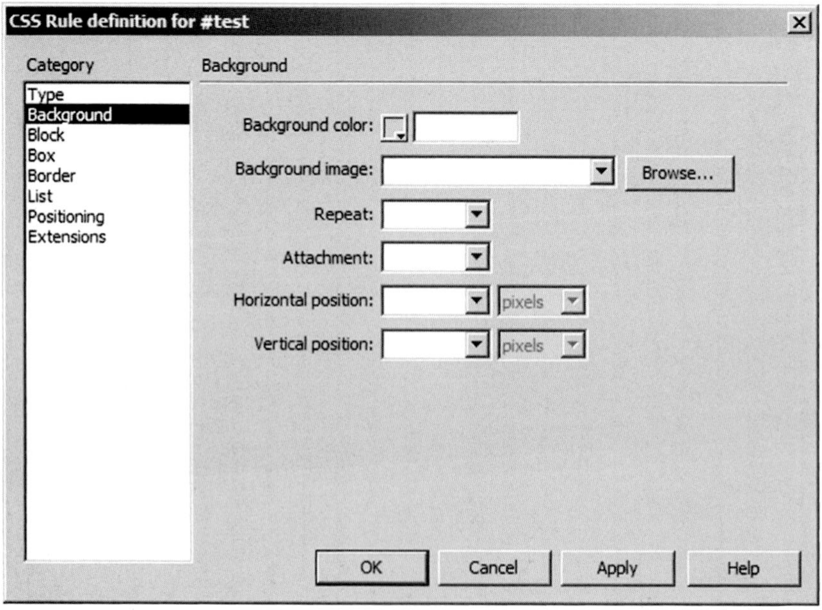

- *Background Color:* This option sets the background color that will appear behind the content area.

- *Background Image:* This option sets the background image that will appear behind the content area. By default, the image will repeat to fill any available space in the background of the content area.

- *Repeat:* This option sets whether a background image will repeat. The available options are Repeat, No-repeat, Repeat-x, and Repeat-y. The Repeat option will tile the image in all directions. The No-repeat option will only display the image once. The Repeat-x and Repeat-y options will tile the background image either horizontally or vertically, respectively.

- *Horizontal Position / Vertical Position:* This option determines where the image will appear if a background image is set to No-repeat. Generally the image can be aligned to the left, right, or center. You can also specify a pixel position that is relative to the top left-hand corner of the element.

## Block

The Block category of the CSS Style Definition dialog box, shown in Figure 10-27, is used to adjust how the content of the DIV elements are presented. The following define two of the available options.

figure | 10-27 |

The Block category of the CSS Style Definition dialog box.

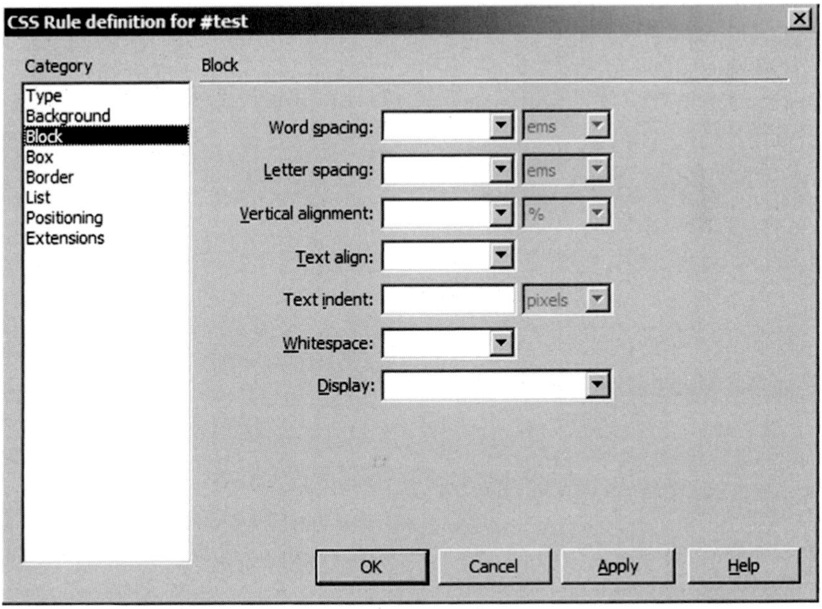

- *Letter Spacing:* This option is used to adjust the space that appears between characters.

- *Text Align:* This option is used to align any text that appears within the content block. The available options are to align the text left, right, center, or justified.

### Box

figure | 10-28

The Box category of the CSS Style Definition dialog box, shown in Figure 10-28, is used to adjust how elements are arranged on the page, and how content is arranged within the element. Earlier we discussed the fundamentals of the box model. This is where you can apply that knowledge. The following define some of the available options.

The Box category of the CSS Style Definition dialog box.

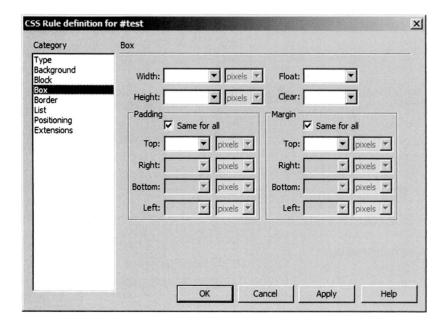

- *Width/Height:* These options are used to determine the physical dimensions of the DIV element.

- *Float:* This option is used to set which way a content block will be aligned, to the right or left.

- *Padding:* This option is used to specify the space that appears between the content and the edge of DIV element. You can set the top, right, bottom, and left padding independently, or all at once.

- *Margin:* This option is used to specify the space between the DIV element and any adjacent elements. Just like the padding, the top, right, bottom, and left margin may be set independently or all at once.

## Border

The Border category of the CSS Style Definition dialog box, shown in Figure 10-29, is used to set how the edge of the content block will appear. Borders are a good way to add visual interest to your page without incurring any real additional file weight. By default, the border around an element is not visible. Also, much like padding and margins the border for the top, right, bottom, or left can be set independently or all at once. The following define some of the available options.

- *Style:* This option sets the line type that will be used as the border for the element. Figure 10-30 shows a few examples of border styles.

- *Width:* This option is used to set the physical width of the border. This value is normally set in pixels.

- *Color:* This option is used to set the color that will be used for the border.

figure | 10-29

The Border category of the CSS Style Definition dialog box.

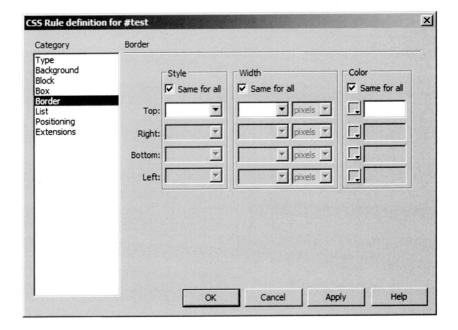

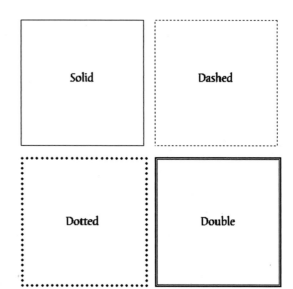

figure | 10-30 |

Borders can be
used to add visual
interest to your
design.

## Positioning

The Positioning category of the CSS Style Definition dialog box,
shown in Figure 10-31, is used to set where DIV elements are
placed on the page. The following define some of the available
options.

● *Type:* This option is used to determine whether the element is
positioned using the absolute, relative, or static positioning.

● *Visibility:* This option can be used to determine a number of
different options for displaying the content block. The most
common use of this style is to turn off the element so that it
does not display in the browser. To do this, set the display
option to None. This setting is typically used in conjunction
with a scripting language such as JavaScript (or behaviors in
Dreamweaver) to turn an element on or off.

● *Z-index:* This option is used to set the z-index value for the
element.

● *Placement:* This option is used to determine the specific location of the element on the page. You can specify a location in
terms of the element's distance from the top, right, bottom, or
left of the page or parent element.

NOTE: If you set the Type property to Absolute, Dreamweaver will
automatically treat this DIV element as a layer. This means that you
can move and resize the element just as you would a layer.

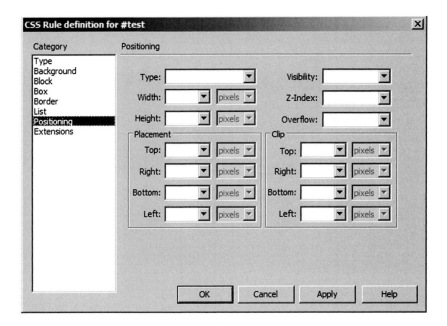

figure | 10-31 |

The Positioning category of the CSS Style Definition dialog box.

## Applying CSS

As we have stepped through this chapter, I have shown you the "cart before the horse" method of building CSS layouts. By that I mean we created DIV elements and assigned them to classes that don't yet exist. Anytime techniques like this are used, there is always the opportunity to make mistakes. So, if you accidentally apply the wrong style to an element, or if you want to apply a different style entirely, the Property Inspector can be used to do it. To apply a style to a DIV element, move your mouse pointer to the edge of the element until the red outline appears. Then click your mouse button. This will select the entire element. Now you can use the Style and/or ID options shown in Figure 10-32 to apply a different style.

figure | 10-32 |

You can use the Property Inspector to adjust what classes or IDs are applied to an element.

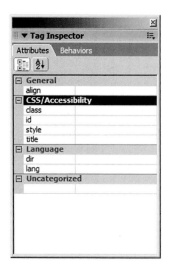

figure | 10-33 |

The Tag Inspector can give you more direct access for tweaking your styles.

# Tag Inspector

The process of laying out all the elements of your design can take a little work. It takes tweaking the size and positioning of each content block to strike that perfect balance. As you can imagine, using the CSS Style Definition dialog box to edit several styles, many times, can get to be a little cumbersome. This is where the Tag Inspector, shown in Figure 10-33, can help out. This panel, which can be summoned via the Window | Tag Inspector menu option, can grant you direct access to fine-tune the properties of a particular style. Once you have the Tag Inspector panel open, click on the Relevant CSS tab if it has not already been enabled.

The Tag Inspector works by showing you two key pieces of information. First, the top of the panel will list all of the styles currently acting on this element. The first column lists the name of the CSS rule and the second shows what HTML tag this rule has been applied to. In the case of CSS positioning, the second column will list the <div> tag. If there is more than one style applied, you can click on the name of the style to gain access to all of that style rule's properties.

The lower portion of this panel displays all of the available properties and all of the properties currently used with this style. There are two ways this information can be sorted. First, you can use the Show Category View button, which will list all of the styles based on the categories used within the CSS Style Definition dialog box. The other option is the Show List View button, which will list all of the properties in alphabetical order. However, in this view any properties that currently have value will be moved to the top of the list for quick access. No matter how you want to sort the properties, they are all edited in the same way. All you need to do is locate the desired property you wish to edit and then click in the right-hand column to modify that property's value. Once the change is made, the Document window will instantly show the change. This direct access will allow you to fine-tune the CSS as needed.

# SUMMARY

In this chapter we have explored how you can design your layouts to use Cascading Style Sheets (CSS). To be completely fair, using CSS for positioning is not without faults. As you have experienced, building pages in this way can take you a little more time. In addition, the CSS positioning features are not supported by every browser. While current versions of the most popular browsers provide support for CSS positioning, some older browsers may have problems. Despite these issues, many web designers are migrating toward using these layout techniques. Modern web design is going the way of CSS because it can accomplish the one thing that HTML alone could never do: draw a hard line between content and presentation.

## in review

1. What is CSS-P?

2. What is the difference between DIV and SPAN? Describe a scenario where you might use each.

3. What are the differences among static, absolute, and relative positioning? Describe a scenario where you might use each.

4. How does z-index apply to CSS positioning?

5. How does floating apply to CSS positioning?

6. How does visibility apply to CSS positioning?

7. What are Dreamweaver layers?

8. What is the practical difference between a layer and inserting a DIV tag?

## ➤ EXPLORING ON YOUR OWN

1. For practice, take an existing design you might have done using tables and reengineer it to use layers. Or, as an alternative, take an existing design and integrate layers to add visual interest.

2. Now that you understand CSS layout, plan and create a simple layout designed to use DIV elements and CSS as the primary layout. Try working with all of the available styles you can use for positioning. You may also want to spend some time working with some of the more visual elements, such as backgrounds and borders.

3. Up for a challenge? Create an entirely unique web design that uses no images. Try developing a design that is visually interesting, but only use fonts, font colors, backgrounds, and borders as the primary visual elements. You may be surprised by what you can accomplish.

**notes**

# ADVENTURES IN DESIGN

## FLOATING CONTENT ELEMENTS

Some web designers believe that creating web pages using a flexible layout is the only way to go. This basically means that the web page will expand to fit whatever size the web browser is set at. So, if someone is running with their browser maximized at a resolution 1280 x 1024, then the page should expand to fill the entire space. I am not here to tell you that this is bad design. In fact, there are certainly times when you want to gear your design in this direction. However, it can be difficult to achieve certain types of layouts because you don't know for sure how wide the window will be. This is where using CSS positioning can help you create "floating" elements.

## Project Example

In the course of your career as a web designer, you may encounter a client that would like a flexible web design at whatever cost. This was the scenario I found myself in with a past client. In this case they wanted a home page that would display several small news items in columns on their home page. The problem with columns is that this typically means you will be using a table for the layout. However, you can't dynamically adjust the number of columns as the page widens, so I had to develop a different approach.

The technique I decided on was to add each news items to its own div area, or container (see Figure B-1). This way, I could use CSS to not only specify how the news item was positioned but how it appeared. In addition, I also nested two additional div elements for the news headline and news brief. This way, I had total control of the news item inside and out— all with CSS.

Now that I had the div infrastructure created, it was time to add the styles. Providing style for the headline and news brief was easy. All I had to do was add the fonts, sizes, and colors. Adding the positioning took a little bit of thought. Remember, my goal here is to make it so that if I have numerous news blocks they will expand horizontally with the browser

Figure B-1. Using DIV elements for layout gives you greater options for styling and positioning.

window. Working vertically with CSS is simple, so how do I work horizontally? This is where I turned to the float attribute. Even though I have several div areas stacked next to each other, I could tell them all to float left. This means that no news item would ever appear any further left than the item before it—which will create the effect that the news items are "floating" within the available space (see Figure B-2).

## Your Turn

Now, come up with your own ideas of how you can use this type of flexible positioning. Instead of using it to deliver small news items, you may want it to deliver other types of content. In addition, you can also use these same techniques to create flexible positioning for the navigation on your page. For example, maybe you want to have a navigation bar that floats on the right instead of the left.

1. Start by deciding what types of elements you want to float dynamically within the page. Will your entire design expand, or just certain elements?

2. Decide on what pieces need to be contained within the div area. In my case, I know that I was working with a headline, image, and story.

3. Create the actual div areas and set their appropriate styles. This may take a little trial and error to get it exactly right.

4. Implement your floating elements within the rest of your page design. Experiment with how scaling the browser in and out affects the positioning of the items in relationship to each other.

Figure B-2. The news items will change their position based on the available space.

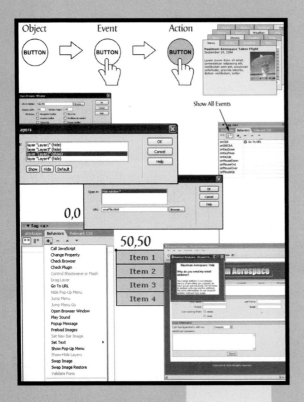

Adding Interactivity with Behaviors

1

*charting your course*

Up to this point in the book we have been focusing on the fundamentals of designing web sites within Dreamweaver. The techniques we have examined thus far have been largely static concepts: designing, building, and maintaining a web site. Now it is time to have a little fun. In this chapter we are going to explore using Dreamweaver behaviors that can add interactive features to your pages. These features range from the purely visual, such as creating a button that changes when your mouse rolls over it, to functional items such as validating information in form fields. Each of the behaviors we examine is an item that will directly contribute to your site's "user experience." Behaviors can be used as techniques to keep the user interested (nobody said your page had to be boring!) or as a method to make your page easier to use.

This chapter has been broken into two parts. It begins by taking a look at some of the concepts behind using behaviors; that is, what behaviors are and how they work. From there, we will roll up our sleeves and get down to adding some behaviors. As we step through this chapter, begin to think about how you can apply behaviors to your design. Just remember that a little bit of interactivity can go a long way.

 *goals*

- **Find out how behaviors work**
- **Learn the fundamentals of JavaScript as it relates to behaviors**
- **Discover how the Behaviors panel can be used to add interactivity to your design**
- **Explore some of the available behaviors**

# ABOUT BEHAVIORS

Many web designers strive to accomplish two things with their design. First, you want to get visitors to your page and keep them there as long as possible. Second, while the users are visiting you want to make their use of the site as easy as possible. Behaviors can help you in both regards. Using behaviors with your site allows you to add interactivity that is not available through HTML alone. Generally speaking, behaviors allow the user to make real-time changes to how a page may appear. For example, you can have a button that will show or hide a particular layer. Behaviors may also be used to perform some type of work. When creating an HTML form to gather information, you may want to ensure that the user has entered their responses in a way you want them. Last, behaviors are used to facilitate navigation. For example, you may want to create a pop-up menu that only appears when the user clicks on a button. No matter how you use them, it always helps to have a little background. Let's take a step back and look at behaviors from a wide-angle lens.

## What Exactly Is a Behavior?

To use behaviors you don't necessarily have to understand how they are built, but it still good information to have. Behaviors are, in one word, JavaScript. Each behavior is essentially a prewritten piece of JavaScript code you can selectively add to your web design. If you are not familiar with JavaScript, it is basically a scripting language that runs on the client side. This means that any JavaScript code included in a page is actually run within the user's web browser, and not on the web server. A noteworthy thing about this is that nearly every user's browser may be configured differently and this can cause some problems when using JavaScript. Fortunately, when Macromedia developed the Dreamweaver behaviors they were generally designed to work with version 4.0 and above of the major web browsers. This constitutes the largest percentage of browsers people currently browse the web with.

Typically, when a behavior is added to a page the accompanying JavaScript is added within the HEAD area of the document. However, some of the more complex behaviors actually create an external JavaScript file, or *JS* file, included with your page. External JS pages accomplish two tasks. First, they greatly simplify the source code of your page. Some of these external *.JS* files can have over a hundred lines of code. Second, having all of the code in an external file allows you to share the code with more than one page. Yet, no matter how the code is added it is important to note that it will never actually appear within the browser; that is, you will only see the results of its labor through interactive components of the page.

## How Behaviors Work

Now that we have discussed a little about how behaviors are put together, let's get down to the nuts and bolts of how they work. Behaviors are based on a simple model of cause and effect; that is, the user interacts with some part of a page, and then something happens. Obviously this is oversimplified, but it is the general concept. To use actual development terms, the element the user interacts with is called the "object." When the user interacts with the object an "event" occurs. This event is used to trigger some type of "action." What is important to understand about the action is that it can be almost anything. In terms of a behavior, a single event may trigger multiple actions.

A good example of the object/event/action relationship is when you have a graphical button that changes when the user moves over it with a mouse. In this scenario the button is the *object*, the movement of the mouse pointer over the button is the *event*, and the changing of the image is the *action*. Usually, when the user's mouse pointer moves off the button the original image is restored. This, too, is an event/action relationship. Figure 11-1 shows a graphic that explains the sequence of this example.

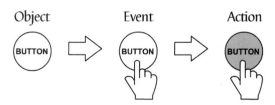

Object        Event         Action

figure | **11-1** |

This chart demonstrates the chain of events in a simple button rollover example.

### Interactive Objects

When you add a behavior to your page, it is applied to a particular object. What is important to understand about objects is that they are not all elements the user will directly interact with. Some objects, such as the body of your HTML page, are indirectly interacted with by the user. The following detail some of the objects typically used when applying behaviors.

- *Hyperlinks:* Obviously anytime we talk about interactivity hyperlinks need to be included in the discussion. If you want a behavior preformed as a result of the user's direct interaction with an object, a hyperlink should be used. What adds to this versatility is that hyperlinks are normally added when you are using behaviors that affect images, sounds, or layers.

- *HTML BODY:* Using the body of your HTML documents (that is, attaching code to the *<BODY>* HTML tag), you can apply behaviors to your entire page. This is useful when using a behavior you want triggered when the page loads.

- *Forms:* Forms are another example of an object a user interacts with indirectly. You can apply behaviors to a form that will be executed when the form is submitted or reset.

- *Form Elements:* Another object users typically interact with is form elements. For example, a user may click on a submit button, checkbox, or radio button. Nearly any form element, even a text field, can cause some type of event that can trigger an action.

**DON'T GO THERE**

While you can apply a behavior to a hyperlink, it cannot be applied to just plain text. The closest you can come is to make your text a hyperlink with a pound sign (#) as the URL value. This will turn the text into a hyperlink that will not take the user anywhere. While this does solve the problem, it is hardly a best practice.

## Common Events

While there are many combinations of actions that can be executed, there is a fixed number of events that can occur within the browser. Each of these events is called an event handler. The event handler specifies what type of interaction has occurred with the object. Going back to our button rollover we discussed earlier, there were two event handlers that were used in that scenario. The *onMouseOver* and *onMouseOut* events occurred as a result of interaction with the button. The thing to understand about events is that the available event handlers will change depending on the type of object the behavior is being applied to. The following explains some of the more common events you will encounter when working with behaviors. This is not an exhaustive list of behaviors, but should give you some idea of the available options. Also, keep in mind that not all event handlers work with all web browsers. The items on this list should work with the popular browsers (generally IE, Netscape, and Opera), version 4.0 or later.

*Mouse Events:*

- *onClick:* This event occurs when the user clicks on the object. The *onClick* event can also be used in conjunction with form elements.
- *onMouseOver:* This event occurs when the user moves their mouse pointer on top of the object.
- *onMouseOut:* This event, which occurs after the *onMouseOver* event, is when the user removes their mouse pointer from on top of the object.

*Page Events:*

- *onLoad:* This event occurs when the page is loaded within the browser. The *onLoad* event creates the appearance that the action is produced as soon as the page appears.
- *onUnload:* This event occurs when the user leaves the page to go elsewhere.

*Form Events:*

- *onSubmit:* This event occurs when the user submits a web form. It is important to understand that the *onSubmit* event occurs not as a result of clicking on the submit button but as a result of attempting to "submit" the form.

*Form Element Events:*

- *onChange:* This event occurs when a form element is changed from its initial value. The *onChange* event is commonly used with the menu form object.
- *onFocus:* This event occurs when the user first interacts with a form element such as a text field.
- *onBlur:* This event, which occurs after the *onFocus* event, is when the user's focus is on another object.

# ADDING BEHAVIORS

Now that we have a little background information out of the way, let's get to work with behaviors. My goal is to tie what you have just read to some of the behaviors Dreamweaver offers. So, if you had a little trouble with the introduction of this chapter many of these concepts will soon make sense. The thing to remember is that the process for applying a behavior is almost always the same: select an object, select an action, select an event. To begin the process of adding behaviors to your design, let's explore the Behaviors panel. After you become acquainted with the Behaviors panel, we can move on to adding a few behaviors.

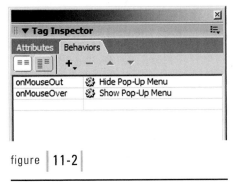

figure **11-2**

The Behaviors panel is used to manage the behaviors added to your page.

## The Behaviors Panel

The Behaviors panel, shown in Figure 11-2, is a tool you can use to add, modify, and manage the behaviors added to your page. This panel can be accessed via the Window | Behaviors menu option. Once open, the Behaviors panel is very straightforward to use. However, its use is predicated on first having some object selected. Once you have an object selected, the next step is to add a behavior. To do this, click on the Add Behavior button to reveal a list of all available behaviors (see Figure 11-3). Now all you have to do is select the desired behavior to open a dialog box that is specific to that behavior. Every behavior will require some degree of configuration; some only require one setting, while others have a wide variety of options. As I go through each individual behavior, I will cover in detail the available configuration options. Once all of the settings have been made, click on the OK button.

When you have applied a behavior to an object, the event and behavior will appear in the lower portion of the Behaviors panel. Figure 11-4 shows an example listing for a simple hyperlink that has a *Go To URL* behavior that will occur when the user clicks on the link. If for any reason you want to reconfigure the behavior to operate differently, you can double click on the behavior's name in this list. Or, if you want to change the default event handler that triggers a particular behavior click on the event handler's name to reveal a pull-down menu. This menu, shown in Figure 11-5, will provide you the entirety of available event handlers that can be used based on the object that has been selected. If you wish to use a different handler, select its name from this list. You can also see a correlation between all of the available events and the applied behaviors by clicking on the Show All Events button near the top of the Behaviors panel (see Figure 11-6).

You may have a situation where you have more than one behavior tied to the same object. When this occurs, you can adjust the order in which the behaviors are performed using the Move Event Value Up button and Move Event Value Down button near the top of the panel. The behaviors that appear toward the top of the list will be executed first. Also, if you have a behavior that has been added inadvertently you can use the Remove Event button to delete it entirely.

NOTE: As we talked about earlier, not all event handlers work in all browsers. So how can you know if you are choosing one that isn't widely supported? You can modify what event handlers are available using the Behaviors panel. To do this, click on the Add Behavior button, and then mouse down to the Show Event For option. From the resulting menu, select the browser or group of browsers you want to target. Remember that targeting the lowest common browser will gain you the widest range of support.

figure | 11-3 |

The Add Behavior button is used to assign behaviors to a selected object.

figure | 11-4 |

The Behaviors panel will display the event handler and behavior that have been applied to a particular object.

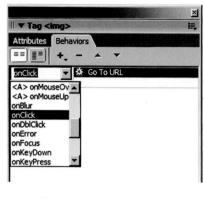

figure | 11-5 |

Using the event handler menu, you can alter when a behavior will be triggered.

figure | 11-6 |

You can use the Show All Events feature to list all of the available events and their applied behavior.

## Exploring Behaviors

As you have surfed the Web you have most likely encountered interactive elements, navigational schemes, or content delivery that was more interesting than the typical static HTML page. Using behaviors, you can include some of these features with your design. We are not going to cover all behaviors in this chapter, but I am going to go over those that can have a direct impact on your design and don't require any direct knowledge of scripting.

### Go to URL

If you remember back to Chapter 5, we talked about how you can design your pages to utilize frames. As you may recall, one of the challenges with frames was that one hyperlink could only target one location (or frame). To solve this problem, the *Go to URL* behavior can be used. This behavior allows you to point the user to separate URLs all at the same time. This behavior isn't only useful when working with frames. You can also use it to direct the user's browser to a particular location based on any number of events. For example, you could apply this behavior to a radio button form element to allow the user to toggle between two pages.

To apply the *Go to URL* behavior, start by selecting the object that will inherit the new functionality. Then open the Go to URL dialog box (see Figure 11-7) by selecting its corresponding option from the Add Behavior menu of the Behaviors panel. At the top of this dialog box you can select the area to target using the *Open in* menu. Then you can add the location using the URL text field. Once you are finished, click on the OK button and the behavior will be added.

figure | 11-7 |

Go To URL dialog box.

## Open Browser Window

If you have spent any time at all browsing the Web you have been exposed to "pop-up" advertising. These ads, which typically appear when a page loads, are presented within a browser window where the navigation, menu, and status bars are all hidden. While these advertisements are usually an annoyance, this same functionality does have legitimate uses. In general, these types of windows can be helpful if you want to present information that is supplemental to the content of the parent window. For example, you might want to provide help information for a person filling out a web form (see Figure 11-8). This way, a user can get help without having to leave the form.

To apply the *Open Browser Window* behavior, start by selecting the object that will inherit the new functionality. Then open the Open Browser Window dialog box (see Figure 11-9) by selecting its corresponding option from the Add Behavior menu of the Behaviors panel. The following detail the options that may be set using this dialog box.

figure | 11-8 |

Providing context help is one example of a legitimate use for opening a new browser window.

figure | 11-9 |

Open Browser Window dialog box.

- *URL to display:* This field is used to specify what page will be displayed within the new browser window.

- *Window width/Window height:* These fields are used to specify the width and height of the new browser window in pixels. It is important to note that these are the dimensions for the viewable area of the window and do not include the title bar, border, or other window-dressing elements.

- *Attributes:* This area allows you to specify what toolbars and functionality will be available on the new window. By default, each of these attributes is turned off.

- *Window Name:* This area allows you to specify a name for the new browser window.

Use caution when applying this behavior to your pages. While it may seem like a good idea at first, opening a new browser window can result in a host of problems. With pop-up advertising becoming so ubiquitous on the Web, many people are resigned to using pop-up blocking software. While this software is intended to block advertisements, it will also block any legitimate uses of this functionality. In addition, opening a new browser window can affect how people with adaptive devices, such as screen readers, are able to view your site.

## Show-Hide Layers

In Chapter 10 we explored how Dreamweaver can be used to create layers. Layers are a great way to contain a chunk of content that can be treated differently from the rest of your design. One interesting feature of layers is that their visibility may be turned on or off. While using the Layers panel, you can set a layer to show or hide, but this is really setting the layer's default value rather than providing a way for the end user to control it dynamically. Using the *Show-Hide Layer* behavior, you can make a layer appear (or disappear) at the request of the user.

There are all sorts of interesting uses for this type of interaction. Adding layers to your design can increase the overall interactivity and visual interest of your design. At the same time, it has practical uses. For example, content can be presented using layers without having to send the user to a different page or go through the process of refreshing the current page. Let's take a look at an actual example of the *Show-Hide Layer* behavior in action.

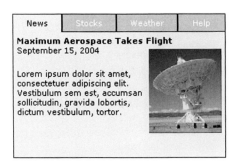

figure | 11-10 |

Using the Show-Hide Layer behavior you can create interesting ways to present content.

Figure 11-10 shows a simple tab-based element that uses layers. In reality, this one element is actually comprised of four separate layers, as shown in Figure 11-11. By applying the *Show-Hide Layer* behavior to each of the tab links, you can create the illusion that this element is being sorted something like a deck of index cards. This can be an effective use of layers because it allows you to present a wide variety of information and not take up a lot of screen real estate.

figure | 11-11 |

This example uses four separate layers to contain content.

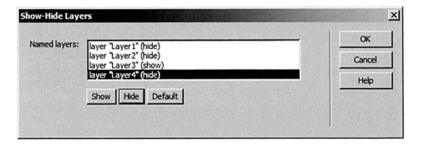

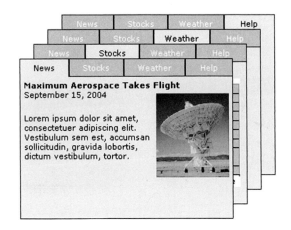

figure | 11-12 |

Show-Hide Layers dialog box.

To apply the *Show-Hide Layer* behavior, start by selecting the object (which is most likely a hyperlink) that will inherit the new functionality. Then open the Show-Hide Layers dialog box (see Figure 11-12) by selecting its corresponding option from the Add Behavior menu of the Behaviors panel. Using this dialog box, you can set which layers will show or hide based on interacting with the selected object. So, in the case of my tab example each tab will show its corresponding layer while hiding all the others. To create this interaction, select the layer's name from the Named Layers area of the window, and then click on the Show, Hide, or Default button. Once you have clicked on one of these buttons, text will be added after the layer's name to indicate the change. Once finished, click on OK.

## Show Pop-Up Menu

If you are designing a web site whose content goes very deep, it can be difficult to create a navigation scheme that makes sense. In addition, a site with a broad set of content offerings may have a navigation system that can take up a significant amount of space on screen. To solve this problem, many web designers have turned to using pop-up menus, like that shown in Figure 11-13. Conceptually, this behavior is very similar to *Show-Hide Layer*.

figure | 11-13 |

Using pop-up menus is a popular way to deliver complex navigational information.

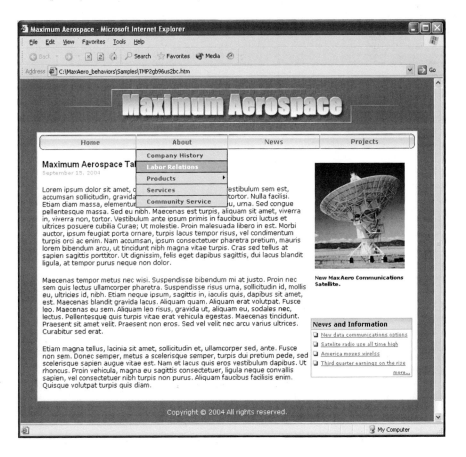

However, it gets a little bit more complicated. For this reason, Dreamweaver has the *Show Pop-Up Menu* behavior. Using this behavior can help you create this functionality in addition to creating and formatting the appearance of the menu.

To apply the *Show Pop-Up Menu* behavior, start by selecting the object that will inherit the new functionality. Then open the Show Pop-Up Menu dialog box (see Figure 11-14) by selecting its corresponding option from the Add Behavior menu of the Behaviors panel. This dialog box is broken into four separate tabs of options. The first tab, Contents, is used to specify the links that will appear as part of the menu. You can use the Text area to specify how the menu option will appear and the Link area to define where that link will send you. Once you have added your first element, you can use the Plus (+) and Minus (-) buttons to add or remove menu options. After you have added a few menu options, there are two more features you can take advantage of. First, you can use the up and down arrows to reorder your items. The order the items appear within this dialog box is the order they will appear within the menu. Your last option is that you can create submenus, or indented menus, using the Indent Item button. Submenu items, like those shown in Figure 11-15, allow you to add hierarchy to your menu

figure | 11-14 |

The Show Pop-Up Menu dialog box's Contents tab.

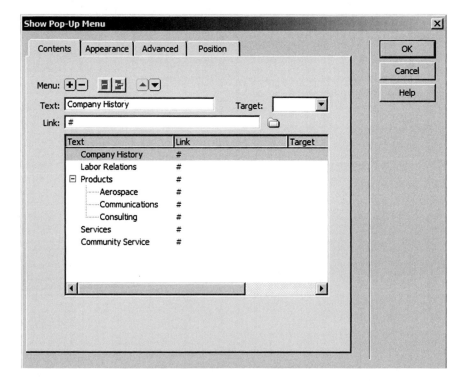

options. If for some reason you want to remove the indent from a menu option, simply click on the Outdent Item button.

The next tab, Appearance, allows you to specify how the menu will actually appear when displayed within the browser (see Figure 11-16). Fortunately, a preview is provided at the bottom of this window

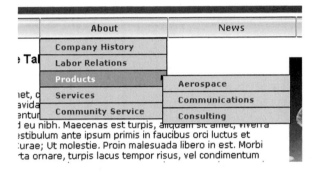

figure | 11-15 |

Using submenus can add hierarchy to your navigational design.

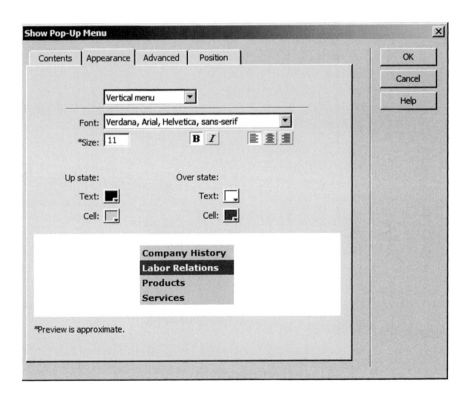

figure | 11-16 |

The Show Pop-Up dialog box's Appearance tab.

to show you approximately what this menu will look like as you adjust the available options. The following detail the options available from the Appearance tab of this dialog box.

- *Vertical/Horizontal:* This option is used to specify the type of menu to create. By default, this will be a vertical menu, but a horizontal menu is also available. Figure 11-17 shows an example of this type of menu.

- *Fonts (and additional formatting):* The Appearance tab allows you to format text using fonts, size, bold, and italics. You can also align the menu options to the left, center, or right.

- *Up State:* The Up State option determines what a menu item will look like when the mouse is not over the link. Using the Text and Cell color selectors you can assign a text color and background color to use for the menu option when it is in the "up" state.

- *Over State:* The Over State option determines what a menu item will look like when the mouse pointer is over the link. Using the Text and Cell color selectors you can assign a text color and background color to use for the menu item when it is in the "over" state.

figure | 11-17 |

Horizontal menus offer an alternative to the vertical style.

The Advanced tab (see Figure 11-18) provides you the option of adjusting the physical parameters of the pop-up menu. Dreamweaver does provide default values for many of these items, so playing around with some of the advanced options is completely up to you. The following detail the available items that may be configured within the Advanced tab of this dialog box.

- *Cell Width/Cell Height:* These options allow you to specify the width of the menu and the height of each menu item. By default this option will be set to Automatic, which means that the menu will expand to fit the menu items.

- *Cell Padding/Cell Spacing:* These options allow you to specify the padding and spacing that will be used for all of the menu

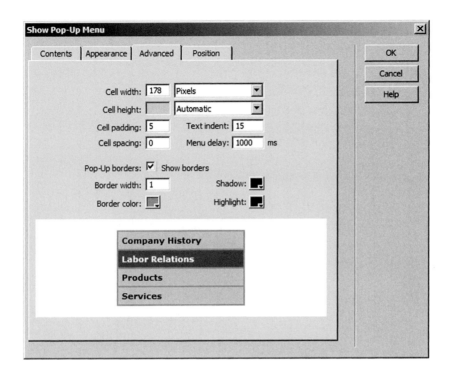

figure | 11-18 |

The Show Pop-Up
Menu dialog box's
Advanced tab.

items. This works just like tables in that the padding is the distance between the content and the border, and the spacing is the distance between items.

● *Text Indent:* This option allows you to specify how much the text will be indented from the left-hand side of the menu.

● *Menu delay:* This option allows you to determine how long, in milliseconds, it will take for the menu to appear after the user's mouse pointer has moved over the trigger object. For those of you who slept during math class (and I include myself in that group), there are a thousand milliseconds in a second.

● *Show Borders/Border Width:* First, the Show Borders option determines if borders will be displayed around and between the menu items. If you choose to display the borders, the Border Width option allows you to specify how wide the border will appear.

● *Border Colors:* There are three different border colors you can specify. First, the *Border color* option allows you to specify the color that will appear on all sides of the menu. The *Shadow color* selector is used to specify a color for the bottom and right-hand side of the menu, just inside border set by the previous option. Finally, the *Highlight color* selector is used to specify a color for the top and left-hand side of the menu.

The last tab of this dialog box is the Position tab, shown in Figure 11-19. The options provided here allow you to adjust where the menu will appear in relationship to the object that triggers its appearance. The four Menu Position buttons should give you some idea of how the menu will appear. I should note that the darker box (cyan in the actual interface) represents the pop-up menu, and the lighter box represents the object that triggers the menu. If you don't like any of these options you can set your own placement information using the X and Y areas. By specifying an X or Y value, you are placing the upper left-hand corner of the menu in relation to the upper left-hand corner of the trigger object. Figure 11-20 illustrates this relationship. The final feature available via this menu is the *Hide menu onMouseOut event* option. This option, which is enabled by default, sets the menu to hide when the user's mouse pointer moves away from the object and/or menu. If you disable this option, the menu will continue to appear until the page is refreshed.

figure | 11-19|

The Show Pop-Up dialog box's Contents tab.

figure | 11-20|

The X-Y relationship between the object and the pop-up menu.

NOTE: Whenever the *Show Pop-Up Menu* behavior is used, the *Hide Pop-Up Menu* behavior will automatically be added. If you wish, you can adjust the event handler for this behavior via the Behaviors panel, just like any other behavior that may have been added manually.

## TRY THIS

Now that we have gone through what it takes to use the *Show Pop-Up Menu* behavior, take a few minutes to practice with it. Simply create a new page, add a hyperlink, and then apply the behavior. Once you create a few menus you will begin to get the feel for what will look best.

## Swap Image

Probably one of the most common interactive features designers have been using for years is the button rollover. The button rollover is a good, yet basic, technique to provide some interactive feedback to the users of your site. In this scenario, you have a button with "up" and "over" states. Typically, each state will have a different appearance. This difference is what makes the button appear that it has been interacted with. To make this interaction work, two separate image files will be needed. The first is the "up" image, or what the button will look like when the user has not yet moved their mouse pointer over the button. The second image is the "over" state, or what the button will look like when the mouse pointer is directly over the button. Figure 11-21 shows

figure | 11-21 |

This is an example of two images you might use for a button rollover effect.

an example of these two button types. Once you have the image files, the *Swap Image* behavior is then used to handle the transition between the two. I should also note that this behavior is not only used for button rollovers. You may have a scenario where the user's pointer moves over one image and another image changes. Or possibly it is several other images that change. In addition, you can change the event handler to enable the image to swap with an *OnClick* (or another event) as opposed to an *onMouseOver*. Fortunately, the *Swap Image* behavior should be flexible enough to meet your design needs.

To create an image rollover effect, start by adding a graphic that will be used as the trigger for this behavior. If you are creating an effect that changes more than one graphic, go ahead and add those images now. The next step is to assign an ID name to each of the graphics involved. This is done by selecting the graphic and editing the ID field within the Property Inspector, shown in Figure 11-22. Now you are ready to add the behavior.

You can add the *Swap Image* behavior by selecting the graphic that will inherit the new functionality. Then open the Swap Image dialog box (see Figure 11-23) by selecting its corresponding option from the Add Behavior menu of the Behaviors panel. Using the Images area of this dialog box you can select the ID that corresponds to those graphics you want to change. Then, use the *Set source to area* option to specify what image should be displayed when the user interacts with the trigger graphic.

Graphic ID

figure | 11-22 |

The ID field within the Property Inspector is used to assign a name to your graphic.

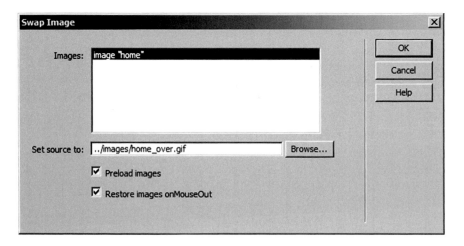

figure | 11-23 |

Swap Image dialog box.

Also in this dialog box are the *Preload images onMouseOut* and *Restore images onMouseOut* options. By enabling these checkboxes, two additional behaviors will be added to this image. The *Preload images* option will download the swapped image with the rest of the page. If you don't enable this behavior, the images will be downloaded when the user interacts with the trigger graphic. This will result in a slight pause in the swapping of images. The length of that pause is dependent on the file size of the graphic and the speed of the user's connection to the Web. The *Restore images onMouseOut* option is what will revert the image back to its original state after being swapped. If you disable this feature, the image will appear in its "over" state until the page is refreshed.

NOTE: The *Preload Images* behavior may actually be used separately from the *Swap Image* behavior. You may want to use it with items such as hidden layers that contain images. Preloading the images will eliminate the delay that can occur with dynamically presenting images that were not displayed when the page was first downloaded.

## Validate Form

There are very few things you can do on the Web that really give the user a chance to express themselves the same way they do when using a web form. It doesn't matter how a text field is labeled, you can almost count on the user typing their last name where their e-mail address should go. Or, even worse, they leave out some key pieces of information you are counting on to receive from the form. Anyone who has created a form for general use can probably tell you of the most boneheaded things that end up in web forms. In an effort to try to correct some of this, the *Validate Form* behavior can be used.

This *Validate Form* behavior can help you do several things with a form that HTML alone cannot handle. First, this behavior allows you to require certain fields within the form. Once a form field has been specified as required, the user will not be able to submit the form until the blank has been filled. In fact, the user will receive an alert, like that shown in Figure 11-24, to let them know that there is missing information. In addition, you can indicate what types of information can exist within a particular field. For example, if you have a

figure | 11-24 |

When the user does not fill in a required form element, they will receive an alert.

field where you are requesting the person's age obviously the response should be a number. Using the *Validate Form* behavior you can help ensure that the data is in a form you expect. In addition, you can use this behavior to specify that the field specifically contain an e-mail address. Although the behavior cannot make sure that the e-mail address is correct, it can check to see if it at least looks like an e-mail address. For example, all e-mail addresses contain the at (@) symbol. Without that symbol, we know it is incorrect.

To use the *Validate Form* behavior, start by selecting the object that will kick off the validation process. For most behaviors it is fairly obvious what this object should be. However, in the case of the *Validate Form* behavior there is more than one way to get this done. You can choose to either apply the validation to a single element or apply it to the whole form. Each has pros and cons.

If you choose to apply the validation feature to just one form element, the validation will occur as soon as the user tries to move on to the next form field. This process is triggered using the *onBlur* event discussed earlier. This technique is good because it gives the user instant feedback on what they have entered. However, this type of constant feedback can get a little annoying if you have a large form. The other technique, which is most common, is to apply the *Validate Form* behavior to the entire form. This way, all of the validation occurs when the user tries to submit the form, which results in a single alert message. Applying the behavior to the entire form is the technique we are going to explore in this chapter.

To apply the *Validate Form* behavior, start by clicking on any element that exists within the form. Next, click on the *<form>* tag within tag selector at the bottom of the Document window (see Figure 11-25). This should select the entire form. Now you can open the Validate Form dialog box (see Figure 11-26) by selecting its corresponding option from the Add Behavior menu of the Behaviors panel. Using the *Named fields* area of this dialog box, you

figure | 11-25 |

The Tag selector is used to select the entire form.

Form Tag

<body> <table> <tr> <td.bodyCell> <table> <tr> <td> <form>

figure | 11-26 |

Validate Form
dialog box.

can select the field you want to validate. Next, you can enable the Required option if this is a form field that must be filled in before the form can be submitted. Now you can use the Accept area to specify what can be entered into a particular blank. The following detail the available options.

- *Anything:* As the name suggests, the user can enter whatever they would like into this form field.

- *Number:* This requires that the response be in numerical form. This will also not allow any other types of characters, such as hyphens.

- *Email Address:* As we discussed earlier, this option will make sure that the user has used an at (@) symbol with their entry.

- *Number from:* This option allows you to specify that the response not only be a number but a number within a certain range. For example, you could ask a question such as "How would you rate this book on a scale of 1 to 10?" The response must be either the numeral 1, the number 10, or anywhere between these two numbers.

Once you have made all of the necessary configurations, click on the OK button to apply the behavior to your form. Once applied, the form will use the *onSubmit* handler to start the validation process.

## SUMMARY

In this chapter we have explored how you can use Dreamweaver's behaviors to increase the interactivity of your design. The thing to keep in mind about behaviors is that they should only be used when design supports such a feature. Also, for behaviors such as pop-up windows or button rollovers a little bit of use can go a long way. The final point to understand is that not everyone can view JavaScript-based behaviors. So, try to use your behaviors in a way that is not critical to the functioning of your page. Or if it is critical, provide an alternative version.

## in review

1. What language is used to build behaviors?

2. What is meant by the term client-side?

3. What browsers are behaviors designed to work with?

4. What objects are commonly used with behaviors?

5. What is an event handler?

6. What are several event handlers and the objects they would typically be used with?

7. Why would you not want to use the Open Browser Window behavior?

8. What are the two ways you can apply the Validate Form behavior?

## ↗ EXPLORING ON YOUR OWN

1. For practice, take an existing design you might have done and add a behavior, or several behaviors, of your choosing.

2. Now that you understand behaviors, plan and create a page designed to use pop-up menus as the primary method of navigation. Try developing an alternative means to offer this same navigation.

3. Create a simple web form, or possibly use one you created in Chapter 4, and add the Form Validation behavior. Take some time to experiment with the different options available.

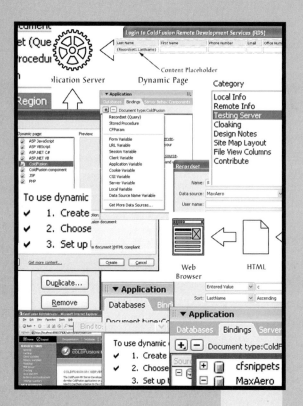

# Working with Dynamic Pages

*charting your course*

Up to this chapter we have been primarily exploring how pages are designed using a static approach. This means that a page will be presented to the user with the exact same content you physically embedded within the page's HTML, and that content will never change unless you modify the file. Now we can build on some of these concepts to develop pages with dynamic content that is stored within databases. By creating a dynamic page, you have a number of different options for how to present content to your audience. Although the learning curve for this process is much steeper than building static pages, adding dynamic content provides a level of functionality that simply isn't available with HTML alone.

In this chapter, I will give you a high-level overview of how dynamic pages work. Once we get the introductory information out of the way, we will then fire up Dreamweaver to create a new dynamic page. It is not my goal to teach everything you will need to know about creating dynamic pages. In fact, we are only going to scratch the surface. As a web designer you will be able to take what you learn from this chapter and use it as a foundation when working with dynamic applications in future projects. Having at least a fundamental knowledge of how dynamic technologies work is essential for modern web designers. Once you get a feel for the available capabilities, you will soon be looking for opportunities to create even more interesting web designs that make use of dynamic content.

 *goals*

- **Learn the fundamentals of how dynamic pages work**
- **Discover how Dreamweaver can be used to work with server technologies**
- **Learn about the options for connecting to a database**
- **Explore how to build pages that use dynamic content**

# ABOUT DYNAMIC PAGES

Building dynamic pages uses a completely different model than you are probably used to. In the past, when you were building static pages you could simply add content to the page and then view it within the browser. All you needed to do static design work was Dreamweaver and a web browser. Now, with dynamic page development several steps have been added to this process. Even though it takes more planning and preparation, there are countless uses for using dynamic pages within your site. Let's explore some of the concepts behind dynamic page development.

## Why Go Dynamic?

Before we get into the nuts and bolts of how dynamic pages work, we should discuss how the technology is used. In a nutshell, dynamic pages should be used in three different scenarios. The first scenario is when you need to deliver a large volume of similar pieces of information. An example would be an e-commerce site that offers hundreds or thousands of different products. If this were built as a static web site, a separate HTML page would have to be created for each product. Could you imagine having to create thousands of pages by hand? And, once the pages are created how could you ever maintain all the content? This is a perfect example of how adding dynamic features to a site can really make maintaining content easier.

The second scenario where dynamic pages are commonly used is with content that changes on a regular basis. Many large sites feature content such as news releases that are subject to change or expansion continually. Having to create a new HTML page every time something new happens can be a cumbersome process. And, just like the e-commerce example it would be extremely difficult to maintain this information over a long period of time.

The final example of where dynamic pages are typically used is with lists of information that may be sorted based on different criteria. For example, your site may contain an employee directory. In this situation, you may want to list all of the employees alphabetically, or you may want to list only those employees whose last names begin with a particular letter. What's more, you can add features to a dynamic page that allows your audience to select how the information is sorted. Possibly they want to see the employee directory in reverse alphabetical order. Adding these types of options can make your web site easier to use.

## The Nuts and Bolts

So how exactly does a dynamic page work? As I mentioned earlier, a static page will contain all of the content and formatting information it will need in order to be displayed in the browser. On the other hand, a dynamic page is different in that it doesn't contain content, but it does have the dynamic code necessary to locate the content within a database. So, how do we go from code to database to browser?

In Chapter 2 I mentioned that anytime you type an address into a web browser you are requesting a file that will be sent back and displayed within the web browser. For static pages, this browser/server relationship is fairly simple. Since a static page already contains its necessary content, there is normally no need to have the server do much but serve up the file so that you can see it (see Figure 12-1). Dynamic pages work in a similar manner, but with two additions. As you can see in Figure 12-2, dynamic pages involve the use of an application server and a database. When a request for a dynamic page is made, an application server will be used to process the code within the page before serving it up to be displayed. While

figure | 12-1 |

Static pages contain everything needed for a web browser to display the page.

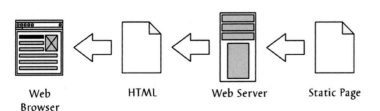

Web Browser     HTML     Web Server     Static Page

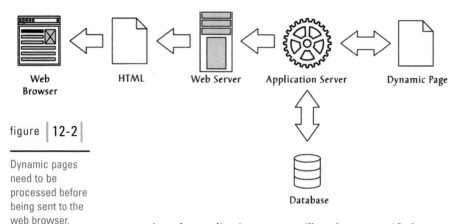

Web Browser

HTML

Web Server

Application Server

Dynamic Page

Database

figure | 12-2 |

Dynamic pages need to be processed before being sent to the web browser.

processing, the application server will suck any specified content from the database and insert it into the page. This way, the page that is returned to the browser is nothing but HTML. If this sounds a little fuzzy, don't worry. We will actually walk through an example of this in the latter half of the chapter.

## Server Technology

Now that you have a feel for the general process, let's take a look at some of the technology you may not be as familiar with. We just discussed how application servers are used to process the code within a dynamic page. This probably left you wondering "What exactly is an application server?" Simply put, an application server is a special piece of software installed on the web server and is used to process dynamic pages. There are several different types of application servers available, and many use different server technologies, or programming languages, which can be used to add dynamic features to web pages.

Unfortunately, building a dynamic web page is not as simple as just deciding what technology you want to use. Because the application server is installed and maintained on the web server, you will need to work with your web hosting company or group to find out what may be available to you. For this reason, Dreamweaver supports several different types of server technologies, including Cold-Fusion, ASP.NET, ASP, JSP, and PHP. It is not my goal to go into the pros and cons of each technology. But, I can assure you that working with each of these within Dreamweaver is very similar. For this chapter, I am going to build an example using ColdFusion because it can be one of the easiest technologies to work with. This is not to say that ColdFusion is necessarily the best choice, but each technology certainly has its advantages and disadvantages.

**NOTE:** For more information on the server technologies mentioned here, visit the following web sites.

- Macromedia ColdFusion: *www.macromedia.com/software/coldfusion*

- ASP.NET: *msdn.microsoft.com/asp.net*

- ASP (Active Server Pages): *msdn.microsoft.com/asp*

- JSP (Java Server Pages):
  - *jakarta.apache.org/*
  - *www.macromedia.com/software/jrun/*
  - *www.ibm.com/websphere*
  - *www.bea.com*

- PHP (PHP: Hypertext Preprocessor): *www.php.net*

## Databases

If you have ever worked with a spreadsheet before, databases are conceptually not much different. Generally speaking, a database is nothing more than a collection of tables that each contains a particular set of information. For example, you might have a table that contains information about all of a company's employees and another that contains news releases. No matter what data it contains, each table is structured in the same basic way. Figure 12-3 shows an example database table we will use for an employee directory later in this chapter.

Every database table is broken into one or more columns, which are actually called fields. Each field name is used to label the nature

| PersonID | FirstName | LastName | Email | PhoneNumber | OfficeNumber |
|---|---|---|---|---|---|
| 1 | Bob | Smith | bsmith@maxae | 555-1234 | 101 |
| 2 | Jane | Jones | jjones@maxaer | 555-2345 | 102 |
| 3 | Carol | Parks | cparks@maxae | 555-3456 | 103 |
| 4 | Todd | Bucher | tbucher@maxa⟨ | 555-4567 | 104 |
| 5 | Alex | Carson | acarson@maxa | 555-5678 | 105 |
| 6 | Sylvia | Snyder | ssnyder@maxa | 555-6789 | 106 |
| 7 | Doug | Carvey | dcarvey@maxa⟨ | 555-7890 | 107 |
| 8 | Abe | Kane | akane@maxaer | 555-8901 | 108 |
| 9 | Sue | Fineberg | sfineberg@max | 555-9012 | 109 |
| 10 | Pete | Peterson | | 555-0123 | 110 |

people : Table — Record: 1 of 10 — (AutoNumber)

figure | 12-3 |

Databases such as Microsoft Access can be used to store content for dynamic pages.

of the information that will be contained within that field. For example, you might have a field to contain a first name, last name, phone number, and so on. Without going into too many technical details, a field can also be set to only contain a certain type and/or length of data. For example, you can specify that a first name contain text that is no more than 20 characters long.

Each time that information is entered into the database it will occupy a row of the table. Each row of data is more commonly referred to as a record. For example, in looking at our employee database each employee is represented by a single record within the database. As a new employee is added, it will be appended to the bottom of the table, thus creating a new record. When you are creating dynamic web pages, it is the database records you will actually output when the page is presented within the browser. The big thing to remember about records is that each needs to contain a unique value, or key. Typically this key is simply a number, which increases by one each time a record has been added, used to separate one record from another. The key value should be stored within its "on" field. Looking back to Figure 12-3, the *PersonID* field contains a unique number for each employee. In this situation, the key value is important because you may have no other way to separate two people who have the same name.

### Available Databases

There are several different types of databases that can be used to store web content. Some databases can be used for small personal sites, whereas others are used to contain millions upon millions of records. In this chapter, I am using Microsoft Access because it is the smallest and easiest database to use. However, dynamic pages can also use other types of databases. Microsoft SQL, Oracle, and MySQL are all examples of databases commonly used when developing dynamic web pages. Fundamentally, each of these structures the information using a model similar to that we just discussed.

# SETTING UP DREAMWEAVER FOR DYNAMIC SITES

Before dynamic pages can be built, we need to first prepare Dreamweaver to work with our application server. As you can already begin to tell, there is a fair amount of preparation work that goes into working with dynamic pages. Fortunately, once everything has been set up you won't have to do it again unless something changes.

# How Dreamweaver Works with Dynamic Pages

As we discussed earlier, an application server is needed to view dynamic pages. This adds a separate layer of complexity when building dynamic pages within Dreamweaver. When we were building static pages, all we needed was a web browser to see the final design. But now that we are working with dynamic pages, this model will simply not work. To get around this problem, there are two different options for developing dynamic pages within Dreamweaver. You can develop and preview the pages on your local workstation, or you can do the development locally and then send the pages out to your web server for viewing. Depending on the type of workstation you use or the application server you are developing for, both options may not be available. Let's take a look at the different options.

## Develop Everything Locally

The optimal way to build dynamic pages within Dreamweaver is to develop and test everything locally. In this environment, you have complete control over all of the variables. In addition, if you work in a team setting you don't have to worry about stepping on any of your co-workers' toes when you are modifying and saving pages. However, for this to work your workstation must actually be set up to function as a web server. If you don't have much experience with this, it can be a little tricky to do. In addition, Macintosh users may not have as many options in this area because many application servers are not designed to run on this platform. But never fear, we will look at another way you can develop dynamic pages within Dreamweaver in a moment.

NOTE: For this chapter, I have set up ColdFusion on my local workstation for development. If you use a Windows computer, the ColdFusion Developer Edition can be downloaded from the Macromedia web site at *www.macromedia.com*. This version of ColdFusion works just like the one used on a web server, but it will only work on your personal computer. If you are the least bit comfortable working with server-based software, ColdFusion is one of the easiest web-servers/application-servers you can install. I should also note that it is possible to install and run ColdFusion on Mac OS X, but it isn't nearly as easy. For more information, consult Dreamweaver help, or the Macromedia web site.

# DEVELOP LOCALLY, PREVIEW REMOTELY

If you don't want to go through the effort of setting up your workstation as a web server, or you don't have the option, you can do your development locally and then send the page to the web server for preview. Fortunately, Dreamweaver does directly support this model of operation. The biggest downside is that you are actually moving files between your computer and the web server anytime you want to view a page, so this can be a little slow at times. This method of using a remote web server is commonly used by designers who work on a Mac, or who use an application server that is not supported by their workstation.

## Setting Up Directories

You are already familiar with the concept of using local and remote sites to handle your web pages. Yet, when building dynamic pages an additional type of site is added to the mix: a testing server. In simplest terms, a testing server is a place where dynamic pages such as ColdFusion, ASP, PHP, and so on can be processed and viewed. If you are running an application server on your local workstation, the testing server and the local site may be the same place. In this case, you will want to make sure the directory that contains your local site is actually within the web root of the application server. This really isn't as technical as it sounds. Anytime an application server is installed, it will add a default folder structure. All you have to do is find the root folder and place your site within it. In the case of this chapter, since I am using ColdFusion my root directory is located at *C:\CFusionMX7\wwwroot\*. Once I add my site within this directory, a web browser can be used to view the pages by going to *http://localhost:8500/mysite*.

NOTE: If you are running your application server locally, it is not a requirement to store your local site within the web root. In fact, you can set up your local site and testing server as two different directories on the same machine. In this case, you should treat your site as if you had remote access to the testing server.

If you don't have the option of running an application server on your local workstation, you can set up a remote testing server. In this case, your web hosting service should be able to provide you with three items you will need: account access information (log-in/password), the root web directory, and a URL to access pages from this account. In the next section we will take a look at how this information can be used to set up a testing server.

## Define a Site

In Chapter 6 we looked at how Dreamweaver can be used to help manage a web site. If you are creating a new site, refer back to Chapter 6 on how to set the Local Info and Remote Info options. In this chapter, we can use the same site definition area to configure Dreamweaver to work in cooperation with an application server. To start this process, summon the Manage Sites dialog box via the Site | Manage Sites menu option. Using this dialog box (see Figure 12-4), either select an existing site and click on Edit or create a new site by clicking on New. This will open the Site Definition dialog box, shown in Figure 12-5. If it is not selected already, select the Advanced tab at the top of this window. Setting up a site to use a dynam-ic server technology is done by selecting the

figure | 12-4 |

The Manage Sites dialog box is used to select an existing site or to create a new one.

Testing Server category of this dialog box. Here you can define a new testing server by configuring the following options.

- *Server Model:* Use this menu to select the type of server tech-nology you will be using. In the case of this example, I will be using ColdFusion. I should note that the other Testing Server options are the same no matter what technology you are using.

- *Access:* Use this menu to select the type of access you have to the testing server. If you are running a testing server locally, you will obviously want to use the Local/Network option. If your testing server is maintained remotely, your type of access will be dictated by the hosting service.

- *Local/Network—Testing Server Folder:* If you are accessing the testing server locally or through a network connection, you will have the option of selecting a folder that resides within your testing server. This is the directory we discussed in the previous

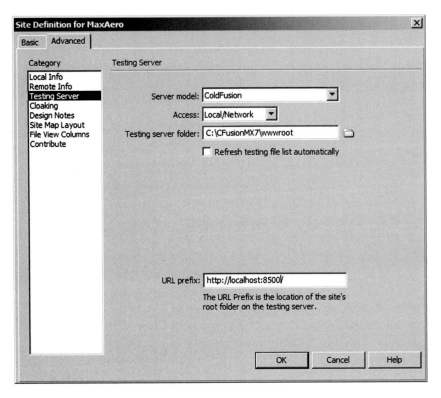

figure | 12-5 |

The Test Server category of the Site Definition dialog box will help you set up Dreamweaver to work with dynamic pages.

section. Since I am using ColdFusion, I will be using a folder within *C:\CFusionMX7\wwwroot\*.

- *FTP:* If you are accessing your testing server remotely, you may be using the FTP option. Once selected, a number of FTP configuration options become available. This information should have been provided by your hosting service.

- *URL prefix:* Use this area to enter the URL that is used for pages on the testing server. If you are running an application server on your local workstation, a "localhost" URL will normally be used. If you are accessing a testing server remotely, your hosting service should provide you with the URL to use.

Once you are satisfied with the configurations made, go ahead and click on the OK button to apply the changes. You are now ready to build dynamic pages.

# BUILD A DYNAMIC PAGE

With all of the preparations out of the way, it is time to get down to business with dynamic pages. In this section I am going to take you through a simple page that will output a series of records from a Microsoft Access database. My intent is not to show you all of the options for creating dynamic pages but to show you just enough to give you an appetite for dynamic web technologies and how they work.

## Start a New Dynamic Page

Creating a new dynamic page works just like any other page. It all starts by selecting File | New to summon the New Document dialog box. Here you can choose the *Dynamic page* option from the Category listing on the left. Once selected, the *Dynamic page* options will appear, as shown in Figure 12-6. Now you can select the server technology you will be designing with. Once again, I will mention that developing dynamic pages within Dreamweaver is nearly the same for each server technology. Even though I am using ColdFusion as the example in this chapter, the same concepts still

figure | 12-6 |

The New Document dialog box offers you a number of different options in the way of dynamic pages.

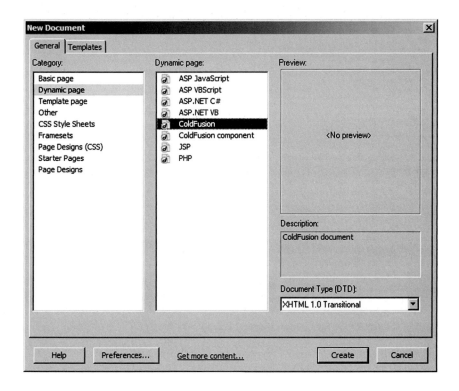

apply with something else. When you have your dynamic page type selected, click on the Create button to start a new page.

On the surface, this page looks no different than a static page within the Document window. In fact, the best way to work with a dynamic page is to go ahead and add all of the design elements first before adding any dynamic information. This way, you can easily integrate the dynamic information with the static pieces of the page. The only real changes come when you want to start working with some dynamic functionality. Next, we will take a look at how you can connect your page to a database.

## Connect to a Database

Before we can begin to pull in some dynamic data, we must first make a connection to a database. Depending on what type of server technology you are using, this may be a little tricky (and somewhat frustrating at times). I just got done reminding you about how Dreamweaver works the same despite the server technology, so what gives? In reality, Dreamweaver works the same with just a few exceptions, connecting to a database being the biggest. However, the good news is that once a database connection is made you will know how to do it the next time.

Unfortunately, most server technologies have different ways of creating database connections. And some, such as ASP, have more than one way of creating the connection. Fortunately, Macromedia has done a pretty good job of documenting the different ways you can connect to different types of databases using different server technologies. So, before you go too much further I would probably take a peek at the Dreamweaver help file (Help | Using Dreamweaver) or the Macromedia support site at *www.macromedia.com/support/ dreamweaver/database.html*.

One of the reasons I picked ColdFusion for use in this chapter is because it is fairly simple to connect with a database. Without getting into too many of the technical specifics, ColdFusion uses something called the ColdFusion administrator (see Figure 12-7) to manage database connections. If you installed ColdFusion on your computer, the administrator is installed at the same time. Using the administrator, making a database connection is as easy as selecting a file on your file system (in the case of Microsoft Access) or specifying an address for a more robust database server else-

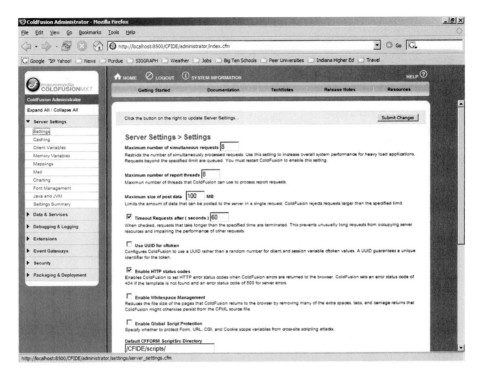

figure | 12-7 |

In case you were curious, this is what the ColdFusion administrator looks like.

where. Once specified, all you have to do is give it a name, which is aptly referred to as a data source. Once a data source has been defined, you shouldn't have to do it again.

It is important to mention that ColdFusion isn't unique in this regard. Actually, other server technologies such as ASP also use a similar connection method called a DSN (or Data Source Name). The big thing to remember about working with named database connections is that the name you use for the local and testing server should be the same as your remote (or live) web site. If you are using a hosting service, you will need to discuss with them what types of database connections they support.

## Hooking It Up

Once you have the connection option figured out, it is time to hook your page into the database. This is done using the Databases panel (see Figure 12-8), which can be summoned via the Window

figure | 12-8 |

The Database panel is used to connect your page to a database.

| Databases menu option. Here, assuming you haven't already made a successful connection, you will see a checklist of items. This checklist may differ slightly depending on what type of server technology you are using. In this case, we have already covered up to step 3 (setting up the site's testing server). If you don't have check marks next to these items, I would go back and revisit some of the information from earlier in this chapter.

The next item on the list, in the case of ColdFusion, is specifying the RDS log-in. RDS, or Remote Development Services, is something ColdFusion uses to provide remote access to the administrator we talked about earlier. If you are running ColdFusion on your local workstation, the RDS log-in is the same as the administrator log-in that was specified during installation. If you are working from a remote ColdFusion server, talk with your hosting service regarding RDS access. With your RDS log-in information, click on the RDS log-in link, and add the password to the resulting dialog box (see Figure 12-9). With that item checked off the list, the last thing to do is to create the data source we talked about earlier. In all likelihood, this will have already been done by the time you reach this point. If so, the last item will automatically be checked off for you. If the data source has not been created, clicking on the data source link will automatically launch the ColdFusion administrator.

figure | 12-9 |

If you are using ColdFusion, an RDS password will be needed here.

## The Databases Panel

After a connection has been made to a database, you see the available data source options within the Databases panel (see Figure 12-10). This panel is primarily used so that you can directly peruse the available database fields. If you work with dynamic pages often, it is easy to forget exactly what types of information are stored in the database. Using this panel, you can check for available fields without having to jump back and forth to the database. To view the available types of data, click on the Plus (+) button next to the data source you wish to inspect. This will expand out, revealing the different database items you can explore. For this book, we are only interested in the Tables option. Next, by clicking on the Plus (+) button in front of the Tables option a list of available database tables will be displayed. Now you can once again click on the Tables option's Plus (+) button to spill out all the fields that are present within this table (see Figure 12-11).

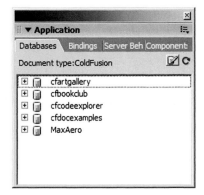

figure | 12-10 |

Once a database connection has been made, the available data sources will appear.

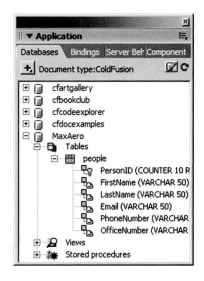

figure | 12-11 |

You can expand a data source's Tables option to view the available database fields.

## Create a Recordset

Now that we have made a connection, and can see the types of data available, it is time to get to the meat of dynamic page development. If there is one skill to master in building dynamic pages, it is database queries. Simply put, a database query is like asking the database to answer a question. For example, in this chapter I am working with a sample database that contains a list of fictional employees. So, I might ask the database to show me everyone whose last name begins with the letter c. In response, the database

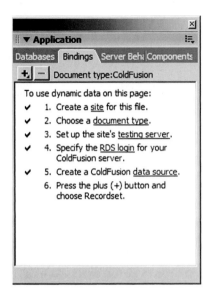

figure | 12-12 |

The Bindings panel is used to create and display recordsets.

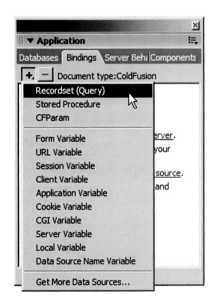

figure | 12-13 |

The Bindings panel allows you to work with more than just databases.

will send back a list of everyone who meets this criterion. This database response is what is called a recordset. As the name implies, a recordset is just a set of records that matched the database query. Technically speaking, these queries are written with a language called SQL (or Structure Query Language). Fortunately, Dreamweaver provides an easy interface to create SQL queries without ever having to write a line of code.

To have Dreamweaver create a recordset, you use the Bindings panel, shown in Figure 12-12. Since the Databases panel is already open, the Bindings tab should be right next to it within the Application panel group. If not, it can be summoned via the Window | Bindings menu option. Before we go any further I should note that the Bindings panel will not work if you have not already successfully created a database connection. Now, to create a recordset click on the Plus (+) button in the upper left-hand corner of the panel. The resulting menu, shown in Figure 12-13, will reveal a number of different types of data you can connect to. Here you select the Recordset (Query) option to open the Recordset dialog box (see Figure 12-14). The following detail how this dialog box's options may be used to create a database query.

1. Use the Name field to specify a name for this recordset. It is critical that this name be unique because it is possible to have more than one recordset on a page.

2. Use the data source menu to select the data source name that corresponds to the database that contains the desired information.

3. Many databases require the use of a login and password to gain access. If so, this information would be added using the User Name and Password areas.

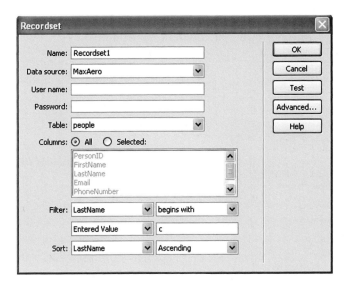

figure | 12-14 |

The Recordset dialog box is used to query information from a database.

4.  Use the Table menu to select the table that contains the desired information.

5.  Once all the previous information has been provided, a list of fields will appear in the Columns menu. Here you can choose to pull information from every column by selecting the All radio button. Or, you can choose a select number of fields when creating a recordset. A good rule of thumb is to not pull any more data than you need to. So, if you only wanted to find first and last names the rest of the data is just a waste of bandwidth.

6.  Next, adjust the Filter options to specify the records you want from the database. This option may seem a little tricky at first but it isn't difficult to use. Remember back to my example of listing all people whose last names begin with c? This is where you specify criteria such as that. How it works is that you use the first menu to select the database field to filter (for example, *LastName*). Next, use the second menu to determine what type of comparison you want it to do. For our example, you may want to use the *begins with* option. Now you need to use the third menu to choose how the filter criteria are to be specified. If you know what you want (such as *begins with c*), use the *Entered value* option. Last, enter the value you want to filter based on. In this case, a simple letter c.

7.  Now use the Sort option to determine the order the records will be returned. For example, you might want the records

sorted by ascending order of last names. This means that you will receive an alphabetical list going from A to Z.

8. Before moving on, make sure to click on the Test button. This will open the Test SQL Statement dialog box, like that shown in Figure 12-15, to show the recordset this query will create. If it isn't what you were looking for, go back and modify the filter or sort options to fine-tune your query.

9. Last, click on the OK button to add the query to your page.

figure | 12-15 |

The SQL Statement dialog box can show you what information your current query will return.

Now that you have created a recordset, it will appear within the Bindings panel (see Figure 12-16). If you click on the Plus (+) button next to the recordset, it will expand to show the database fields available within this recordset. This will be extremely handy as we move onto the next section about adding information from the recordset to our dynamic page.

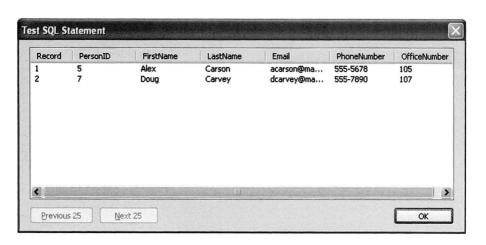

figure | 12-16 |

The Bindings panel will show you the available recordsets.

## Output Dynamic Information

As I mentioned earlier, one of the best ways to build a dynamic page is to start with the static design elements and then add the dynamic information. Once a recordset is created, you can also use the Bindings panel to embed the database information into your page. For this example, I want to create a table that will be filled with the dynamic information. So, I will start by adding a new HTML table in the typical manner we discussed way back in Chapter 3. With my new table on the page, I can now being to add dynamic content.

To start this process, place your cursor on the page where you want to insert the information from a particular database field. For my example, I am going place my cursor in a table column that corresponds to a fictional employee's last name. Next, move to the Bindings panel and click on the Plus (+) button in front of the desired recordset to reveal the list of database fields. Now select the content source you want to add to the page. For example, I want to insert content from the *LastName* database field. Then, to drop in the content click on the Insert button at the bottom of the panel (see Figure 12-17). In the Document window, dynamic content will appear as a placeholder showing both the recordset name and the field name with a light blue background (see Figure 12-18). After you have added one, it takes no effort to continue to fill out the rest of your page with dynamic content.

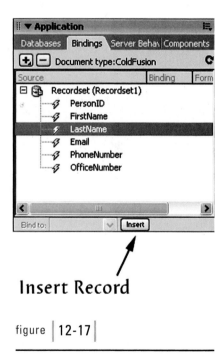

**Insert Record**

figure | 12-17 |

The Insert button on the Bindings panel.

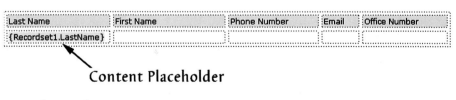

**Content Placeholder**

figure | 12-18 |

Placeholders will be added where there is dynamic content.

### Live Data View

Adding dynamic content placeholders to your design may seem a little lackluster after all the work you had to go through to get there. The real excitement doesn't happen until you view the page with some live data. Using the Dreamweaver live data view, you can take a look at the dynamic content as it will appear within the design of your page. To enable this view, select the View | Live Data menu option, or click on the Live Data View button within the Document toolbar (see Figure 12-19). Once this option is turned on, your page will become alive with dynamic information.

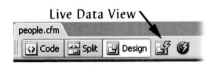

figure | 12-19 |

The Live Data View button on the Document toolbar.

While in live data view, you can continue to work with your page. Feel free to adjust some of the design elements, or to add dynamic content to the page. About the only thing you can't do is click on a hyperlink.

NOTE: In addition to the live data view, you can preview a page within the browser. This is done by selecting the File | Preview in Browser | (select browser) menu option. Using the preview option with dynamic pages is a little different than usual because it will make a temporary copy of the page on your testing server so that you can see it. So, if you are using a remote server for testing you will need to make sure a connection is available before previewing a page.

# SERVER BEHAVIORS

To this point we have really only output just one record. What happens when we want to present all records from our query? This is where server behaviors come into play. Server behaviors work a little like JavaScript behaviors we talked about in Chapter 11, but they are designed to use server-side technology. In a nutshell, server behaviors are prewritten snippets of code (using whatever server technology you are working with) that are used to accomplish a particular task. Dreamweaver provides several of these via the Server Behaviors panel. This panel, whose tab is right next to the Bindings tab, is used to associate a behavior with a record or set of records. In this case, I want to take a set of records (my fictional employee information) and replicate it for every record that exists within my recordset.

To apply this functionality, I am going to use the *Repeat Region* server behavior. This behavior will take a specified set of records, and any corresponding HTML such as a table row, and repeat it over and over for every record within in a recordset. Start by selecting the dynamic content, or HTML object that contains the dynamic content, as it appears within the Document window. In the case of my example, I am going to select the entire row of my HTML table. Next, if it is not already open summon the Server Behaviors panel. Here you can click on the Plus (+) button and select Repeat Region from the resulting menu (see Figure 12-20). This will open the Repeat Region dialog box, where you can specify what recordset to repeat, and how many records to show. You can choose to only show a certain number of records, or it can repeat to display everything within the recordset. Once satisfied with the settings, click on the OK button to apply the behavior. Now use the live data view to preview your page (see Figure 12-21). Now we are working with some live data!

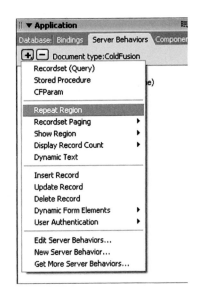

figure | 12-20 |

The Server Behaviors panel is used to select the *Repeat Region* behavior.

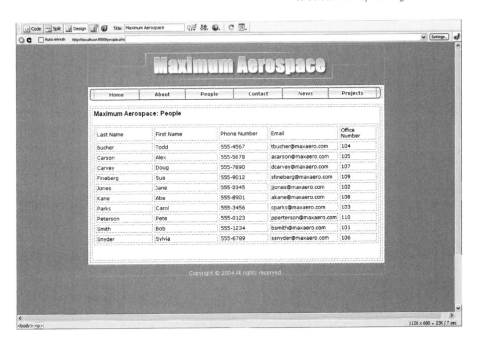

figure | 12-21 |

An example page with a repeating region in the live data view.

# GIVE IT SOME STYLE

The last step when working with dynamic content is to give it some style. Believe it or not, information you add from a database is treated much the same way you would treat static content. The general rule is that when dynamic content is displayed within the browser it will inherit whatever formatting has been applied to the containing element. In practice, CSS is an excellent tool to control the formatting of a dynamic page. Back in Chapter 10 we talked about how CSS can be used to not only add style to your page but to add structure. This is done by specifying styles for headings, links, paragraphs of text, and so on. Using this same strategy is very helpful when working with dynamic pages, because they too require you to give structure to the information on your page.

As you continue to work with dynamic content, keep an eye on the dynamic content placeholders. These will give you a good idea of how the content will appear. So, if the placeholder text is bold the corresponding dynamic content will be bold when displayed within the browser. In addition, don't forget that you can flip on Dreamweaver's live data view to see what the "real" page will look like with the dynamic components added.

# SUMMARY

In this chapter we have explored how Dreamweaver can be used to create dynamic pages. The key thing to remember about this chapter is the sequence of events that lead to building dynamic pages. First, figure out what application server and server technology you are going to work with. Next, configure Dreamweaver to work with that application server. Now you can design a page to contain the dynamic content. Then connect your page with a dynamic data source such as a database. Last, add the dynamic content. I know that this chapter may seem a little difficult at times. However, I can't stress enough that it helps to have a little background on working with server-based technology. What you have just learned will make you a more well-rounded web designer in the future.

## in review

1. What is the difference between a dynamic page and a static page? Describe a few reasons why a dynamic page may be used.

2. Generally speaking, what is an application server?

3. How is a database used in conjunction with dynamic web pages?

4. What are the two models for developing pages within Dreamweaver?

5. If I wanted to develop a dynamic page using Dreamweaver, what am I going to need?

6. What is a database query? Explain how a query is used and its relationship to the recordset.

7. What are the three Dreamweaver panels discussed in this chapter? Describe how each is used when building a dynamic page.

8. How is Dreamweaver's live data view used with dynamic pages?

9. Why is CSS a good technology to use when applying formatting to dynamic text?

## ✗ EXPLORING ON YOUR OWN

1. Developing dynamic pages takes a fair amount of work to find all of the technical elements that will be needed. As your first task, prepare a testing server you can use to process dynamic pages. This may mean setting up your local workstation as a small development server. Many of the application servers mentioned earlier in this chapter offer a free development version for personal use. The Macromedia web site, and the Dreamweaver help file, can offer you a number of tips for creating a testing environment.

2. Take an existing design and modify it to utilize dynamic content. For example, you may have a page that was intended to list employee information, jobs postings, or news releases. Once you have identified the page, take some time to lay out the structure of the content as it will appear on the page. You may also want to create corresponding CSS styles for the areas of content.

3. Using a preconfigured testing server, in addition to an HTML layout designed for dynamic content, create a new page that will display the dynamic content of your choice. To do this, you may need to create a database in Microsoft Access (or similar product) to store your information.

# ADVENTURES IN DESIGN
## BUILDING INFORMATION WIDGETS

If there is one thing I will encourage you to do with your web designs, it is to find new and interesting ways of presenting content. Anyone can build a page where the information flows in from top to bottom, but it takes creativity to do something different. However, take caution. Don't be so creative that you confuse or disorient the user. Be just different enough so that your audience will appreciate that you took the time to make their experience better.

## Project Example

As part of a past project for a residential construction company, I needed to design a web page that would deliver several small chunks of content, but I didn't want them to take up much space on the screen. So, what I needed to do was develop an interactive "widget" that would deliver content to the user. I use the term *widget* because there is no other word to describe small interactive components that are custom built for any particular project.

So, what I decided to do was create a small tabbed element that used an index card metaphor. As the user clicked on or moused over each of the tabs, the "card" would rotate to the front and display the requested content. To make this interaction as fast as possible, I used layers to contain each piece of content. This way, I could show or hide the layers based on the user's interaction. Not only is my custom widget functional but it creates a slight bit of interactive interest (see Figure C-1).

To create this effect I started by identifying the pieces of content that would appear with each of the tabs. This determined two things: how many tabs would be needed and how large the widget would need to be. Next, I created several new layers, one of each tab. It was important that the layers be the exact same size and lined up exactly, so I used Dreamweaver's Property Inspector to enter in the pixel values of size and location.

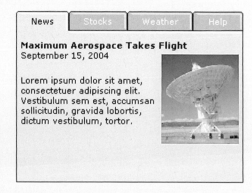

Figure C-1. Always look for new or interesting ways to deliver content.

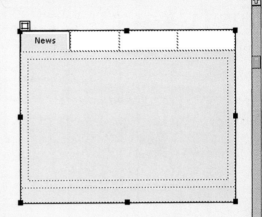

The next step was to design how each card would actually appear. For this I used tables that were the exact same size as the layer. In this table, the top row was used to contain each of the tabs and the lower row was used to contain the content. To create the effect of having an "active" tab, the current card is made a different color from the rest. Each of these tabs contains either text or graphics that are to be used as hyperlinks for triggering the show/hide behaviors (see Figure C-2).

Figure C-2. You can use separate images or text as each of the tabs within the table.

Now that the basic design is down, the remaining cards are created by simply replicating the fist table for each additional layer. Then, the tabs and content are changes for each of the individual cards. With all of the assets in place, the Show-Hide Dreamweaver behavior is applied to each of the "inactive" tabs. As an extra twist, I set the tabs to show and hide based on the *onMouseOver* event.

## Your Turn

Now it's your turn to try something like this. The key to being successful when developing interactive elements is to not go too far. With all of the available options, this is easy to do. Try to focus on the best way to display particular content. Once you solve this, everything else is just getting the technology to work.

1. Start by examining the content you want to deliver. How many different types of content are there, and how long are they?

2. Devise an interactive way of presenting the content. Put yourself in the shoes of your audience. If you came looking for this content, how would you want it presented to you? Is there any way that it can be accessed more quickly?

3. Once you figure out how to deliver the content, design an interface that makes sense. In my case, I used the tabbed index card as a metaphor for the design. This makes it easier for the audience to interact because they are already familiar with the concept. Remember, this is all about making things better for the user, Simple is better.

4. Build and implement the widget based on your design. This will take a little work, and possibly a little experimentation. Try to break some new ground with your design. However, try not to stray too far too fast.

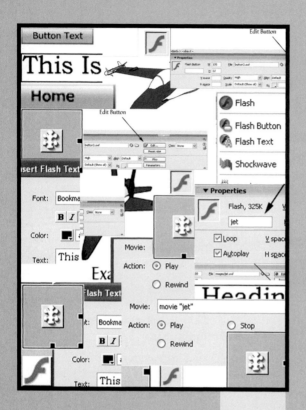

Working with Macromedia Flash and Multimedia

13

*charting your course*

There is only so much you can do with HTML, CSS, and JavaScript. To achieve an exciting web design, many times you will need to reach beyond what the web browser alone can display for you. This is where many multimedia elements come into play. In the early years of the Web, there were very few options for the types of media that could be displayed within the browser. Today, we are able to use Flash, video, and other multimedia as elements that may appear seamlessly within your design. The increase in multimedia options means that you have a greater number of alternatives when designing an immersive web site that can enhance the user's experience.

In this chapter we are going to focus primarily on how you can embed and work with Macromedia Flash files within the pages you design with Dreamweaver. Although there are many options for adding multimedia to your pages, Flash offers you unparalleled versatility. Once you have a feel for how to work with Flash, we will also explore a few other options for adding other types of multimedia, such as video, to your design. With that said, let's get rolling.

 *goals*

- **Explore how Dreamweaver can be used to add Flash elements to a web page**

- **Discover some of the tools available for creating Flash elements within Dreamweaver**

- **Learn the options for working with video**

# WORKING WITH MACROMEDIA FLASH

If you are not familiar with Macromedia Flash, chances are that you have already interacted with it on many web sites. In a nutshell, Flash is a multimedia file format used to develop movies that contain text, graphics, animations, or even video. Much like most other multimedia elements you use on the Web, using Flash within your web designs requires that you have a specific browser plug-in installed on your computer. This plug-in is a special piece of software used to play the movie within the browser once downloaded. Fortunately, Macromedia Flash is one of the most common plug-ins among web users. And if a user doesn't already have the flash plug-in, it can be downloaded from the Macromedia web site.

In this section we are going to explore a little background on Flash, and how you can add it to your designs within Dreamweaver. There are also tools you can use to directly create small Flash-based objects that can be added to your pages. In addition, I am also going to show you a few behaviors, like those we explored in Chapter 11, that are commonly used in conjunction with Flash elements.

## The Nuts and Bolts of Flash

Macromedia Flash elements are designed and built using a software package of the same name. What makes Flash a little different from other multimedia formats is that it is a generally a vector-based format. If you remember back to your high school geometry class, a vector is basically another name for a line. Therefore, vector-based graphics (and text) within Flash are based on points, lines, and curves that are combined to display the visuals you see on screen. Flash is special in this respect because multimedia formats are typically based on raster graphics, or what some people generically refer to as bitmap graphics. Raster graphics are simply composed of a grid of colored pixels. Figure 13-1 shows the same graphic in both vector and raster forms to illustrate the difference. The one on the right is a bitmap (if you look closely you can see some of the pixelation happening around the edges of the jet).

So why is this important? Using vector graphics offers you a number of advantages – the primary being that vector graphics have a much smaller file size. This means that you can add graphics, animation, or stylized text to your web designs without having to worry about the heavy file weight associated with GIF or JPG

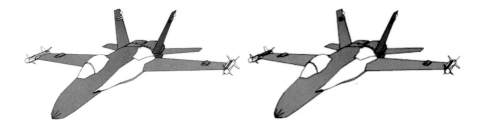

image files. The other major advantage to working with vectors is that you can push, pull, enlarge, or shrink the graphic to your heart's content and it will not degrade in quality. This allows you to create interesting animation effects without having to use something as clumsy as an animated GIF.

figure | 13-1 |

Here you can see the difference between vector (left) and raster (right).

## File Formats

When working with Flash there are two predominate file formats you will interact with: FLA and SWF. The FLA file format is used to save the Flash movie as you are still working on it. This allows you to open the file into the Flash application and make changes. If you are designing a web page to use Flash content, you will be using the SWF format. This format, which stands for Small Web File, is different from the FLA in that it is a compressed version of the movie. This means that only those elements needed to display the movie within the browser are contained in the file. In addition, the SWF file is often protected. This means that the SWF file cannot be reopened into the Flash application.

# Designing with Flash

As I mentioned earlier, Flash is a highly versatile way of delivering multimedia content on the Web. One of the most common misconceptions of Flash development is that you create one big Flash file and throw all of your content into that file. While this is certainly possible, it is not the only way to work with Flash. In reality, this is somewhat dangerous because it means that your entire site is reliant on a single piece of technology. In addition, building a Flash site such as this can really take a fair amount of effort to build and maintain.

Another common method of using Flash content is to create smaller movies and then use them as component pieces of your web design. For example, you might use Flash as the banner of the page, a navigational component, or some interactive widget used to illustrate a concept. The key is not to approach Flash as the only solution to creating great web designs. Flash should be used as a supplemental element in delivering content in ways that could not be accomplished by other means.

**DON'T GO THERE** When Flash was first beginning to proliferate across the Web, many web designers created animated introductions for their web sites. Chances are that you have already experienced this phenomenon. While these "intros" do provide interesting visuals, they have become one of the most clichéd concepts in web design.

## Inserting Flash Movies

Now that you have a little background on Flash, let's take a look at how you can use Dreamweaver to embed Flash movies into your web design. This process all starts by creating a new page, or opening an existing HTML page that will contain the Flash content. Once open, place your cursor on the page where you want the movie to appear. Now you can insert the movie by selecting the Insert | Media | Flash menu option, or you can use the Media | Flash option in the Common category of the Insert bar (see Figure 13-2). By selecting either of these options you can use the Select File dialog box to choose the SWF file you wish to insert. Once you click on OK, a placeholder graphic (shown in Figure 13-3) is dis-

figure | 13-2 |

The Common category of the Insert bar contains the Media options that can be used to add several types of media.

figure | 13-3 |

When adding Flash movies, a placeholder is displayed within in the Document window.

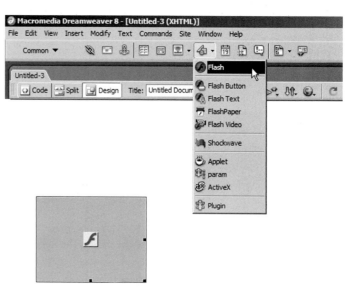

played within the Document window. By default, this placeholder will be the same size and shape as the Flash movie you just embedded. If you want to actually view the Flash movie within the context of the page, simply click on the Play button within the Property Inspector (see Figure 13-4).

**Play Button**

figure | 13-4 |

Clicking on the Play button within the Property Inspector will show the Flash movie.

After you have inserted a Flash movie, there are several Flash-specific settings that can be made using the Property Inspector. The following detail the available options.

● *W (Width) and H (Height):* As you could probably guess, this setting is used to determine the overall width and height of the movie as it will appear within the page. Unlike working with GIF or JPG images, Flash's vector graphics can be scaled in or out without affecting the quality of the image.

● *Loop:* When enabled, this will set the Flash movie to play over and over again. If disabled, the movie will play once and then stop.

● *Autoplay:* When this option is enabled, the Flash movie will play once it is loaded within the web browser.

● *Quality:* This setting is used to determine the smoothness of the vector graphics when displayed. A Low setting will decrease quality, but increase the speed of the movie. Conversely, a High setting will increase quality, but may decrease the speed of the movie on slower computers. Figure 13-5 illustrates the difference between settings. In reality, you may never need to use anything other than the High setting.

figure | 13-5 |

You can adjust the quality of a Flash movie from Low (left) to High (right).

● *Scale:* This setting is used to determine how the movie will scale to fit within the height and width specified. By default, this will be set to display the entire movie. However, there are two additional options. The No Border option will crop the movie so that it will be displayed at its native aspect ratio. The Exact Fit option will scale the Flash movie to fit the Height and Width at all costs. Figure 13-6 illustrates the differences between settings.

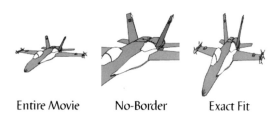

Entire Movie     No-Border     Exact Fit

figure | 13-6 |

The different scale options that can be used with a Flash movie.

## Adding Flash Buttons

If you don't own a copy of the Flash authoring application, you can still use Flash objects within your web designs. One way is to use Dreamweaver's Flash button object to create simple navigational elements. In Chapter 11 we explored behaviors that could be used to create button rollovers. Using Flash buttons, you can create similar effects without having to create multiple GIF or JPG images.

To add a Flash button object to your design, place your cursor on the page where the new button will appear. Now you can insert the object by selecting the Insert I Media I Flash Button menu option, or you can use the Media I Flash Button option in the Common category of the Insert bar. This will open the Insert Flash Button dialog box, shown in Figure 13-7. Using this dialog box you can modify the text, font, font size, and background color of the button. In addition, you can use the Style list to select from a number of available button styles that come with Dreamweaver. As you select each button style, you can preview and interact with it using the Sample window. Once you are satisfied with your settings, click on the OK button to add the object to your page (see Figure 13-8). Once the button has been added, you can edit the features of the Flash button object by selecting the item and then clicking on the Edit button within the Property Inspector (see Figure 13-9).

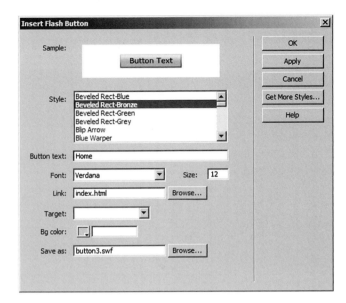

figure | 13-7 |

Insert Flash Button
dialog box.

figure | 13-8 |

Flash buttons may be viewed within the Document window.

**Edit Button**

figure | 13-9 |

A Flash button's settings may be modified by clicking on the Edit button within the Property Inspector.

## Adding Flash Text

If you remember back to Chapter 2, we talked about how you have a limited choice of fonts when working on the Web. This is because your audience must have the same font that is used within your design resident on their computer. To overcome this problem, at least in part, Dreamweaver offers the Flash text object. Much like Flash buttons, Flash text is created without having to own the Flash authoring application. As the name implies, Flash text is a simple

Flash object that contains nothing but text. This provides you a lightweight solution for times when you want to add text using any special fonts.

To add a Flash text object to your design, place your cursor on the page where the text will appear. Now you can insert the object by selecting the Insert I Media I Flash Text menu option, or you can use the Media I Flash Text option in the Common category of the Insert bar. This will open the Insert Flash Text dialog box, shown in Figure 13-10. Using this dialog box you can modify the font, font size, style, color, alignment, and so on. You can also turn your Flash text object into a hyperlink by adding a URL or file path to the Link area. The last item in this dialog box is the name of the SWF file that will contain your flash text. Once all of the options have been set, click on the OK button to add the object to your page (see Figure 13-11). Just like Flash buttons, if you want to edit anything about the Flash text object you can select the item and then click on the Edit button within the Property Inspector.

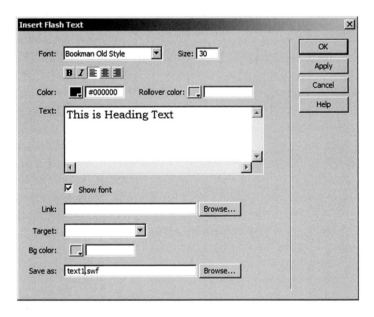

figure | 13-10 |

Insert Flash Text dialog box.

figure | 13-11 |

Flash text may be viewed within the Document window.

This is Heading Text

# Using Behaviors with Flash

Back in Chapter 11 we explored some the options for using JavaScript behaviors to create interactive web designs. In this chapter, we are going to take a look at two additional behaviors that are commonly used in conjunction with Flash objects. The *Control Shockwave or Flash* and the *Check Plug-in* behaviors can be helpful when building web designs that utilize Macromedia Flash.

## Control Flash Movies

One of the interesting features of Flash is that you can "talk" to it using JavaScript. This communication is made possible by using the *Control Shockwave or Flash* behavior that comes with Dreamweaver. Using this behavior you can add hyperlinks or buttons that will interact with the buttons in different ways. For example, you can create a link that will play, stop, or rewind the flash movie. In addition, you can have the Flash movie jump to a specific frame within the movie. If that doesn't make much sense, you can think of Flash just like video, consisting of a series of frames that creates the illusion of motion over time.

To add these interactive controls, start by inserting a Flash movie using the instructions from earlier in this chapter. Once the movie is added, you should now provide a name for the Flash object using the Property Inspector (see Figure 13-12). With a flash movie added and named, you now need some type of object that can be clicked on to trigger the behavior. For example, you may want to use a text link with a pound sign (#) as the link location. If it is not already open, go ahead and summon the Behaviors panel by selecting the Window | Behaviors menu option. Now you can highlight your link object, click on the Add Behavior button (see Figure 13-13), and select Control Shockwave or Flash from the resulting menu. This will summon a corresponding dialog box, where you can use the Movie pull-down menu to select the Flash movie you

figure | 13-12 |

Use the Property Inspector to add a name to the Flash object.

Object Name

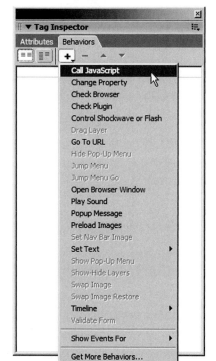

figure | 13-13 |

The behaviors are
added using the
Add Behavior but-
ton on the
Behaviors panel.

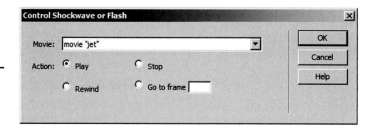

figure | 13-14 |

Control Shockwave
or Flash dialog box.

want to control (see Figure 13-14). Next, choose what you want the
movie to do from the remaining options. Once satisfied, click on
the OK button to apply the behavior.

### Check for Plug-in

Anytime you work with Flash the thing to remember is that not
everyone will have the Flash plug-in. This means that you need to
do one of two things. First, you can provide alternative non-Flash
content. So, if you are delivering some content using Flash, you
might have a plain HTML version for those people without the
plug-in. Your second option is to simply tell the user that some elements of the site require the use of Flash and they need to down-

load it from the Macromedia web site. Whichever option you use, you will need to do some type of detection to find out if the user has the plug-in or not. The *Check Plug-in* behavior is used to detect whether the Flash plug-in is present and can then route the user to a different page based on the result. For example, if a user comes to your Flash page and they do not have the plug-in, you can send them to a page that doesn't require Flash.

You can add the *Check Plug-in* behavior by selecting the corresponding option from the Add Behavior menu of the Behaviors panel. Once selected, this will open the Check Plug-in dialog box, where you can define how this behavior will function (see Figure 13-15). The Plugin pull-down menu allows you to select what plug-in the page should search for when loaded. In this case, we are going to detect the Flash plug-in. Next, you can specify two different URLs. The first is the location the user should be sent if the plug-in is found. The second is where the user should be routed if no Flash plug-in is available. Finally, enabling the *Always go to first URL if detection is not possible* option will send the user to the first location if the JavaScript is not able to determine whether or not the plug-in is installed. Once you have selected the desired option, click on the OK button to apply the behavior.

figure | 13-15 |

Check Plugin dialog box.

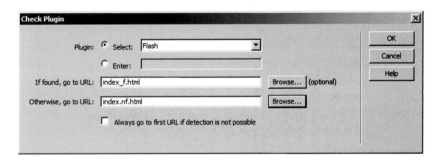

NOTE: The *Check Plug-in* behavior not only works for Flash but can detect Shockwave, LiveAudio, QuickTime, and Windows Media Player applications.

## Shockwave

A few times in this chapter I have made mention of the Shockwave multimedia file type. You can think of Shockwave as Flash's older brother. This format, which is generated from the Macromedia Director application, is used to develop interactive movies that function in a manner very similar to Flash. There are many differences between the two, but generally Shockwave elements are used to create very robust applications, video games, or 3D content that can be viewed through the web browser. In addition, I should also mention that Shockwave movies can actually contain Flash movies, but not vice versa.

Shockwave movies can be added to your web design in very much the same way Flash elements are added. However, instead of adding a SWF file you will be inserting a DCR file. To do this, place your cursor on the page where you want the Shockwave movie to appear. Now you can insert the object by selecting the Insert | Media | Shockwave menu option, or you can use the Media | Shockwave option in the Common category of the Insert bar. By selecting either of these options you can use the Select File dialog box to choose the DCR file you wish to insert.

# WORKING WITH MULTIMEDIA

In addition to adding Flash movies, you can work with video and audio within your web design. However, using video with your design is not nearly as seamless as working with Flash. The primary difference is that Flash can be used to extend the functionality of your web design, whereas video and audio are normally used to provide some type of visual (or audible) interest to the site. For this reason, it is important to make certain that including video is something you really want to do. In this section, I will give you a very high-level overview of using video and audio within your web design. In reality, working with these types of media elements is an extremely broad topic, so what I discuss here is by no means the entire story.

## About Video on the Web

During the early years of the Web, there were few if any options for delivering any type of media. The first types of video that were available on-line required the user to download the file to their computer before playing using some type of player application. Within the last several years we have seen a proliferation in the number of options for publishing video on the Web. However, even though there is a large number of options anytime you work with video on the Web the same challenges are present. The first obstacle to designing with video is simply that it must first be created. Developing an original video can be a complicated and highly expensive process. For example, to capture and edit video you are going to need a camera, a computer with some sort of video connectivity, and video-editing software. Fortunately, recent developments in digital video technology have given rise to low-budget alternatives for developing video.

Another major consideration for delivering video over the Web is file size. Even a small video (i.e., of short length) can have a fairly heavy file weight. And as you know, the larger the file weight the longer the download time for the user. To combat this problem, technical improvements have been made in several different areas. First, new video compression schemes have been developed to help squeeze every last byte out of the video files. These schemes work by throwing out some of the data that is used to describe each frame of the video. The result can lead to a slightly lower-quality video, but the drop in file size may be well worth the effort. Another major change to affect download times is the expansion of video streaming technology. Video streaming is basically where video is played as it is downloaded. This way the end user doesn't have to wait for the entire move to download before watching. The caveat to this is that it requires the presence of special software on your web server. Real, QuickTime, and Windows Media are all examples of video streaming technology that can be used.

The last consideration to make when working with video on the Web is your audience. Much of successful web design hinges upon knowing and understanding your intended audience. Is your site the type of site where someone would expect to find a video? One of the biggest mistakes of new web designers is to use new technology just for the sake of using it. Also, think about the technology your audience has available. While many of today's web users have some type of broadband Internet access, it is still far from the majority. Before including video, think about whether or not your users are accessing the Web using a telephone modem. By making this consideration early, your audience may keep coming back to your site for more.

## Working with Video

There are two predominate ways you can add video to your web site: linking or embedding. Each method certainly has its advantages and drawbacks. Remember to consider how your audience is bound to interact with your web site. This will help you determine the best course of action.

**DON'T GO THERE**

Although Dreamweaver is an excellent tool for web design, it doesn't natively have all of the options for working with video. If you are going to be using video as part of a professional design, I suggest checking with the video software manufacturer (such as Real, Apple, or Microsoft) to find the best way for implementing their file types within a web page.

## Linking to Video

Creating a link to a video file is the easiest way to add video to your site. In this method, you are simply creating a hyperlink to a video file that will either open and play within the web browser or launch an external video player such as QuickTime or Windows Media Player. In the case of Internet Explorer on Windows, the user will actually be asked which option they prefer. The primary advantage to this technique is that opening video in an external player will allow the visitor to continue browsing the Web while the video is playing. However, not everyone's browser is configured the same way. If the browser does not recognize the file type, it may prompt the user to download the video to their computer before playing.

Creating a link to a video file is really no different than creating any other type of hyperlink. Start by selecting the object that will be used as the link (possibly text or an image) and then use the Property Inspector's Link area to add a path to the video file. Depending on what type of video you are linking to, the file extension may be different. Common video formats for this technique include AVI or MPG.

## Embedding a Plug-in

figure | 13-16 |

When embedding a plug-in, a placeholder graphic will be displayed within the Document window.

Besides linking to a video file you can also embed it directly into your design. Using this technique, the video will appear and play inline with the rest of the design elements on your page. To do this, you will need to embed a plug-in into the web page. Start by placing your cursor on the page where the video will appear. Now you can insert the plug-in by selecting the Insert I Media I Plugin menu option, or you can use the Media I Plug-in option in the common category of the Insert bar. This will open the Select File dialog box, where you can select the video file to play. Common video formats for this technique include MOV (QuickTime) and WMV (Windows Media). Once you click on OK, a small placeholder graphic will be added the page (see Figure 13-16). Unlike Flash elements, this placeholder will not immediately appear the same size as the video file. You will need to use the resize handles to manually adjust the video's size. With the file now embedded, I have found that it is best to preview the page within the browser. Dreamweaver does provide a Play button within the Property Inspector, but I have found that previewing video within Dreamweaver to be problematic.

## Working with Audio

Before closing out this chapter, I am going to give you a quick look at how to add audio to your web page. I want to preface this by saying that I will show you how to do it as long as you promise not to add audio unless you have a *very* good reason. While you may enjoy hearing your favorite song play in the background of your page, most people will find it irritating.

There are two ways you can add audio to your web page. First, you can use the exact same embed plug-in procedure we just used with video. All you have to do differently is select an audio file instead of a video file. Common audio formats include WAV, MP3, and MIDI. The other way you can add audio is by using the *Play Sound* Dreamweaver behavior. To do this, start by selecting an object that will trigger the sounds to play. For example, you may want to have a button that makes a click noise when the user moves their pointer over it. Next, continue by selecting the Play Sound option from the Add Behavior menu of the Behaviors panel. Once selected, this will open the Play Sound dialog box (see Figure 13-17), where you can specify the sound file to play. After choosing a file, click on the OK button to apply the behavior. To preview (or pre-hear as the case may have it), view the page within a web browser.

figure | 13-17 |

Play Sound dialog box.

# SUMMARY

In this chapter we have explored how you can use Dreamweaver to add multimedia elements such as Macromedia Flash. We also spent some time exploring how digital video and audio can be used in conjunction with your site. The key points you should understand are what flash is, how it can be embedded, and your options for working with digital video.

While these multimedia elements add a degree of excitement to your design, remember that they all require some type of plug-in or helper application on the end user's computer. Also, don't forget that successful web design is contingent upon knowing and understanding your audience. It is your audience that will dictate whether it is acceptable to use multimedia as part of your design.

## in review

1. What is Macromedia Flash?

2. What is the difference between vector and raster? Describe the advantages to using vector graphics.

3. What is the difference between the FLA and SWF formats?

4. What is the advantage to using Flash text objects? Describe some reasons you may not want to use this feature.

5. What is Shockwave?

6. What are some considerations to make when working with digital video?

7. What are the two ways for using video with your web page?

8. Why is video streaming important as it relates to web design?

## ↗ EXPLORING ON YOUR OWN

1. Take an existing design you might have done and augment it using Flash buttons and Flash text. Take some time to experiment with each of the options.

2. Just for practice, locate or create a digital video file. Try to use the file as both a linked and embedded piece of media.

# Integrating with Macromedia Fireworks

*charting your course*

As great as Dreamweaver is at facilitating web design, we must admit that it can't do everything. Anytime you embark on a new web project, there are many pieces and parts that must be coordinated into the final pages that hit the Web. One way to think about Dreamweaver is that it is a coordinating agent for the elements created within other tools. One of the best examples of this relationship is considering how Dreamweaver works with graphics. One of the big things Dreamweaver really doesn't do is images. Sure, you can add images to your page, but by the time the graphic has been inserted what you see is what you get. Many times this isn't enough.

As you work through the design process small iterative graphic changes will be needed. Often this just means adjusting color, dimensions, or possibly even adjusting how it behaves when handling interaction. While simple, such things do involve the use of tools other than Dreamweaver. In this chapter I am going to give you an overview of how Macromedia Fireworks can be used to help extend Dreamweaver. Since Dreamweaver has little in the way of graphic editing ability, a tool such as Fireworks makes a great companion when doing web design. In addition, because Dreamweaver and Fireworks are from the same company these two products enjoy a level of integration that can help you become a more efficient web designer.

 *goals*

- **Learn how you can make adjustments to images on the fly**
- **Explore how to optimize images for best performance**
- **Learn how to integrate Fireworks pop-up menus**

# ABOUT FIREWORKS

If you are not familiar with Fireworks, or are just getting started with it, I can give you a little background. Generally speaking, Fireworks is a graphic editing tool that is used by many web designers because it has several features geared toward web designers. In addition, Fireworks uses a fairly unique environment in that you can work with graphics that are both in raster and vector formats (refer to Chapter 13 for a discussion of raster versus vector). As I mentioned earlier, one of the biggest advantages that Fireworks offers is its ability to work in concert with Dreamweaver.

In this section we are going to explore a little background on Fireworks, and how you can use it to add graphical and interactive design elements within Dreamweaver. In addition, I am going to show you a few techniques for creating interesting visual effects. My goal isn't to teach you all the ins and outs of working with Fireworks but to touch on a few of those features that can help you create more effective web designs with Dreamweaver.

## The Nuts and Bolts of Fireworks

Before we hop right into editing graphics using Fireworks, let's talk for a moment about some of the details that will help us be successful when integrating with Dreamweaver. When working with Fireworks, the primary format you are working with is the PNG. The PNG file is to Fireworks what the FLA file is to Flash. PNG is the file format used to save the Fireworks image as you continue to work within it. This allows you to open the image back into Fireworks and make changes. If you are designing a web page to use images made with Fireworks, you will probably be using the GIF and JPG web graphic files we discussed earlier.

The difference between the Fireworks PNG file and these web graphics is that PNG has not yet been compressed. This means that the GIF and JPG files only contain enough information needed to display the image within the browser. While these files can be reopened into Fireworks, you will be limited to working with them at a purely raster level. This means that all of the Fireworks-specific information is no longer available for this file. To take full advantage of Dreamweaver/Fireworks integration features, it helps to not only save your PNG files but to save them somewhere within your local site.

In addition to saving images within your site folder, you should also consider using Dreamweaver's site management options to enable Design Notes. As you begin to create and edit graphics with Fireworks, Design Notes can be used to automatically maintain a relationship between a web graphic and the Fireworks source PNG that created it. This way, anytime you want to edit a graphic using Fireworks the original source PNG will be used. Going back to the original graphic means that you can take advantage of the Fireworks-specific features inherent in the PNG file, in addition to not having to worry about the "double compression" of your web graphics.

> ▶ **TRY THIS**
>
> Now that you have a little background on how Fireworks works with Dreamweaver, go ahead and either configure a new site or use an existing site that has Design Notes enabled (see Chapter 6 for details on enabling Design Notes). You can use this site through the remainder of the chapter for working with both Dreamweaver and Fireworks.

## Round-trip Graphic Editing

If there is one point of integration that can save you development time on a regular basis it is Dreamweaver's ability to use Fireworks when modifying a graphic that has been added to your page. This type of interaction is commonly referred to as round-trip editing. This means that you take a graphic from Dreamweaver, move it into Fireworks, make your changes, and then send it back to Dreamweaver. This allows you to streamline the process of working with graphics because you don't have to worry about opening, saving, or managing external files—all of which goes on behind the scenes.

The process of enabling round-trip editing within Dreamweaver is simple. All you need to start with is a graphic that has been inserted within a Dreamweaver page. Now you can perform the following steps to go round-trip with your graphic.

1. Select the image you want to edit within Fireworks.

2. Within the Property Inspector, locate and click on the Fireworks Edit button within the Edit area of the inspector

(see Figure 14-1). By clicking on this button, Fireworks will automatically start up, so that you can edit the selected image.

**Edit**

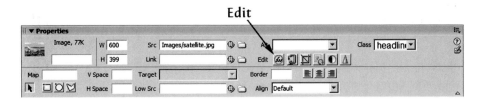

figure | **14-1** |

The Edit button within the Property Inspector will automatically start Fireworks so that you can edit the image.

figure | **14-2** |

The Find Source dialog box pops up when the location of the source PNG file is not known.

If this graphic wasn't originally created within Fireworks, or Design Notes is not enabled for your site, you will be presented with the Find Source dialog box (see Figure 14-2). Using this dialog box, you can choose to edit the PNG source file (if the graphic originated from Fireworks) or use the actual graphic file that was selected within the Dreamweaver page. As a general rule, you should try to use the Use a PNG option if the graphic was created in Fireworks and you have the PNG source file. Otherwise, you really have no other option than to select the Use This File option to edit the graphic file that is a part of your site.

**Find Source**    [x]

Editing "satellite.jpg".

Do you want to use a Fireworks PNG as the source of "satellite.jpg", or edit this image file directly?

| Use a PNG |
| Use This File |

To set a preference for the future, choose an action below.

Fireworks source files:

| Ask When Launching ▼ |

Now that the graphic is open within Fireworks, use the available tools to make any changes or additions you desire. Once satisfied with your alterations, click on the Done button in the upper left-hand corner to return the graphic back to Dreamweaver (see

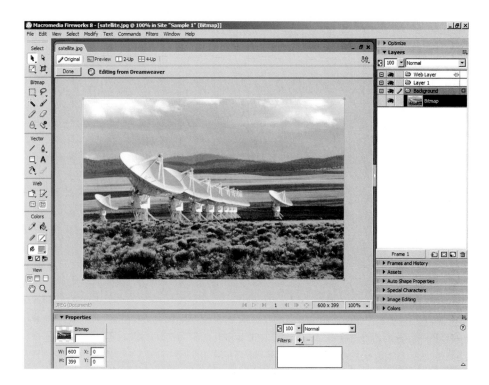

Figure 14-3). The new modified image will now be displayed within the Document window.

figure | 14-3 |

The Fireworks Done button is used to send the image back to Dreamweaver.

## Placeholder Graphics

Fireworks is not only used to edit existing images, but can be accessed from Dreamweaver to create new images. This is helpful when you are working with a new design and you know you need a graphic to go in, but aren't quite sure what it should be. In this scenario, image placeholders are used. How this works is that you add a placeholder image, and then use Fireworks to create a graphic that will replace it. This is similar to round-trip graphic editing. However, you aren't actually opening an image within Fireworks. Using this process will create a new graphic file within Fireworks that has the same dimensions as the placeholder. The following are the steps for making this happen.

1. Using a new web page, or opening an existing page, add an image placeholder by selecting Insert | Image Objects | Image Placeholder.

2. Use the Image Placeholder dialog box (see Figure 14-4) to specify the name, dimensions, color, and alternate text for the "purposed" image. It is important to note that the name and dimensions you use here will automatically be used for the new image. This doesn't mean that you are stuck with them, but it can save you a little time later. Once satisfied with your settings, click on the OK button to add the placeholder to your page (see Figure 14-5).

figure | 14-4 |

The Image Placeholder dialog box is used to specify the attributes of the placeholder that will appear within the Document window.

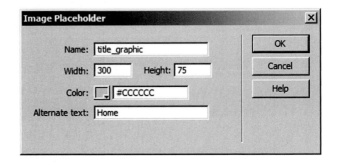

figure | 14-5 |

The image placeholder as it appears within the Document window.

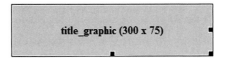

3. With the placeholder graphic added to your design, we can use Fireworks to create a replacement graphic. To do this, select the placeholder, and then click on the Create button within the Property Inspector (see Figure 14-6). This will automatically open Fireworks with a new blank graphic with the same dimensions as the placeholder.

figure | 14-6 |

The Property Inspector's Create button will automatically open Fireworks with a new blank canvas.

4. Using the available tools within Fireworks, compose the new graphic.

5. Once your graphical masterpiece is complete, click on the Done button in the upper left-hand corner. This will start the process of saving the new file.

6. The first file you will need to save is the source PNG file. As I mentioned earlier, Fireworks will automatically name the file with the name you selected for the placeholder. If necessary, change the file name, select a location for the file, and click on Save.

7. Next, you will need to save the file that will be used within the web page. Once again, Fireworks will automatically use the name that was assigned to the placeholder. If necessary, modify the file name, select a location for the file, and click on Save.

8. Now the new image will appear in place of the placeholder within the Dreamweaver Document window.

## Optimize Images

Way back in Chapter 2 we talked about some of the file format options you have when working with images on the Web. The key to working with many of the web graphic formats is to finely tune the image in order to obtain as small a file size as possible. This process is often referred to as optimization. By optimizing an image, you can strike a balance between file size and image quality, creating the "optimum" experience for the user. For example, maybe you have a JPG image that could be compressed to give it a smaller file size. Or, you may have a GIF image where you would like to add a transparent color. There is any number of operations that can be performed when optimizing a graphic for the Web.

Because Dreamweaver is not a graphic editing package, it must rely on external tools to handle image optimizing activities. Taking advantage of the integration between Dreamweaver and Fireworks, you can optimize the graphics within your page on the fly. To do this, select the image as it exists within Dreamweaver's Document window. Now move down to the Property Inspector and click on the Optimize in Fireworks button, shown in Figure 14-7, within the Edit area. Once the button has been clicked, Fireworks will

figure | **14-7**

The Property Inspector's Optimize in Fireworks button will summon the Fireworks Optimize dialog box.

**Optimize In Fireworks**

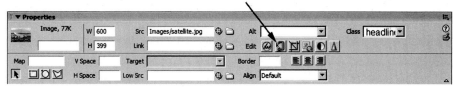

automatically open the image within the Optimize dialog box (see Figure 14-8). This dialog box is broken down into three separate areas that are represented by the tabs at the top of the window: Options, File, and Animation. The Options tab is used to adjust how the graphic file is saved. Here you can adjust the format, and the compression settings for each of the options. The next tab, File (see Figure 14-9), is used to edit the physical size of the graphic. For example, if you wanted to shave a few pixels from the edge of an existing image you could do that here. The final tab, Animation (see Figure 14-10), is used to adjust the parameters of an animated GIF image. This can be helpful if you want to adjust the duration

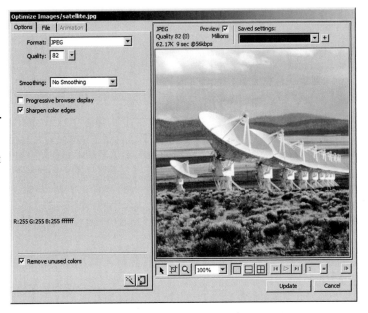

figure | 14-8 |

The Options tab of the Optimize dialog box is used to adjust the file format and compressions settings for the selected image.

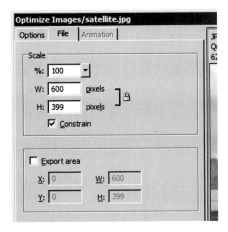

figure | 14-9 |

The File tab of the Optimize dialog box is used to adjust the physical dimensions of the selected image.

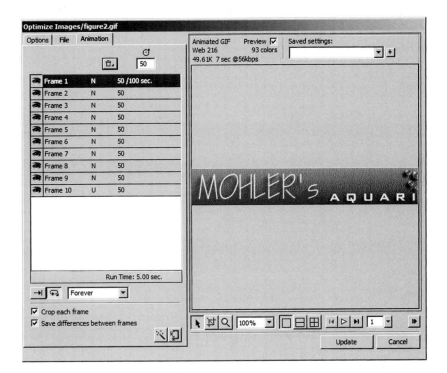

Optimize Images/figure2.gif

Options | File | Animation

Animated GIF   Preview ☑   Saved settings:
Web 216        93 colors
49.61K 7 sec @56kbps

| Frame 1 | N | 50 /100 sec. |
| Frame 2 | N | 50 |
| Frame 3 | N | 50 |
| Frame 4 | N | 50 |
| Frame 5 | N | 50 |
| Frame 6 | N | 50 |
| Frame 7 | N | 50 |
| Frame 8 | N | 50 |
| Frame 9 | N | 50 |
| Frame 10 | U | 50 |

Run Time: 5.00 sec.

Forever

☑ Crop each frame
☑ Save differences between frames

Update    Cancel

MOHLER'S AQUARI

figure | 14-10 |

of the animation, or possibly remove an extraneous frame. For more specifics on the features and functionality provided by the Optimize dialog box, you can access the help area via the Help | Fireworks Help menu option within Fireworks.

The Animation tab of the Optimize dialog box is used to adjust the parameters of animated GIF images.

NOTE: If the Find Source dialog box appears after you click on the Optimize button, this means that the Fireworks source PNG file cannot be found, your current site does not have Design Notes enabled, or the image was not originally created using Fireworks. If available, you can use this dialog box to locate the PNG source file, or the actual web graphic file can be used.

## Working in Fireworks

In addition to working back and forth between Dreamweaver and Fireworks, you can build graphical elements within Fireworks and then export them to Dreamweaver. This can be helpful when you want to build visual page elements using a graphical editing package instead of Dreamweaver. Then, by exporting the graphics directly to Dreamweaver you can avoid having to build everything twice. In this section we are going to explore two popular features of Fireworks: slices and pop-up menus. My intent is not to teach you all about graphical development within Fireworks but to give you just enough of an appetite for building interactive graphical elements that can be utilized within Dreamweaver.

## Slices

There are many design techniques that call for taking one large graphic and making it function as several smaller ones. The best example of this would be some type of graphical menu bar like that shown in Figure 14-11. In this example, we have one big graphic, but we want each button to be its own image so that we can interact with it individually. The easiest way to achieve this effect is by taking the one image, carving it up into pieces, and then inserting them all into a table that will hold them all together. If you have ever done this manually, you know that it can be an extremely tedious process. This is where the Fireworks Slice tool comes into play. Using Fireworks, you can both divide up the graphics and create the associated HTML code at the same time. Then, once finished you can dump it all into Dreamweaver.

figure | 14-11 |

Graphical menu bars are a great example of images that can be sliced up.

1. Either create a new graphic or open an existing graphic within Fireworks.

2. Use the Slice tool, shown in Figure 14-12, within the Web area of the Fireworks toolbar on the left.

3. Once enabled, use the Slice tool by clicking and dragging outlines around the areas of the image you would like to convert to individual graphic files (see Figure 14-13). Use special care to make certain you only include portions of the image you want to include. The size and shape of the box you draw will determine the dimensions of the final graphic file.

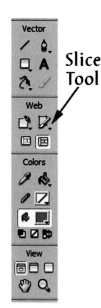

figure | 14-12 |

The Slice tool is located within the Web area of the Fireworks toolbar.

4. After you have chopped up the image, and are ready to move into Dreamweaver, we can now export the graphics and HTML. Do this by using the Quick Export button in the upper right-hand corner of the window (see Figure 14-14). Here you can select the Dreamweaver I Export HTML option. Selecting this option will open the Export dialog box, where you can define the location where the graphics and HTML will be stored. When working with Dreamweaver, this location should be somewhere within your local site directory. Once you click on the Save button, the graphic files and an HTML file will be created within the folder you specified.

NOTE: At this point you may want to save the source PNG file for later. This way, if you need to make any alterations you don't have to start over from the beginning.

5. Once all files have been created, it is time to go back to Dreamweaver. When working with HTML from Fireworks you have two different options. You can either open the HTML file directly or insert into a new or existing document.

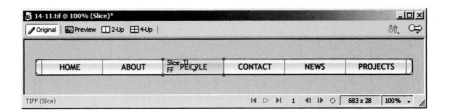

figure | 14-13 |

Outlines will appear around the areas of the image that will be converted into individual files.

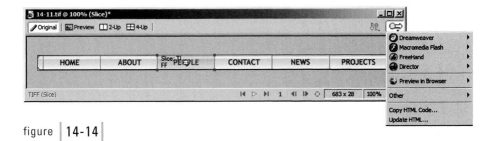

figure | 14-14 |

The Quick Export button is used to dump out the graphics and HTML from Fireworks.

A good practice is to go ahead and insert the Fireworks HTML into a new document right away (and then delete the Fireworks HTML). To insert your new graphical element from Fireworks, use the Insert I Image Objects I Fireworks HTML menu option.

figure | **14-15** |

The Insert Fireworks HTML dialog box is used to select the HTML file that was exported from Fireworks.

**6.** Using the Insert Fireworks HTML dialog box (see Figure 14-15), select the HTML file we just created within Fireworks. You may also want to select the *Delete file after insertion* option, to automatically delete the HTML file. This can be helpful so that you don't have any extra files to manage as part of your site. Once you have the file selected, click on the OK button to add the elements.

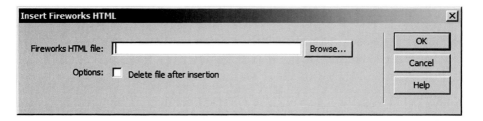

**7.** Now that the graphics and associated HTML have been added to a page within Dreamweaver, you can select and work with each of the graphics individually. For example, you might want to attach a hyperlink or behavior to one of the graphics.

## Building Pop-up Menus

While we are on the subject of building menus, Fireworks can also be used to create pop-up menus like we built in Chapter 11. What is nice about this is that Fireworks uses the exact same *Show Pop-Up Menu* behavior that Dreamweaver uses. This way, you can build the menu and associated effects using Fireworks and then implement the graphics, HTML, and JavaScript behaviors within Dreamweaver. In addition, you can make some adjustments to the pop-up menu using Dreamweaver's Behaviors panel.

In a nutshell, this effect works by first taking a menu image and separating it into slices just like we did in the previous section. Once the image has been cut apart, you can attach the pop-up menu behavior to each of the slices. Then, once finished it can all be dumped into Dreamweaver. The following details how you can get this done.

NOTE: Creating a pop-up menu starts out the exact same way as when we were slicing an image in the previous section. For this task, I am going to assume that you have already separated the image into slices. Essentially, I will be picking up after step 3 of the previous section.

1. Once you have the image carved up into slices, use the Pointer tool (located in the Select portion of the Fireworks toolbar; see Figure 14-16) to select one of the slices that corresponds to a button that will trigger the pop-up menu effect.

2. Now, with the slice selected use the Modify | Pop-up Menu | Add Pop-up Menu menu option to summon the Pop-up Menu Editor (see Figure 14-17). This dialog box works almost exactly like Dreamweaver's Show Pop-up dialog box that we explored in Chapter 11. For this chapter, I am only going to touch on some of the more unique features Fireworks offers.

3. One of the big differences with the Fireworks pop-up menu is that you can use graphics to punch up the visual design of the menus. This is done by selecting the Pop-up Menu Editor's Appearance tab. Here you can adjust the Cells option to use the Image feature. This will reveal a few new options (see Figure 14-18).

4. Using the Up state and Over state you can add a graphical style that will be used as the backgrounds for the menu items. This is done by selecting a graphic thumbnail within the Style box. As you choose different styles, the change will be reflected in the Editor's

Pointer Tool

figure | 14-16 |

The Pointer tool is located within the Select portion of the Fireworks toolbar.

figure | 14-17 |

Although it looks slightly different, the Fireworks Pop-up Menu Editor works just like the one in Dreamweaver.

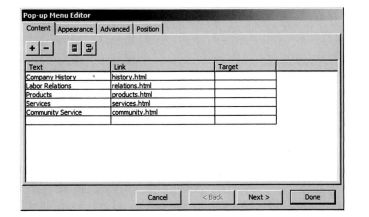

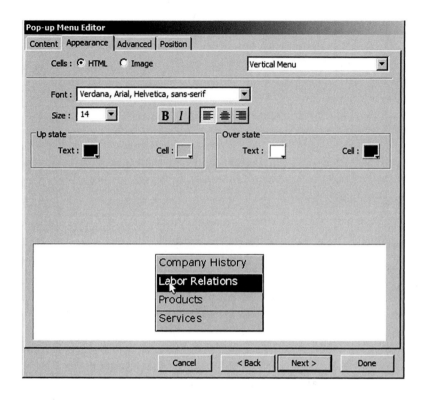

figure | 14-18 |

The graphics options of the Pop-up Menu Editor.

preview window. In addition to adjusting style, you can also adjust the Cell color to determine the color of the menu options in either Up or Over states.

5. Once you have set all of the desired options, click on the Done button to apply the behavior.

6. If you have multiple menu options, repeat steps 1 through 5 for the remaining buttons.

7. With all of the behaviors added, the Quick Export button is used to export all of the graphics, HTML, and JavaScript behaviors. Once again, select the Dreamweaver | Export HTML option to summon the Export dialog box, where you can define the location where the graphics and HTML will be stored. Once you click on the Save button, the graphic files and an HTML file will be created within the folder you have specified.

8. Now we can go back to Dreamweaver and use the Insert Fireworks HTML menu option to select the HTML file we just created within Fireworks. Once the file has been selected, click on the OK button to add the elements.

9. Once all of the graphics, HTML, and JavaScript behaviors have been added to your page in Dreamweaver, you can make any adjustments that may be necessary. If you missed a menu option, or want to make some minor changes, the Dreamweaver Behaviors panel can be used to make alterations to the pop-up menus. Also, make sure to save the Fireworks PNG source file for later use. You may want to make more drastic changes later on.

# SUMMARY

In this chapter we have explored how Fireworks can be integrated with Dreamweaver to help manipulate the graphics used as part of your web design. The key items to remember are how you can go round-trip, from Dreamweaver to Fireworks and back, with many of your graphic changes and how effects and graphics built within Fireworks can be exported and further manipulated within Dreamweaver. As you move forward with future projects, keep in mind that web design is not mastering any one tool. Great design means knowing and understanding the options for integrating one technology with another. Dreamweaver is the glue that holds the technology pieces together.

## in review

1. What is Fireworks generally used for?

2. What is the native file format used for Fireworks source images?

3. Why should Design Notes be used when working with both Dreamweaver and Fireworks?

4. How does round-trip graphic editing relate to Dreamweaver?

5. What are placeholder graphics used for?

6. What does it mean to optimize an image?

7. What are slices?

8. How can effects created in Fireworks be exported for use within Dreamweaver?

## ↗ EXPLORING ON YOUR OWN

1. Just for practice, take an existing design and use Fireworks to optimize an image. Take some time to test out the different compression options for each graphic format.

2. Using Dreamweaver, create an image placeholder that will be used for a graphic title heading. Now use Fireworks to fill in the text and generate the final image. Experiment with the round-trip editing features to modify the text within the graphic.

3. Create a graphic using Fireworks that can later be used as some type of menu system. Once you have the graphic created, use the Slice tool to chop the image into several distinct pieces. Move the graphics and HTML into Dreamweaver so that it can be integrated with an existing design.

**notes**

# index

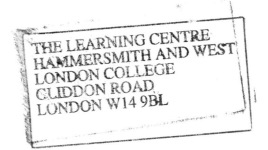